PUTIN'S MASTER PLAN

TO DESTROY EUROPE, DIVIDE NATO, AND RESTORE RUSSIAN POWER AND GLOBAL INFLUENCE

DOUGLAS E. SCHOEN
WITH EVAN ROTH SMITH

ENCOUNTER BOOKS
New York • London

INTRODUCTION

At five in the morning on Thursday, February 27, 2014, unidentified gunmen stormed the Supreme Council of Crimea in Simferopol, the capital of Ukraine's semiautonomous Crimea region. A local pro-Russian activist camped outside the Supreme Council told journalists that the gunmen "didn't look like volunteers or amateurs, they were professionals. This was clearly a well-organized operation. . . . Who are they? Nobody knows. It's about 50–60 people, fully armed."[1] The mysterious gunmen took down the Ukrainian flag that flew over the Supreme Council and raised a Russian flag in its place. All across the Crimean peninsula, taking advantage of the early morning light, dozens of teams of unidentified, heavily armed soldiers seized key government, military, and infrastructure sites; raised Russian flags; and rebuffed all questioners.[2] Soon, the world had a name for these uniformed but unidentified soldiers who had materialized to take control of Crimea in a matter of hours: "Little Green Men."

They didn't come from Mars but from Russia, on the direct order of Russian president Vladimir Putin. Analysts who have observed Putin's decadelong pattern of aggressive interference in Ukraine quickly recognized his hand in Crimea's seizure. The rapid and violent escalation of Russian military and political involvement in Ukraine opened a new chapter in Putin's bloody project to reestablish Russia as a regional and global power.

Soon, it became clear to the world that the Little Green Men were Russian Spetsnaz forces, and Putin himself would eventually admit as much.[3] Putin moved quickly to consolidate control of Crimea and annex it to Russia. Within a month, Crimea had switched its clocks to Moscow time.[4] Putin's illegal invasion and annexation of Crimea would be followed by Russian sponsorship of a violent separatist movement in Eastern Ukraine.[5] As of this writing, Russian-backed separatists continue to do battle with the Ukrainian military in and around Donetsk and Lugansk, costing thousands of lives and threatening to plunge Ukraine into political, economic, and social catastrophe.

While Putin's forces were still establishing control of Crimea, before most media or politicians had fully acknowledged or grasped the seriousness of Russia's speedy land grab, Poland's then foreign minister, Radosław Sikorski, warned prophetically that "this is how regional conflicts begin. This is a very dangerous game."[6]

Sikorski is right. By invading Ukraine, Putin has plunged Europe into a perilous state of conflict and turmoil not witnessed since the darkest days of the Cold War. Since seizing Crimea and starting the war in eastern Ukraine, Russia has conducted cross-border raids into the Baltic States,[7] ordered its fighters to buzz US Navy ships,[8] and sent nuclear-capable bombers into the airspace of neighboring countries.[9] Indeed, Putin has become so aggressive that he risks pushing Russia into a full-blown nuclear confrontation with NATO.[10] During the Cold War, the world was lucky to avoid a nuclear war between America and the Soviet Union. We may need to be that fortunate again.

Putin's ambitions are not limited to the territory of the former Soviet Union, though he has begun to question whether former Soviet states are even legally independent of Russia.[11] Putin has targeted countries like Bulgaria[12] and Slovakia[13] for expanded Russian influence as well. Never one to miss an opportunity, Putin has taken advantage of the long-running feud between Greece and its European creditors to position Russia as an alternative ally and potential financial savior for the beleaguered, bitter Greeks.[14] Putin's vision extends beyond Europe, too: he has intervened in Syria to support Bashar al-Assad[15] and transferred nuclear technology to Iran's ayatollahs,[16] and he has cut trade deals with North Korea's lunatic Kim dynasty.[17]

To some, Putin may seem like an unpredictable tyrant, obsessed with power, violence, and conquest, who lashes out at neighboring countries impulsively and spasmodically. We believe the truth is much more subtle, and even more formidable, than either of these characterizations: Putin is a calculating master of geopolitics with a master plan to divide Europe, destroy NATO, reestablish Russian influence in the world, and, most of all, marginalize the United States and the West in order to achieve regional hegemony and global power. And his plan is working.

While many observers are now waking up to Putin's single-minded hostility in Europe and the threat he poses to security on the continent and around the world, no one has yet documented and analyzed Putin's far-reaching plan, why it is so dangerous, and why the United States and its allies must take decisive steps to roll back his agenda. Putin still has defenders in Europe and America, some of whom are bought and paid for by Kremlin petrodollars and others who simply don't believe that Putin is an existential threat to the West. In this book, we intend to make it clear just how pernicious Putin's plan is, and why he must be stopped.

American and European leaders have failed to respond adequately or forcefully to Putin's challenge. They propose weak half-measures—like storing American tanks in Polish warehouses[18]—while Putin builds more nuclear missiles[19] and opens military bases on conquered Ukrainian territory.[20] Indeed, Russia is set to double its strategic nuclear arsenal, in direct violation of the 2010 New START Treaty naïvely negotiated by the Obama administration.[21] No less of an authority than former US national security advisor and grizzled Cold Warrior Zbigniew Brzezinski says flatly that "we are already in a Cold War" with Russia.[22] Yet our politicians equivocate and explain away Russia's blatant pattern of internationally destabilizing military aggression.

This book is the first comprehensive attempt to systematically explain Putin's global strategy, which could lead to the breakup of the NATO alliance and potentially to war with the West. The West currently has no strategy, no plan, and no tactics to confront Putin's offensive other than limited economic sanctions and token gestures.

We are neither alarmists nor alone in our concern over Putin's aggression and the damage he has done to Europe's future. Thomas Friedman, remarking on how quickly the situation in Europe has deteriorated, asks rhetorically, "Did someone restart the Cold War while I was looking the other way?"[23] The *Economist* goes further: "Nearly a quarter-century after the collapse of the Soviet Union, the West faces a greater threat from the East than at any point during the cold war."[24] Edward Lucas provides a chilling laundry list of Putin's most egregious behavior: "The Kremlin provokes and intimidates its neighbors with aggressive espionage, corruption of political elites, propaganda onslaughts, cyberattacks, economic sanctions, coercive energy policies, surprise military exercises, and violations of airspace, territorial waters and even national borders."[25]

There is no shortage of evidence that Russia poses a clear and imminent threat to the West and its allies, to Western values, and to liberal democracy in general. To be sure, the Poles and Lithuanians—along with the Estonians, Latvians, Bulgarians, and Romanians—understand this threat, which is why they're urging America to station heavy military equipment on their territory.[26] We can and should do much more. It can't be reassuring that Yevgeny Lukyanov, deputy secretary to the Russian Security Council, recently made it clear that if the Baltic States voluntarily host NATO missile defense sites, "they become our targets."[27] No warehoused battle tank or unused artillery piece will deter a Russian strike on these countries. Only real consequences for Russia, a more robust American presence in Eastern Europe, and clearheaded, decisive Western leadership can halt Russian aggression.

Unfortunately, Western leaders haven't gotten the message. The European Union has shown no spine, failing to stand by its Eastern neighbors or to take on Putin. Indeed, the European Union has grown so weak that it now faces the prospect of disintegration, driven by the ongoing refugee crisis and the United Kingdom's "Brexit" referendum to leave the EU. Both the refugee crisis and Brexit are wins for Putin that increase Russia's power in Europe. America has little better than Europe. Walter Russell Mead is right when he observes that "the Obama administration failed to understand just how important Europe is to the United States, and it has never appreciated how important the United States is to Europe . . . not since the 1930s has America been this absent when its vital interests were this critically engaged."[28] Whether by intent, ignorance, or incompetence, Western leaders have simply failed to understand or address the storm clouds gathering over Europe. Scholar Stephen Blank correctly diagnoses "a continuing Western and U.S. failure of nerve" when it comes to recognizing, confronting, and defeating Putin's master plan.[29]

THE PLAN

By fracturing the transatlantic relationship between America and its European allies, undermining or even destroying the NATO alliance, dividing the European Union, and establishing Russian hegemony in Europe both within and beyond the former borders of the Soviet Union,

Putin seeks to usher in a new world order that recalls the bipolar rivalries and tensions between political systems during the Cold War. It is an order in which America will be unable to defend or promote, either rhetorically, diplomatically, or militarily, our core Western values of human rights, liberal democracy, and free markets. If left unchecked, Putin and his network of loyalists will wield enormous power within Russia and continue to enrich themselves at the expense of the Russian people and the economies of neighboring countries; Russia will continue to collaborate with the worst authoritarians and tyrants, from Iranian theocrats, to Chinese bureaucrats, to Latin American autocrats; the global expansion of rights and commerce that followed the end of World War II and the Cold War will cease and even reverse; and America and the West, cowed into isolationism, will give up the global fight for a freer world.

Russia's neighbors, especially Ukraine and Georgia, have been living with the reality of Putin's master plan since at least 2008. The countries of the former Soviet Union, militarily weak and economically vulnerable, have been easy targets as well. But Putin has set his sights on larger prizes. NATO itself is under threat.[30] The EU is growing more wobbly by the day, with the UK's shocking Brexit vote an ominous harbinger of future European disintegration.[31] Western values are under constant assault by the Kremlin's "weaponized propaganda."[32] Russian submarines slip into Swedish waters[33] as easily as Russian hackers crack into President Obama's e-mail.[34] It is vitally important to connect the dots and recognize the narrative that makes Putin's pattern of outrages and provocations a carefully crafted plan, and not just repetitiously bad behavior. A thorough accounting of Russian aggression illustrates how dangerous Putin's regime has become. Russia has purposefully provoked a series of wars and crises in neighboring countries, including Georgia, Ukraine, those in the Baltics, and Moldova. Russia invaded Georgia in 2008, in the midst of the Beijing Olympics, with Putin peeling off the regions of South Ossetia and Abkhazia, issuing Russian passports to their residents, and beginning a soft annexation of Georgian territory into the Russian Federation.[35] In 2014, as previously noted, thinly disguised Russian forces seized Crimea and began an ongoing war against the Ukrainian government in the eastern Donbas region, where the breakaway people's republics of Donetsk and Luhansk continue to fight and kill Ukrainians with Russian arms and assistance.[36] The Baltic states of Estonia, Latvia, and Lithuania suffer frequent interference in the form of massive cyberattacks, airspace violations, and even the 2014 cross-border abduction of an Estonian Internal Security Service official.[37] In Moldova, more than one thousand Russian combat troops prop up the tiny separatist state of Transnistria, which is unrecognized by any member of the United Nations.[38] This arrangement has not benefited Moldovans or the residents of Transnistria, who must live under effective Russian occupation. As a leading Ukrainian businessman patiently explained in a private conversation: "Putin is the sole decision maker in the Kremlin, that's for certain. He waits, he postures, and he looks for opportunities. And when he sees weakness he acts." Certainly, Putin's nonstop pattern of provocations and interventions bears this out. "Make no mistake," the Ukrainian continued, "Putin has his eye on the Baltics, north Kazakhstan, wherever Russians are living in the near abroad. He will wait as long as it takes, and he will act decisively."[39] Westerners gravely underappreciate the seriousness of Putin's regional ambitions.

Putin has also struck beyond Russia's immediate borders, deploying the Russian military in Syria in support of his longtime ally Bashar al-Assad in October of 2015.[40] The Russian air force pounded ISIS and rebel positions, bailing out Assad's struggling Syrian Arab Army and, as Russian state media put it, managing to "profoundly reverse the situation."[41] Putin's sudden strike in Syria was a master class in interventionism and a stark counterpoint to failed Western efforts in Iraq, Afghanistan, and Libya. Russia leveraged overwhelming air power to strengthen Assad's position, seriously weaken ISIS and al-Qaeda, and expand its own military presence in Syria and the Eastern Mediterranean.[42] Yet Western leaders were smugly confident that Putin had acted too boldly; Obama predicted that Russia's intervention was "just going to get them stuck in a quagmire and it won't work."[43]

Just six months later, Putin defied this prediction and declared his mission in Syria accomplished as the Russian military began withdrawing forces and turning its focus to building out permanent bases in Syria.[44] America's leaders were blindsided, and the "quagmire" narrative demolished. Obama and his advisors had been certain that Syria would turn into Putin's Vietnam, but instead it became his Grenada: a surgically precise military action with limited goals that were accomplished swiftly, and with little loss.

Putin's Syrian success was epitomized by Assad's recapture of Palmyra, an ancient and historically significant city that had earlier fallen to ISIS. When the Syrian Arab Army retook Palmyra, it proved that Putin had reenergized Assad, beaten ISIS, and was now a global actor of broad influence and historic importance. Putin surely didn't mind that in rescuing Palmyra from the clutches of ISIS, he and Assad had deeply embarrassed the United States and Europe. Over the course of the Syrian campaign, Putin mortally wounded Assad's moderate opposition; became a global leader in the fight against ISIS terror; deepened his relationship with Iran; and promoted Russia's own military, political, and even commercial interests in the Middle East. No Western military action in the last two decades can boast anything comparable to this degree of success. It is critical to understand just how brilliantly effective Putin's intervention in Syria has been. As one columnist starkly puts it, "Putin has attained all that he wanted."[45]

Putin's power play in Syria has advanced his agenda in Europe as well. By arming Assad and aggressively deploying Russia's own forces, Putin has prolonged the Syrian conflict, made it considerably bloodier, and driven millions of refugees into Europe. Europe's struggle to deal with the social, political, and security ramifications of the mass Muslim migration has not only distracted the world from Putin's invasion of Ukraine but also strengthened Putin's hand against an increasingly fractured European community—and further weakened the EU as an institutional force. Indeed, the EU's failure on Muslim migration was a direct cause of the Brexit vote, which threatens to unravel the entire European system. Independent of these developments, Western and Central Europe are learning just how expansive Putin's plan might be, as he fans the flames of Euro-skepticism and backs radical Far-Left *and* Far-Right parties that have become "Putin's fifth column in the EU."[46] The parties he supports go from the National Front (France) and the Northern League (Italy) to the National Democratic Party (Germany) and Jobbik (Hungary). "Pro-Russian parties currently hold 76 of 751 seats in the European Parliament," according to a report in the Ukrainian magazine *Novoye Vremya*.[47] A senior Western diplomat frankly admitted that "the Russians are looking for ways to break the unity of Europe, and they are targeting the weaker states."[48] Just as worrisome as Putin's growing political influence is the situation of Europe's economy having proven unable to free itself from its addiction to Russian oil and gas. Indeed, Europe has inadvertently bankrolled much of Russia's military expansion and rearmament. Separatist bullets and artillery shells in Ukraine are paid for by Germans and Italians heating their homes.

Europe has also become less committed to the fundamental premise of NATO: mutual defense. A Pew Research Center study conducted in spring of 2015 finds that "at least half of Germans, French and Italians say their country should not use military force to defend a NATO ally if attacked by Russia.... Americans and Canadians are the only publics where more than half think their country should use military action if Russia attacks a fellow NATO member."[49] These public attitudes demonstrate how close the NATO alliance is to becoming a paper tiger that will crumple if Russia strikes. Indeed, Edward Lucas warns ominously that we must "fix NATO or risk WWIII."[50]

The victims of Putin's aggression understand just how underprepared the West is to respond to Russian aggression. In a private conversation, a Ukrainian industrialist explained: "There's a simple way to analyze this that you Westerners don't understand. Putin is ready for war and nobody else is. And he's not going to stop until he is rebuffed. So far no one and nothing is standing in his way."[51] Another highly positioned Ukrainian agreed that Putin was ready for war, and that unless "the West comes to grips with that reality, it will never be able to develop a workable plan to stop him."[52] It's astonishing that Putin has gotten away with such flagrant disregard for international norms and the sovereignty of neighboring countries. But save for the outright invasion and annexation of Crimea, Putin has gone to great lengths to avoid directly implicating the Kremlin, thereby maintaining at least a veneer of deniability when it comes to conducting plainly Russian acts of interference and violence. He has only recently conceded that Russian intelligence operatives are in Ukraine, but he continues to deny the full extent of Russian military intervention in eastern Ukraine, and he has signed an order "making the deaths of Russian troops lost during 'special operations' a secret."[53] Instead of overt military aggression, Russia unleashes an asymmetric arsenal of separatists, cyberwarfare, espionage, and special forces to disrupt and destabilize his neighbors. Some analysts have called this approach "hybrid warfare," in which traditional hard power is married to misinformation, propaganda, and cybercampaigns that overwhelm not only a target country's military capabilities but also its media, politics, and social cohesion.[54] Chatham House's James Sherr describes Russia's hybrid wars as "a model of warfare designed to slip under NATO's threshold of perception and reaction."[55] It worked in Georgia, and it's working in Ukraine. Unless the West learns how to respond, it will continue to work the next time that Putin chooses to expand his growing empire.

At the same time that Putin targets his neighbors with hybrid warfare, he uses a deep and often-underappreciated soft power arsenal to keep the rest of Europe at bay. Putin- and Kremlin-loyal oligarchs leverage Russian oil, gas, and corporate assets to neutralize European opposition to Russia's strategic goals, while giving European elites motive to accept absurd Russian denials of responsibility for events bearing clear Kremlin imprimatur. Much of Central, Northern, and Eastern Europe depends heavily on Russian energy to heat homes and power industry, a critical vulnerability that Putin keenly understands.[56] Putin has shut off energy supplies to entire countries before, most notably to Ukraine in the mid-2000s, and no one doubts that he would do so again. Europe's shaky economy would be crippled by even a weeklong shutoff of Russian energy to the Netherlands or Poland—let alone to Germany, Italy, or France. One shudders to think what would happen if Greece lost access to the 40 percent of the energy supply that Russia provides it for even a day or two.[57] Putin understands the advantage Russia's energy resources provide, and his bare-knuckle brand of petropolitics has dissuaded or co-opted more than a few European critics of Russian aggression.

Putin remains fixated on his ultimate goal: Russian hegemony in Europe, but not in the old Cold War sense. He doesn't seek a Soviet-style, Moscow-centered megastate on the European continent, or even a Warsaw Pact–like formalization of Russian supremacy. Rather, Putin aims to neuter Europe politically, to make it concerned only with commerce and comfort, so that muscularly enforced Russian interests will dominate the political fate of the continent. By way of analogy, during the Cold War, Finland was compelled by its location between NATO countries and the USSR to remain neutral in the conflict and deferential to both sides, officially uninterested in the outcome, and at least in theory comfortable with either Soviet or Western victory. Today, Russia aims to "Finlandize" all of Europe to the point where it is simply uninterested in saying no to Putin—and where no Kremlin act of domestic oppression or international provocation would merit a European response. In Putin's plan, European leaders will shake their heads, shrug, and sign another round of Russian energy–import deals. America, an ocean away, will watch dejectedly, its objections meaningless without committed European allies.

PROSPECTS

This frightening future is no longer as far away as it once appeared. Putin has proven that he is determined to get there and is willing to expend Russian blood and treasure on the effort. This is no pipe dream, no revanchist delusion. This is real. It is no longer such a stretch to imagine Russians dashing across open fields in Lithuania or shelling towns in Poland—instead of in Ukraine.

There's just one problem with that scenario. Poland and Lithuania, unlike Ukraine, are NATO members. That means that under Article 5 of the North Atlantic Treaty, an attack on Poland or Lithuania is considered an attack on *every* NATO country, from America to Germany to Greece. Indeed, it was Article 5 that allowed America to rally European allies to its side in the aftermath of 9/11 and mount a joint effort against the Taliban in Afghanistan. In the event of a Russian attack on a Baltic state or on Poland, we should expect our allies to make a similar demand of us.

Russian direct action against NATO looms on the horizon as Putin ratchets up his provocations in the Baltic States. Putin is betting that even if he were to attack Poland or a Baltic country, NATO and Europe would fail to respond, just as they failed to respond to the attacks on Georgia and Ukraine—even though in the case of Ukraine, the Budapest Memorandum of 1994 guaranteed the country's territorial integrity.[58] NATO members, especially the United States, must ask themselves the following questions: Are we willing to risk the lives of our sons and daughters to protect far-flung European countries that border Russia? Will Peoria really fight for Poland? Putin is determined to test the limits of the NATO alliance and push the partnership past its breaking point, leaving Europe defenseless against a re-armed Russia. Eventually, a miscalculated Russian attack on a NATO country could provoke a major European war—or even a world war.[59]

American and European leaders have been blindsided by Putin's ruthless pursuit of power and influence. There has been an across-the-board leadership failure in the West. Sanctions against Russia have not gone nearly far enough and have not forced Putin to change course in Ukraine or warned him off from future aggression.[60] Putin has provided separatists in Ukraine with a seemingly unending supply of tanks and heavy weapons, but President Obama prevaricated for months before offering Kiev nonlethal military assistance and a handful of advisors.[61] Our European NATO allies, who have never carried the full burden of their own defense, have little to offer the Ukrainians in the way of hardware. What Europe *can* offer is financial relief and assistance as Ukraine's economy continues to collapse, but so far, "the sums on offer from the outside world have been pitifully small," as the *Economist* accurately notes.[62] Meanwhile, sanction-strapped Russia has managed to direct millions of rubles to prop up the separatists.

Western leaders have demonstrated a near-total lack of political courage in the face of Putin's rampage across what the Kremlin disparagingly calls its "near abroad." Even the cold-blooded murder by Russian-backed separatists of 298 civilians, including 211 EU citizens, aboard Malaysian Airlines flight 17, or MH17, using a Russian-made missile system was not enough to rally Europe.[63] The Netherlands, which lost 198 of its citizens aboard MH17, continues to receive 34 percent of its energy supplies from Russia.[64] No wonder Putin feels emboldened: American and European leaders never give him reason to fear serious consequences for his behavior.

The West and the United States need to do much better. In this book, we will outline a set of policies to protect America and Europe, roll back Putin's aggression, and promote the free development and integration of Eastern Europe into European and global institutions.

Putin's single-minded bid for regional hegemony, global influence, and a dramatic reorganization of the world order threatens Russia's neighbors as well as the security of the Western world and the survival of Western values. Putin is pushing us toward the disturbing prospect of a new global struggle for power—with the locus of the struggle once again centered in Europe. The war in Ukraine is Russia's latest and boldest assault on European stability. While Putin may no longer be aiming to establish full Russian control over Ukraine, his actions show a consistent logic and strategic coherence. Putin seeks to foment low-level conflict to undermine stability and ultimately promote expanded Russian influence, either directly or through proxies. This approach has worked in Georgia; it appears to be having great success in Ukraine; and there is every reason to believe, as we will show, that it could work in Moldova, the Baltic States, and anywhere else that Putin sets his sights.

We in America and Europe must directly confront the stark truth of open Russian aggression toward the West and the real threat that it could lead to a major war in Europe. We must understand what the West stands to lose if Putin gets his way: a legacy of peace and prosperity; our values of liberty and human rights; and centuries-old democratic and civil institutions. From overt annexations of territory to covert support for separatists and radicals, Russia is actively undermining the stability of Europe in ways not seen since the fall of the Soviet Union. It is abundantly clear that Vladimir Putin is determined to undo the hard-won peace and triumph of liberal democratic values in Europe and to remake the continent in Russia's image. We in the West must be equally as determined to preserve our security, defend our values, and put a stop to Putin's dark, bloody vision for Europe's future. To do that, we will have to reaffirm and reinvigorate the transatlantic alliance between the United States and Europe—the partnership that won the Cold War and that stands even now as the main obstacle to the fulfillment of Putin's vision.

CHAPTER 1

The Transatlantic Relationship in the Twenty-First Century

In times like this, when the security of the Euro-Atlantic area is challenged, the North Atlantic Alliance has not wavered. And it will not waver. For 65 years, we have been clear in our commitment to one another as Allies.

—NATO SECRETARY GENERAL ANDERS FOGH RASMUSSEN[1]

Today, the situation in Europe and America is grim. The transatlantic relationship, forged in the aftermath of World War II to resist Soviet expansion, has deteriorated to a breaking point. Russia has invaded Ukraine and is challenging American power around the world. Migrants from the Middle East and North Africa are streaming across the Mediterranean and up through Turkey, driving a crisis of identity and culture that threatens to end the European Union as we know it, and already appears to have driven Britain from the EU. Economically, the postrecession "new normal" of slow growth and declining labor force participation has left millions of working Americans and Europeans struggling to make ends meet. Politically, far-right nationalists and far-left socialists are gaining in Europe, while in America the Democratic and Republican parties are failing to inspire an increasingly dissatisfied electorate. The transatlantic community is in worse shape than at any point since the end of the Cold War, and we have almost certainly not seen the worst of it yet.

No one has taken a keener interest in the West's weakness than Vladimir Putin. He has seized the opportunity that Western vulnerability presents, driving internal and external crises, leveraging Russian advantages, and rebuilding the Kremlin's global power and importance. Putin has struck at the core of the transatlantic alliance, breeding Euro-skeptical parties that want to do away with the EU and encouraging anti-American politicians who advocate for the dissolution of NATO. Putin has fostered and fomented crises from Syria to Ukraine and beyond, starting fires faster than the West can put them out, while exhausting our resources and willpower. Putin has even gone after American and European allies, cutting arms deals with Washington-aligned Arab nations and rekindling old Soviet connections in Latin America and Africa. Putin and Russia have launched nothing less than a full frontal assault against the transatlantic alliance.

Of course, Russia faces many challenges of its own, not least of which are the demographic implications of a shrinking, graying population and the persistent challenges of an economy that depends almost entirely on oil and gas exports. In many ways, Russia remains, per German chancellor Helmut Schmidt's famous formulation, "Upper Volta with missiles."[2] Putin is a strongman dictator who has short-circuited Russia's democratic system, ruling over a deeply troubled and divided society that has used petrodollars to paper over the unresolved political, economic, and psychological scars of the Soviet collapse. At a fundamental level, America and Europe are far-stronger societies with considerably greater resources, stability, and potential than Russia. But far from being a comfort, this disparity should make us even more concerned that we have been unable to confront Putin's propaganda, warmongering, and aggression. It raises troubling questions about the consequences of Western peace and prosperity and whether we have become so complacent in our success that we no longer understand the need to defend it—let alone possess the nerve or courage to do so.

THE WESTERN INHERITANCE

The situation was not always so dire. At the turn of the millennium, the transatlantic community seemed reinvigorated and poised for a century of success. The shocking events of September 11, 2001, shattered the post–Cold War peace but gave new purpose and a sense of mission to institutions that had floundered in the 1990s, bereft of the Soviet foe that they were built to oppose. Victory over the Soviet Union had seemingly enshrined the West as the unchallenged political and economic leader of the world community; now the threat of violent Islamic extremism represented a new opportunity for NATO to flex its muscles against an enemy that only understood force, while leaders in Europe and America banded together in defense of human rights and universal values. When America invoked Article 5 of the North Atlantic Treaty on October 4, 2001, obliging other NATO members to join in its response against al-Qaeda and the Taliban, no one was eager to go to war. But the Western allies understood the seriousness of the threat and stood shoulder to shoulder in support of common values.

Indeed, in the early 2000s, we possessed so much clarity of purpose that the very definitions of "the West" and "the transatlantic community" expanded to include historically Western countries that had been trapped behind the Iron Curtain but earned their way into our community through hard-fought political reform, tough economic sacrifices, and unwavering dedication to replacing Communism with liberal democracies. Poland, Hungary, and the Czech Republic became NATO members in 1999 and were joined by Bulgaria, Estonia, Latvia, Lithuania, Romania, Slovakia, and Slovenia in 2004. All these countries went on to join the European Union, with integration efforts ongoing today.

The process of including former Communist countries in Western institutions has frequently been contentious, but debate and indeed profound disagreement are all hallmarks of open, democratic decision making. When NATO and the EU opened their doors to the countries of the former Eastern Bloc, no one expected a painless integration process. But the United States and its European allies put in the work to get it right, confident that Western values were worth defending and promoting. Today, this commitment is no longer evident. Putin has noticed our wavering devotion to Western values and our lackadaisical defense of core Western ideals.

America and Western Europe share many political and cultural values and a deep generational bond forged in the fires of twentieth-century history. Even today, any American or European crossing the Atlantic for business or pleasure senses the closeness between our societies. It is a remarkable outcome of history that a Wisconsinite can travel thousands of miles to Germany and find values, churches, and even beers that are familiar. Similarly, a culturally minded resident of London, Paris, or Milan feels at home in the chic cafes and arthouse cinemas of Manhattan's

Greenwich Village. This common cultural expanse of the West, internally diverse but profoundly united, underpins the transatlantic project. As important as the political and economic institutions of the West are, we must remember that they are not ends in themselves: they exist to preserve and protect our civilizational values. It is worth reminding ourselves what these values are and what they mean.

First and foremost, these values transcend the Left-Right political divide, excepting the radical fringes on both sides. Western values are the arena within which our political discourse occurs. Indeed, the values themselves make democratic politics possible.

Human rights are the foundation of all the other rights. The most succinct, direct explication of these rights is found in America's Declaration of Independence: "All men are created equal, . . . endowed by their Creator with certain unalienable Rights, that among these are Life, Liberty and the pursuit of Happiness." Jefferson's words, over two centuries old, were revolutionary not only for their assertion of these rights but also for their contention that they were God given, not government created; governments could not *give* or take them away. What governments could do, and what they continue to do today, is fail to observe these rights. Recent years have seen Vladimir Putin's contempt for human rights and liberties, whether through shooting down a plane full of civilians, jailing journalists and activists, or outlawing free speech for homosexuals. A similar disregard for human dignity is shown by the North Korean, Chinese, and Iranian governments, as well as by ISIS, al-Qaeda, and Boko Haram, among other flagrant violators of human rights around the world. The West must remain committed to promoting these rights and defending vulnerable people and populations, from imprisoned journalists to persecuted minorities.

Free economies—allowing individuals to trade, contract, and create with one another on their own terms, for their own benefit, and in whatever role or capacity they choose—are another cornerstone of Western societies. In Europe, the many varieties of a free economy have yielded democratic-socialist societies in Scandinavia, entrepreneurial capitalism in Poland and the Baltics, and resilient industrial societies in Western Europe. In America, we have built the wealthiest society in history through a spirit of restless invention and innovation. But in corrupt petrostates like Russia, government elites and Kremlin-dependent oligarchs control the nation's hydrocarbon-dependent wealth, while entrepreneurs and the highly educated flee to the West, where their talents can be rewarded.

Liberal democracy ensures popular control of government, holds public officials accountable to the citizenry through free and fair elections, and sets clear limits on the power of the state to interfere in the lives of private citizens. The forms liberal democracies take vary, from two-party republics like America's to multiparty parliamentary monarchies like the United Kingdom's. In these societies, governments exist for the sake of the population they represent, not for the sake of preserving and perpetuating their own rule. The ultimate good is considered the good of the people, rather than the preservation of a royal family, the enrichment of oligarchs, or the creation of an ideological utopia. Churchill famously said that democracy was the worst form of government except for all the others, and this remains the case. To be sure, democracy rarely produces results quickly or resolves disputes decisively or neatly—and over the last decade or so, political discontent in the West, including in the United States, has led many to doubt the integrity of governing institutions and even the future of democracy itself. Clearly, Western citizens and political leaders must work to improve the political institutions that ensure representative government and open societies. But one need only contrast admittedly imperfect American and European democracies with Putin's authoritarianism, Iran's theocracy, or China's communist totalitarianism to understand what the other choices are.

Putin's attempts to subvert the progress of liberal democracy in Europe and co-opt European political parties to serve Russian strategic ends, which we detail in later chapters, should alarm anyone who believes in democratic values. (His efforts are unwittingly aided by many well-meaning Europeans at the top echelons of the EU, who have lost their taste for liberal democracy, preferring bureaucratic top-down control.) The West's key values of human rights, a free economy, and liberal democracy have made our societies the envy of the world in living standards, education, political liberty, and personal happiness. But since the Soviet Union's collapse, many have taken Western values for granted. At the outset of the 1990s, political scientist Francis Fukuyama went as far as to predict the "end of history" and the global triumph of Western values.[3] But history itself intervened, spoiling this hopeful forecast.

UNDER ATTACK

A quick scan of the headlines demonstrates the precarious state of our world: Putin's neo-Tsarist Russia is establishing imperial zones of influence in Europe, Central Asia, and the Middle East; radical Islamic extremists are attempting to rebuild the caliphate in Iraq and Syria; China's totalitarian communist regime remains globally ascendant; Bolivarian Socialists are in power in nearly a dozen Latin American countries; the ayatollah's theocracy in Iran is on track to become a nuclear state; the Taliban retains control of large areas in Afghanistan and Pakistan; the countries of West and Central Africa are beset by intercommunal violence and public health nightmares. Outside of the West itself, human rights, free economies, and liberal democracy appear to be in retreat. And even in Western Europe and the United States, political correctness is undermining our commitment to these values.

Vladimir Putin certainly does not believe in human rights, at least not according to any recognizable Western conception of them. Nor do many among the Russian elite and the majority of the general populace. Putin does not preside over a free economy, and he has proven himself a committed enemy of liberal democracy. He understands, perhaps better than we do, that the West's military power, economic strength, and political will are dependent on our core values. If we allow our commitment to these values to waver, and Russian aggression to undermine our confidence in the West's ability to overcome challenges while remaining true to its core principles, then Russia will gain at our expense. If we fail to defend human rights, Russia will continue to disregard them. If we don't promote free economies, then Putin and his obedient oligarchs will continue to direct the lives and livelihoods of hundreds of millions of people. If we don't stand up for liberal democracy, then Putin will continue to govern Russia with an iron fist until the day a handpicked successor inherits his authoritarian regime.

Western values matter. They have made us happy, prosperous, and free. The transatlantic alliance can and must do more to protect and promote them, both internally and around the world.

Together, the two sides of the North Atlantic—the United States on one side and Western Europe on the other—constitute the greatest political, military, economic, and cultural force in human history. While exact definitions of "the West" vary, and no single institution or organization should be taken to represent the full breadth and depth of the transatlantic relationship, there is doubtless a common civilizational space spanning Alaska to the borders of Eastern Europe, with outposts in places like Australia and Japan. This area accounts for just under one-seventh of the world's population but about half of its global economic output[4] and the overwhelming preponderance of the world's military strength, and it is where many globally influential centers of culture reside, including New York, London, Los Angeles, and Paris. What happens in the West reverberates across the world. This can be a problem, as it was when the bursting of the American housing bubble precipitated a global economic recession. But it is also a key strength that the West can leverage to the betterment of humanity, as it does when the Nobel Peace Prize is awarded to someone like Malala Yousafzai, or when Western economies produce world-changing technologies like the Internet.

Cultural and economic advantages have limits, however, when posed against a determined adversary like Putin, along with his anti-Western allies in Beijing, Tehran, Pyongyang, and elsewhere. They're not especially useful in the effort to combat Putin's power grab in Eastern Europe and the Middle East. The Nobel Peace Prize is influential precisely because it is largely apolitical (at least in principle), and inventions like the Internet come about when brilliant minds are free to innovate without political interference. So it is difficult to bring Western culture or economics to bear in a systematic way against authoritarians like Putin without compromising our own values and handing him a moral victory. Economic sanctions against Russia have had some effect, but Putin has been adept at evading them and finding other less scrupulous trading partners in Asia and the Middle East. Our European partners can still do considerably more to abide by the sanctions they have agreed to. Russians may like Western culture, but there is plenty of Russian-language media to keep them happy. It seems unlikely that we would ever go so far as to restrict Russian tourism to the West altogether.

That leaves one Western strength that can be brought unambiguously into the fray against Putin's aggression, and that stands explicitly at the command of our political leaders: military power. NATO countries account for slightly more than half of global military spending,[5] or about $893 billion in 2015.[6] Our militaries are not as strong as they should be, and the Russian military is making gains, but there is little doubt that NATO possesses the most powerful military in history. It is especially remarkable that this unequaled force was created not by a conquest-mad dictator or power-hungry warlord but by largely peaceful, democratic countries whose primary interest was self-defense. Imagine what Vladimir Putin would do with just one of America's ten *Nimitz*-class aircraft carriers. Imagine what the Iranian Revolutionary Guards would do if they had a tank as good as the M1 Abrams. Imagine what the People's Liberation Army of China would do if it had special operations forces as well trained as Delta Force or Seal Team Six. America and its allies maintain these forces with the hope that we will never have to use them.

But Putin has put the West in a position where we must make it clear that all options are on the table. Putin has been unafraid to kill civilians and invade his neighbors. He represents the antithesis of Western values. Western leaders may be able to stop him through the effective application of coercive diplomacy and economic pressure, though up to now, our efforts in these areas have been mostly unavailing. Undergirding any successful approach must be a credible threat of Western military action—particularly united NATO military action—should Putin threaten a NATO country like Estonia or Poland or pursue open war against the citizens of Ukraine, Georgia, or any other sovereign nation that resists Russian pressure. The West spends billions on its armed forces, and we should make it clear that we maintain them precisely to protect Western countries from aggression.

Unfortunately, our political leaders have been caught flatfooted. They have failed to formulate a coherent response to Putin's aggression. They have yet to define the scenarios where the use of force would be justified. For years, we have conceded the initiative to Putin, who controls the outcome of conflicts in Ukraine and Syria since he is the only one willing to back up his words with the threat or application of military force. He knows that the West's feckless leaders are so worried about being blamed for starting a war that they will not do what it takes to prevent one.

PUTIN'S CHALLENGE

Although the transatlantic relationship has been tested many times before, it now faces its gravest threat from a Russia determined to sever the ties that bind the West together. And the West's internal social tumults are providing plenty of fodder for Putin to draw upon. Putin has been explicit in his condemnation of contemporary Western values, claiming that "many of the Euro-Atlantic countries are actually rejecting their roots, including the Christian values that constitute the basis of Western civilization. They are denying moral principles and all traditional identities: national, cultural, religious and even sexual."[7]

Indeed, statistics show that in Western Europe and the United States, religious practice has been on the decline for decades, and it is dropping off more sharply among the young. At the same time, movements for gay rights, especially gay marriage, have redefined Western social arrangements—and for some in the West, this is not to their liking. Thus, Putin's themes find a sympathetic audience even among a portion of Westerners. Putin also appeals to nationalist identity politics, undermining the European integration project, when he says that "one must respect every minority's right to be different, but the rights of the majority must not be put into question."[8] These words resonate with many in Europe today, especially in light of the migrant crisis. Thus in multiple areas, Putin positions himself as the champion of what he portrays as traditional values. The West, Putin insists, has lost its way, and he is here to save it.

Of course, Putin has no intention of saving the West. Rather, Putin aims to shatter the internal European consensus that has brought about the longest period of peace and prosperity since the Roman Empire. The European Union has many flaws, but its fundamental purpose of better relations, free trade and travel, and coordinated solutions to shared challenges is admirable and worthy. But a successful, prosperous, and broadly cooperative Europe is Putin's worst nightmare, since it provides him with no window to pursue his own political or territorial ambitions on the continent. A Europe united in its commitment to Western values will not find Putin's brand of neo-Tsarist authoritarianism appealing, and European countries that coordinate their defense policies through NATO or the EU will not fall to Russian military pressure. The more division and discord Putin can spread within Europe, and the more doubt he can plant in the minds of Europeans when it comes to Western values, the more opportunities he will have to achieve his goals.

Putin is also doing his best to spread anti-American sentiment in Europe, hoping that he can precipitate the internal collapse of the American-European partnership while also dividing the Europeans. However, since our own leaders have often proved so inept, it's not always easy to distinguish between what Putin is responsible for and what damage we have done to ourselves. It was American military strength that held the line against the Soviets and prevented a land war in Europe during the Cold War, but today there are fewer American forces in Europe than there are cops in the NYPD.[9] Our military officers commanding forces stationed on the Continent are "forced to rely on weapons shipped back temporarily or hardware borrowed from allies in the expanding effort to deter the latest threats from Russia."[10]

Putin can afford some uncertainty about the outcomes of his aggressive push into Europe and the Middle East. He does not need to predict exactly how every move will play out, because chaos and confusion are as much to his benefit and the West's detriment as more predictable outcomes. It seems unlikely that when Putin began supporting Bashar al-Assad's regime in Syria in 2011,[11] he knew or hoped that the Syrian civil war would produce a large-scale migrant crisis in Europe. But it did, in no small part because of Assad's brutality and the Russian military support that enabled it. The migrant crisis benefits Putin by fostering division among Western allies and showing Europe's inability to deal with a major challenge to its political and economic systems. By precipitating the United Kingdom's exit from the EU, the migrant crisis struck a blow to European unity that may even be fatal. Putin didn't plan for it, but he didn't have to—unintended consequences and unforeseen crises damage the status quo that he seeks to overturn. Similarly, the accidental downing of Malaysian Air flight 17 by Russian-backed rebels in Ukraine was unintentional but demonstrated the impotence of NATO, even after hundreds of European civilians were killed with Kremlin-supplied weapons. The pattern is clear: Putin acts, a series of chaotic and unpredictable events ensue, innocent civilians suffer—and the West dithers.

Because Putin is driving events, he has the opportunity to shape the narrative and the outcome. Western leaders continually fail to appreciate this simple logic. When Obama claimed that Putin's intervention in Syria will "get them stuck in a quagmire,"[12] the president was trying to draw parallels between Putin's Syrian campaign and American misadventures in Vietnam and more recently in Iraq, but the comparison is fundamentally flawed. Vietnam became a quagmire for America because the Soviet Union and China gave the North Vietnamese the funding and military equipment they needed to drag out the conflict.[13] In Iraq, Iranian aid to Shi'a militias[14] and a global network of Islamic terror funding achieved the same effect. Quagmires don't just happen; they arise as the result of concerted actions from multiple players. Syria will not become a quagmire for Russia just because Obama wishes it to happen. If Obama wants to see Putin bogged down in a Syrian commitment that imposes real costs on Russia, then the president must take substantive action to accomplish that goal. Unfortunately, the American opportunity to shape a favorable outcome in Syria has already passed. Putin got there first.

STANDING UP

It is no exaggeration to say that Putin's ambitions pose a threat to the lives of tens of millions of innocent people in Eastern Europe and the Middle East. At least eight thousand dead Ukrainians,[15] 250,000 dead Syrians,[16] and more than four million Syrian refugees[17] are a testament to that. Add to that the diplomatic, military, and economic assistance that Putin provides to China, Iran, North Korea, Cuba, and Hezbollah, and the scope of his pernicious influence becomes clear.

There is no inherent reason why Russia should have to play the role of global villain. The dream of Russia and the West sharing a "common European home," as Mikhail Gorbachev puts it,[18] may seem far off, but it is not impossible. But if the West is to have any chance at halting and reversing Putin's gains in Europe, the Middle East, and elsewhere, the first step is to redouble our commitment to the transatlantic partnership and to defend a political consensus that keeps America and Europe united behind a set of common values and strategic goals. Preserving and strengthening the alliance should be the paramount foreign policy goal for both the United States and Europe. Our partnership does not only provide far-reaching mutual benefits; it is also the foundation to confront and address global crises, from those in the Middle East to those in Asia. For all our faults, the countries of the transatlantic alliance remain the most powerful political, economic, cultural, and military force for good in the world—but only if we act accordingly.

CHAPTER 2

The Russian Century
Putin's Plan for the Future

First and foremost it is worth acknowledging that the demise of the Soviet Union was the greatest geopolitical catastrophe of the century.

—VLADIMIR PUTIN[1]

If I wanted, in two days I could have Russian troops not only in Kiev, but also in Riga, Vilnius, Tallinn, Warsaw and Bucharest.

—VLADIMIR PUTIN[2]

Vladimir Putin is many things—KGB officer, master politician, multibillionaire, ruthless autocrat—but, above all, Vladimir Putin is a man with a plan. His plan is to unmake the world order that has stood since the end of the Cold War, especially in Europe, and replace it with one where Russia has the power, influence, and military strength to get its way on any issue. This means subjugating Russia's immediate neighbors and integrating them into a Russia-centric political and economic system, neutralizing Europe and ending the transatlantic relationship with America, and seeding an endless series of global crises that drain the West's ability and desire to influence global affairs while promoting the interests of Russia and its allies. In short, Putin plans to make the twenty-first century the Russian century.

To hear Putin tell it, Russia of course has no ambitions beyond its borders.[3] But Putin's vision for the future of the world is made plain by a consistent pattern of disruptive behavior, targeted use of force, and diplomatic intrigue that demonstrates his single-minded strategy to resurrect Russia as a regional hegemon. Putin envisions an Eastern Europe firmly under the control of Moscow and fully integrated into Russia's economic, political, and cultural sphere of influence, alongside a Western Europe that is dependent on Russian energy, complacently isolationist, and most importantly anti-American. Putin's determination to achieve this vision should not be underestimated.

Western leaders appear blind to Putin's far-reaching plan. Barack Obama responded to Russia's seizure of Crimea by warning Putin that he is "on the wrong side of history."[4] On the contrary, Putin is writing history. As author, commentator, and retired US Army lieutenant colonel Ralph Peters pithily puts it, "Obama talks, Putin kills."[5] Indeed, international wars and conflicts started by Putin have claimed the lives of about ten thousand people, both military and civilian.[6] Putin shows no signs of letting up, as the war in Ukraine enters a bloody period of attrition and the Kremlin trains its sights on the Baltic States.[7]

It is vital to understand in depth exactly what Putin has planned for his neighbors, Europe, and the world. In this chapter, we will lay out what Putin's master plan is, country by country, region by region. In each instance, we will explain what Putin has accomplished so far, what he is doing now, and what he appears to be planning next. Should Putin achieve his goals in just a few of these targeted countries and regions, the world will become a drastically different place, remade in Putin's vision, and the consequences for global peace, security, and prosperity will be dire.

UKRAINE

Ukraine is the lynchpin in Putin's strategy for Europe. The second-largest European country, with a population of over forty-five million, Ukraine is a valuable strategic prize positioned astride the major transit corridor for Russian oil and gas into Europe.[8] But Putin's interest in Ukraine is more than strategic—it is also cultural, historical, and ultimately imperial. Over seven million ethnic Russians live in Ukraine,[9] primarily in the east and south, and Ukraine has been part of the Soviet Union or Russian Empire, unofficially, since the 1700s.[10] Indeed, *New Yorker* editor David Remnick contends that "in Putin's mind, Ukraine is not a nation" but rather a part of Russia that is only independent due to an accident of history.[11] In this belief, Putin's attitude echoes that of the tsars. Putin occasionally refers to parts of Ukraine as "Novorossiya," or "New Russia."[12] For Putin, control over Ukraine represents the resurgence and renaissance of Russian civilization, the righting of an historic wrong, and the vitality of Russian regional and global power. The only problem? Most Ukrainians have no interest in being part of Putin's project.

Because most Ukrainians have no immediate desire to be governed as a puppet of Moscow, Putin has undertaken a concerted effort to ensure that Ukraine remains too politically and economically unstable for integration into the EU or NATO. In Putin's thinking, if Ukraine is too volatile for the West to embrace, then Ukrainians will be left with only one option for their future: Russian domination.

It is difficult to overstate just how ruinous Putin's master plan has been for the people of Ukraine. They have endured gas shutoffs in the dead of winter;[13] repeated political and economic interference; and finally, a bloody, violent invasion of their country in an ongoing war that has claimed thousands of Ukrainian lives and destroyed the country's economy, which is rapidly "turning Greek."[14] So long as the West does nothing to help Ukraine fend off Russian attacks, repair its economy, and clean up its corrupt institutions, all Putin has to do is wait for the nation's political will to crumble under the pressures of war and growing poverty. If that happens, then Putin will likely succeed in making Ukraine into "Novorossiya."

BELARUS

Although it gained independence at the same time as Ukraine, Belarus is Europe's last tin-pot dictatorship, continuing a Soviet-style communist government today.[15] Since 1994, Belarus has been ruled by Alexander Lukashenko, who once defended his autocratic, totalitarian regime by declaring that it is "better to be a dictator than gay."[16] Lukashenko has been a reliable Russian ally since the 1990s and serves as president of the largely aspirational Union State of Russia and Belarus, a supranational organization that, at least in theory, will eventually bring Belarus and Russia together in a commercial, military, and currency union.[17] While the Union State project is far from complete, in 2014 Lukashenko became a founding father of the Eurasian Economic Union, a customs union and political integration project that now includes Russia, Kazakhstan,

Kyrgyzstan, and Armenia, in addition to Belarus. It has been seen as a key component of Putin's vision of creating an alternative alliance to rival the EU.

It's easy to write off Belarus as a mismanaged backwater, economically unimportant and politically doomed. But that's not what Putin sees. To Putin, keeping Belarus in the Russian sphere of influence and control is a preliminary but necessary step on the journey toward Russian regional hegemony. Like Ukraine, Belarus was part of the Russian Empire and Soviet Union, and its history is inextricably linked to that of Russia through centuries of shared linguistic, political, and religious heritage. For Putin, there is little reason for Belarus to chart its own course in Europe, and he certainly does not intend to give Belarussians that option. Putin's plan for Belarus is to enforce ever-closer integration with and dependence on Russia. He may pretend that the political projects joining Russia and Belarus are equal partnerships, but it is clearly Russia that is in the driver's seat, with Belarus along for the ride. Moscow will steadily exert more control over Belarussian affairs, likely through the Eurasian Economic Union, until Belarus becomes indistinguishable from a province of the Russian Empire—as it once was.

MOLDOVA

A tiny, impoverished country tucked between Romania and Ukraine, Moldova is nonetheless overflowing with complexities and beset by unsolved political riddles. Moldovans are linguistically and culturally close to Romanians, and much of Moldova was part of the Kingdom of Romania before World War II. But Moldova spent fifty years as part of the Soviet Union, and today about 30 percent of the country is ethnically Ukrainian, Russian, or another non-Moldovan minority.[18] As a result, contemporary Moldovan politics is fraught with existential questions about whether the country's future lies with the West, with Russia, or in reunification with Romania.

Putin has no intention of letting Moldovans make that choice themselves, and he holds a trump card: the unrecognized breakaway state of Transnistria, which violently seceded from the rest of Moldova in 1990 and continues to be propped up by more than a thousand Russian troops who have been stationed there for over twenty years.[19] Moldova's large Russian minority and the presence of Russian troops are eerily reminiscent of Ukraine and Crimea. Indeed, some have already warned that Moldova is "the next Ukraine" and that it is only a matter of time before Putin attempts to leverage his Transnistrian foothold and perhaps swallows a chunk of Moldova along with it.[20] That day may indeed come, and sooner than many might imagine. In the meantime, Putin is spreading anti-European propaganda to ensure that Moldovans don't grow too enamored of the West. Russian-language television, which is hugely popular in Moldova, encourages rumors that "if you join the E.U., everyone becomes gay," or that European regulators "won't let you keep animals around your houses."[21] Putin and his surrogates lavish attention on Moldova, while few Western leaders can be bothered to visit. The Kremlin's intentions are clear: leverage existing divisions and anxieties within Moldova to derail any chance at European integration and eventually return the country to direct Russian control.

THE BALTIC STATES

Estonia, Latvia, and Lithuania are quite possibly the greatest success stories to come out of the old Soviet Union. All three are NATO and EU members with vibrant democracies and market economies that have produced globally competitive companies such as Skype. Of course, Putin can't stand it. He has made life difficult for the Baltic States in innumerable ways, including a massive 2007 cyberattack on Estonia,[22] aggressive misinformation and propaganda campaigns in all three countries,[23] and even the threat of nuclear war.[24] In 2014, Russian agents slipped across the border and abducted Estonian security officer Eston Kohver,[25] who was held in Moscow for more than a year before being released in an exchange for a Russian spy.[26] Alarmingly, Russia has launched a "review" of the "legality" of the independence of the Baltic States after the 1991 collapse of the Soviet Union.[27]

The Baltic States have much to lose if Putin's master plan comes to pass. After a century marked by war and totalitarian Soviet rule, Estonians, Latvians, and Lithuanians have finally carved out a decent life in their corner of the world. Only a few hours from St. Petersburg, democracy and free markets thrive in the region, citizens vote in European parliamentary elections, and tourists from around the EU travel freely and spend euros. The Baltic States are a thumb in the eye of Putin's autocracy and a constant reminder to Russians across the border that Putin and his cronies are denying them the fruits of European integration. Indeed, the ethnic Russians living in the Baltics are better off than their compatriots in Russia proper, though many are bitter about being ruled by non-Russians. That is why Putin has turned his relentless "hybrid" warfare on the Baltics, and why these countries may yet prove to be the flashpoint that ignites a wider conflict between Russia and the West. It is one thing for Russia to bully Ukraine or exploit and manipulate the Belarussians and Moldovans. But the Baltic States are NATO members, and a Russian attack against them would trigger Article 5 of the North Atlantic Treaty, obligating America and its Western European allies to assist.

THE CAUCASUS

The Caucasus region, where a towering mountain range divides Europe and Asia, has been a key success for Putin's designs. Putin has utilized his full playbook to get what he wants in the Caucasus, from energy politics and interethnic rivalries to hybrid war and "frozen" conflicts—that is, struggles in which armed hostilities have ended but no peace agreements or political resolutions have been reached, meaning that the situation can enflame again at any time. The Caucasus is strategically vital to Russia, as it serves not only as a gateway to the Middle East but also as a transit route for abundant Central Asian oil and gas on its way to thirsty European markets.[28] And Putin has more control there now than ever before. Wedged strategically between Turkey and Iran, Armenia is a member of Putin's Eurasian Economic Union and hosts Russian troops. It is essentially a Russian client state, dependent on Moscow for its economy, national security, and political stability. Oil- and gas-rich Azerbaijan is more wary of Putin, due in part to its simmering conflict with Armenia and close ties with Iran, but Moscow is pushing hard for Azerbaijan to join the Eurasian Economic Union as well.[29] Arastun Orujlu, head of the Center for East-West Studies, warns that "Azerbaijan is going to be next after Ukraine,"[30] while ordinary Azeris believe that "if the West doesn't do anything to stop Russia, they will be emboldened to take back Azerbaijan by force as they did a hundred years ago."[31] Putin already has a toehold here, as Russian-backed Armenian forces already control the Nagorno-Karabakh region in southeastern Azerbaijan. This flashpoint, dormant since the early nineties, could be reignited by Putin, just as Crimea was.

Georgia has put up more of a fight than its Armenian or Azeri neighbors. In 2007, newly elected Georgian president Mikheil Saakashvili was openly defiant of Putin and vowed to plot a new course forward out of Georgia's Soviet past, flirting with NATO and even EU membership. In 2008, Putin invaded, seized, and eventually annexed Abkhazia and South Ossetia, two ethnically (and religiously) distinct regions in Georgia. (Abkhazians are Sunni Muslim, and Ossetians are religiously mixed but mostly Christian, like other Georgians.) Even after the war ended, Putin continued a propaganda and economic campaign against Georgia, and against Saakashvili personally. Today, less than a decade after Moscow invaded Georgia, the country is moving closer to Russia and away from the West.[32] Saakashvili has been replaced by politicians friendlier to Russia.

Putin has been unambiguous about what the future in the Caucasus holds: "As for the Trans-Caucasus region, Russia will never leave this region. On the contrary, we will make our place here even stronger."[33] Indeed, in the region, Putin has things going his way: Armenia has acquiesced, Azerbaijan sees few alternatives, and Georgia is drifting back into Russia's orbit.

SCANDINAVIA, FINLAND, AND THE ARCTIC

Putin has two key objectives in Scandinavia: cowing the countries into accepting Russian regional dominance and securing valuable Arctic energy resources and shipping lanes. Putin knows he will never absorb Sweden or Denmark into the Eurasian Economic Union or any of his other thinly veiled imperial projects. Rather, his goal is to convince them to sit on the sidelines while he makes his move on the nearby Baltic States, and as he stakes aggressive Russian claims to the oil-rich Arctic seabed, where as much as 20 percent of the world's undiscovered oil lies.[34] The Swedes and Finns, though not NATO members, are armed to the teeth, and Putin would rather not challenge them head on. Instead, he has developed a set of intimidation tactics designed to demonstrate just how vulnerable Scandinavia is to Russian attack. These have included numerous violations of national airspace by Russian fighters and bombers on a scale not seen since the end of the Cold War. In one incident, a Russian jet fired a flare at a Swedish fighter, an unsubtle reminder that it could just as easily be a missile next time.[35] There have even been sightings of what many suspect are Russian minisubmarines off the Swedish coast, just miles from Stockholm, though the Swedish navy denies that the Russians can sneak up on them so easily.[36]

So long as the Scandinavians live in fear of a sudden Russian attack, they will be unwilling to intervene if Putin attacks the Baltics, and half-hearted in their competition with Russia for lucrative Arctic drilling rights. Putin has even gone as far as to plant a titanium Russian flag on the North Pole seabed, staking a claim to billions of dollars of oil and gas.[37] And while Green-minded Scandinavians worry about climate change, Putin eagerly awaits melting Arctic ice caps that will open up new shipping lanes on Russia's northern coast, providing a speedier route to Asia for European exports as well as access to Russia's vast (and dubious) Arctic territory claims.[38] If he can neutralize Scandinavia and Finland with his over-the-top scare tactics, Putin will open the door to Russian domination of the Arctic and increase his odds in the Baltics. If Russia encounters resistance—especially from the non-NATO Finns and Swedes, who would have to fight on their own—Putin may very well go beyond the use of mere flybys and minisubs.

THE BALKANS

Russia has had interests in the Balkans for centuries, and deep religious, linguistic, and cultural connections will always exist between Russia and the countries of the Balkan Peninsula. But Putin's interest in the Balkans is not academic or benign; the Balkan countries are Europe's weakest flank, beset by shoddy economies, corrupt politics, and a legacy of ethnic conflict. The EU and NATO have worked hard to achieve progress in the Balkans, expanding their membership and the promise of a European future to much of the region.[39] Now, Putin is working to undo all that progress. Leveraging long-standing Russian ties to the Balkans, Putin is attempting to turn countries such as Greece, Bulgaria, Macedonia, and Serbia into Russian allies within Europe. If he succeeds, as he appears to be doing, he will have snuck a Trojan horse into NATO itself and compromised the EU's consensus-based decision-making process.

Plainly dissatisfied with European institutions and teetering on the brink of economic ruin, Greece is the most vulnerable of the Balkan states. Putin has been quick to position Russia as Greece's last true friend, hosting Greek prime minister Alexis Tsipras in Moscow and allowing rumors to circulate that Russia would bail out Greece's economy if the EU refused to.[40] The Greeks, understandably starved for positive reinforcement from abroad, like what they are hearing from Moscow.

Bulgarians, meanwhile, are less enthused about the interest Putin has taken in their country, but a political system dogged by corruption and an oligarch-run economy provide precisely the sort of environment Putin can exploit.[41] Macedonia and Serbia are less integrated into the European system and have strong nationalist movements that view Russia as a traditional ally and natural protector.[42] Putin has high hopes that he can convert these relationships into lasting political influence that secures Russian interests in the heart of the Balkans and guarantees him a say in all European discussions.

CENTRAL EUROPE

Putin's strategy for Central Europe is focused on exploiting institutional weaknesses in former communist states, such as Hungary and Slovakia, while neutralizing wealthier and more powerful countries, such as Germany and Austria. Hungary's president, Viktor Orbán, who has vowed to create an "illiberal state"[43] and openly repudiates the European and Western values at the center of the European Union, has become Putin's closest ally in Europe and a dangerous threat to the future of the EU.[44] Slovakia's economy is dominated by oligarchs who do considerable business with Russia, making the country a prime target for Putin's intrigues.[45] Slovak politicians have little desire to become Russian puppets, but they're wary of alienating a vital trading partner.[46] Putin has taken advantage of Slovakia's hesitancy to rail against EU sanctions on trade with Russia, where Slovakia or Hungary are both capable of ending the EU's consensus-based sanctions. It would be a political coup for Putin if they did so.

The Germans may be more wary of Russia than any other country in the world, having fought two devastating wars against Russia in the past century. As such, Putin's goal is not necessarily to encourage a close relationship between Germany and Russia, though he will take anything he can get, but rather to rupture the close relationship that Germany has with the United States. By encouraging far-left and far-right strains of anti-American politics and rhetoric in Germany, Putin hopes to drive the two countries far enough apart that NATO becomes functionally inoperable and America's military presence in Europe is compromised. The Germans continue to depend heavily on Russian energy to power their economy,[47] which in turn drives the European economy. Putin hopes to set up a choice whereby Germany pursues its economic relationship with Russia over its political relationship with America. If Putin succeeds, he will be that much closer to "Finlandizing" the European continent and ending the transatlantic relationship.

WESTERN EUROPE

Putin sponsors a range of insurgent political organizations in Western Europe—extremists, nationalists, separatists, and anti-Western and anti-American groups—in order to promote anti-EU policies and disrupt the ability of Western European leaders to formulate a cohesive response to Russian aggression further east. In Britain, the UK Independence Party, or UKIP, received 13 percent of the vote in the 2015 elections[48] despite openly endorsing Putin's illegal invasion and annexation of Crimea,[49] and subsequently championed the Brexit vote to leave the EU. France, Britain, Spain, Italy, and Belgium all have populist political parties that are "committed" to Putin.[50] The right-wing National Front party in France has been loaned tens of millions of euros by a Kremlin-connected bank, and Putin has hosted the National Front's leader, Marine Le Pen, in Moscow.[51] A January 2015 poll finds that between 29 and 31 percent of French voters would support Le Pen if she runs for president in 2017, putting her ahead of all other contenders.[52] Radical pro-Putin parties are poised to grow in popularity in Europe as economic woes, dissatisfaction with immigration policy, and frustration with the status quo discredits mainstream political parties on both the left and right.

For a glimpse of the future of Western European politics, just look at Greece. The country's far-left SYRIZA party and neofascist Golden Dawn party disagree on just about everything—but they both love Putin.[53] What Putin hopes to offer the voters of Western Europe is just that: a choice on everything except whether to stand up to Russia and defend their own own values. He figures that if core European states such as France and Britain elect governments that include Putin loyalists, NATO will be as good as dead. The thinking is that a Le Pen government that is pro-Putin would never send its troops to protect Estonia from a Russian invasion or endorse another round of sanctions on Russian-backed separatists. Pro-Putin Western European governments would also roll back efforts to reduce reliance on Russian energy and happily send their euros and pounds east to fill the Kremlin's coffers. Putin, of course, will be generous enough not to turn off the gas during cold European winters, so long as his customers keep playing by his rules.

It follows that Western Europe's pro-Putin politicians would also undermine their nations' foundational relationship with America, closing military bases and ending long-standing cooperative defense arrangements. We may even see a repeat of France's Cold War–era decision to decline participation in mutual defense arrangements with America. If that were the case, how could the United States trust pro-Putin politicians on basic matters of political decency and respect for human rights? It is one thing when politicians hold their noses for the sake of national commercial benefit, as many countries do with China. But when politicians throw in their lot with Putin, whose chief export has been war and bloodshed, they put at stake their very existence as liberal democracies, to say nothing of forfeiting any claim to a moral high ground. Simply put, Putin's meddling in Western Europe poses a threat to the future of the Western alliance—and with it, the future of Western civilization.

THE MIDDLE EAST

Putin has many reasons to be interested in the Middle East, including global oil supplies and Russia's lucrative arms sales in the region. But Putin's overriding strategic priority in the Middle East concerns Iran, the world's largest Shi'a Muslim nation. Not that Putin has any special love for Iran or its particular brand of Shi'a theocracy. What Iran represents is

the gravest threat to American interests in the Middle East and the ability
to shatter America's regional alliance system. Moreover, Iran stands as a
counterweight to Turkey, and has the power to destabilize the Caucasus
region, where Shi'a Muslims in Azerbaijan and southern Russia look to
Tehran for religious, cultural, and even political leadership. For these reasons, Putin supplies Iran with arms, nuclear technology, and diplomatic
support that continue to be a decisive factor in the country's emergence
as a regional power.

Russia's direct support for Bashar al-Assad in Syria has been conducted in clear collaboration with Iran, and Iranian military advisors on
the ground direct Syrian troops armed by Putin. Today, Iran is in effective
control of coastal Syria, Lebanon, the Shi'a regions of Iraq, and areas of
Yemen ruled by Tehran-backed ethnic Houthi rebels. A member of Iran's
parliament has declared that the country now controls four Arab capitals:
Baghdad, Damascus, Beirut, and Sana'a.[54]

Understandably, America's Arab allies are alarmed by Iran's rise,
which has deeply upset the balance of power in the Middle East. Egypt
and Saudi Arabia, two powerful Arab nations and natural rivals with
Iran, are determined to reassert their influence and roll back Iranian
gains. But they aren't turning to America for help. Instead, they're running straight into Putin's arms. The Saudi royal family, who have become
"disillusioned with President Obama and his policies in the region,"
recently dispatched Deputy Crown Prince and Minister of Defense
Mohammed bin Salman to Moscow to negotiate deals with Putin on "oil
cooperation, space cooperation, peaceful nuclear energy cooperation,
and nuclear technology sharing.[55] In addition, Egypt recently signed a
sweeping military cooperation agreement with Russia, and Cairo plans to
buy billions of dollars of arms from the Kremlin.[56] Egyptian and Russian
officers will train together, and their navies will hold joint exercises in the
Mediterranean.[57] Putin is working all sides of the conflict in the Middle
East, to the detriment of American security interests—and no one is bat-
ting an eye in Washington.

America's Middle Eastern allies can no longer rely on Washington for
material or diplomatic support. Instead, they're flocking to Putin for arms
and technology. Putin's alliance with Iran demonstrated the value of the
Kremlin's friendship, and is upending a regional order that has persisted
largely unchanged for decades. Iran is now on the verge of achieving

effective regional hegemony with Russian help, and the rest of the Middle East is scrambling to be on the right side of history: Putin's side.

In Iraq, meanwhile, any positive benefits that may have resulted from America's decade-plus war there now belong to Tehran. There is plenty of blame to go around for allowing the Middle East to slip into such chaos, and surely America's politicians of the last fifteen years must shoulder a considerable portion of it. But we cannot forget that Putin has worked tirelessly toward exactly what we are witnessing today: a rising Russia-backed Iran; a disintegrating American alliance system; and growing Russian influence in Arab countries. On all counts, Putin is getting what he wants.

CENTRAL ASIA

To many in the West, and especially in America, Central Asia is most familiar as the land of Borat and America's grinding Afghan quagmire. For most Russians, however, Central Asia is the land of the *Osterns*, massively popular Soviet-era movies inspired by America's Westerns but set on Central Asia's endless steppes and bone-dry deserts, with Turkic nomads filling in for Native American braves and clever Russian frontiersmen replacing stiff-spined sheriffs.[58] To Vladimir Putin, Central Asia is a land of opportunity, bursting with oil and natural gas begging for export and crisscrossed by well-worn Silk Road trade routes that cry out for high-speed freight trains and intercontinental superhighways. Russian control of Central Asia would hand over to Putin some of the world's largest natural gas fields, and thereby consolidate Russian control of an energy market vital to both European and booming East Asian economies.

So far, Kazakhstan and Kyrgyzstan have signed on to Putin's Eurasian Economic Union, with Tajikistan poised to follow suit. Uzbekistan and Turkmenistan are likely to acquiesce eventually as well. These countries may be among the poorest in the world, but their vast reserves of natural resources make them strategically priceless. Beyond oil and gas, they have coal, uranium, gold, iron ore, and manganese. Tajikistan and Kyrgyzstan, nestled up against the Tian Shan mountains just west of the Himalayas, have enormous stores of fresh water frozen in their glaciers. Soviet-era mismanagement means that the region remains underexplored, with major discoveries of resources worth billions of dollars having occurred within the last ten years. Putin is already working with the Chinese to build high-speed railways that will ship Central Asia's riches to the hungry economies of Asia.[59] Putin has built Russia into the power that it is today on the back of commodities extraction and energy exports. If Putin can consolidate control over Central Asia through political alliances and economic links, it will deepen his purse for military expenditures and secure the Kremlin's position astride strategic trade routes from Europe to Asia.

EAST AND SOUTH ASIA

By now, it's no secret that Putin has built a powerful alliance with China, as one of this book's coauthors describes in detail in *The Russia-China Axis: The New Cold War and America's Crisis of Leadership* (2014). China is a key market for Russian energy, and Chinese funds are also a major source of foreign direct investment in Russian infrastructure, especially in oil-rich Siberia. Chinese president Xi Jinping was Putin's guest of honor in Moscow during the 2015 Victory Day celebrations, where the two signed approximately $6 billion in infrastructure deals to knit the economies of the two countries closer together.[60] The relationship between Russia and China is mutually beneficial and pragmatic: Putin denounces American power and promotes a multipolar world, while China cheerily trades with all that approach it. In return for pulling the weight of China's strategic interests and playing the bad cop, Putin gets to ride shotgun on the Chinese economic bandwagon. Putin delivers China-funded infrastructure projects to his constituents, and the Chinese get improved access to the abundant natural resources of the Russian hinterland.

The formal vehicle for coordinating relations between China and Russia has been the Shanghai Cooperation Organization, which also has as members most of the Central Asian states. In July 2015, India and Pakistan announced plans to join the SCO as full members.[61] India, perennially on edge about the behavior of its traditional rival, Pakistan, and concerned over growing Chinese power, is also a major customer of Russian arms. As in the Middle East, Putin is happy to sell weapons to both sides of a conflict, so long as the checks don't bounce. A similar motivation applies to Putin's unseemly relationship with North Korea and its murderous Kim dynasty. In March 2015, Putin welcomed North Korea's Kim Jong-un to Moscow and pronounced a "year of friendship" between Russia and North Korea.[62] Putin's plan for Asia obviously doesn't discriminate against Stalinist dictatorships.

CONCLUSION

Vladimir Putin's master plan is designed to make the twenty-first century a Russian century. His vision reaches from the United Kingdom to the United Arab Emirates, from Korea to Kyrgyzstan. He is unleashing hybrid warfare against Russia's immediate neighbors in Ukraine, Belarus, and the Baltics, and has fired warning shots at the Scandinavians and the Finns. Putin backs pro-Russian populist political parties in Central and Western Europe, thereby disrupting continental politics and threatening to undermine NATO and the EU. In the Middle East, Putin is backing Iran's bid for regional power, but he also has no problem selling arms to disillusioned American allies. Putin is integrating Central Asia into a Russia-centric political and economic system, pursuing an ever-deeper strategic partnership with China, and backing the North Korean regime. Taken together, this amounts to a comprehensive strategy to break apart the world order that has governed the last twenty-plus years of global affairs, which will be much to the benefit of Russia's regional and global positioning. And so far, it's working.

CHAPTER 3

How NATO Is Failing Itself, Europe, and America

America's commitment to collective defense under Article 5 of NATO is a sacred obligation in our view—a sacred obligation not just for now, but for all time.

—VICE PRESIDENT JOE BIDEN[1]

The Russians will keep probing until they meet resistance. If we don't stand up to small provocations, eventually they will reach Article 5.

—SENIOR EUROPEAN DIPLOMAT[2]

There is a high probability that [Mr. Putin] will intervene in the Baltics to test NATO's Article 5.

—FORMER NATO SECRETARY GENERAL ANDERS FOGH RASMUSSEN[3]

The core mission of the North Atlantic Treaty Organization had always been to defend Europe from Russian aggression. When the Soviet Union collapsed, it appeared that this mission had been a success, and that Russia would no longer pose a military threat to Europe. Indeed, in the two decades since the end of the Cold War, NATO has invented new missions for itself, from attempting to mitigate the violent breakup of Yugoslavia in the 1990s to its more recent operations in Afghanistan and Libya. But a resurgent Russia, invading its neighbors and threatening the security of NATO members, means that NATO must return to its roots: deterring and defending against Russian aggression. Unfortunately, NATO, in part because its members are more preoccupied with Islamic terrorism, has failed to address the Russian threat and has put the safety of Europe and the United States in jeopardy as a result.

It is clear that Russia poses a direct threat to NATO countries. The cross-border raid in Estonia may be the only time, at least that we know of, that Russian ground troops entered NATO ground territory, but Russian violations of NATO airspace are far more frequent and just as alarming. In 2014 alone, NATO members scrambled jets 442 times in response to Russian activity. Russian fighters and bombers have flown into Norwegian and Polish airspace,[4] been intercepted over the English Channel,[5] and were caught forty miles off the coast of California on the Fourth of July.[6] These threats are not idle: Russian bombers can carry nuclear weapons capable of killing hundreds of thousands with a single strike. When Putin directs these planes into Western skies, he sends a clear message: "I can get to you, and hurt you, whenever and wherever I want." It is NATO's job to prove otherwise. But so far, Russia has been given no reason to discontinue these sorties.

During a private meeting in August 2015, a senior European diplomat who oversees his country's policy on Russia and Eastern Europe put it simply: "The Russians are back on stage, and they are here to stay." When we pressed him on what has changed in Russia's stance in the last few years, he contended, "After the end of the Cold War, there was an abnormal twenty year period when the Russians did not have the resources or capabilities to achieve their desired level of influence in Europe and the world."[7] That period has come to an end. Russia's renewed capabilities are plainly evident every day that Russian arms flow to separatists in eastern Ukraine, Russian jets crisscross Western airspace, or Russian troops kidnap NATO military officers. What is not evident is NATO's ability to respond effectively to these actions and guarantee the security of its member states.

Alarmingly, NATO has become so impotent that some member states are taking steps to build defense and security relationships outside of the alliance. In Northern Europe, NATO members Denmark, Iceland, and Norway are meeting and directly coordinating security policy with non-members Sweden and Finland.[8] These new mutual-defense arrangements are directly driven by Russian aggression in the Arctic and Scandinavia.[9] Latvia and Lithuania, two countries toward which Putin has shown considerable hostility, are set to begin joint weapons acquisitions in order to encourage "development of joint military capacities," according to Lithuanian president Dalia Grybauskaite and Latvian president

Raimonds Vējonis.[10] Poland and Estonia, two countries with much to fear from Russia, may also join the arrangement. Lithuanian defense minister Juozas Olekas has made it clear that "regional defense cooperation of the Baltic states is more critical than ever, [and] our security assurance is our solidarity."[11]

The Western powers show a clear lack of willpower when it comes to confronting Putin. But there is also the looming possibility that NATO may not be able to do enough to stop Russia's naked military adventurism even if it tried. Putin's invasion of Ukraine and his interference in other Eastern European states has put NATO's capabilities to the test, and they have been found wanting. In recent years, NATO has been more concerned with counterinsurgency operations in Afghanistan or cruise-missile strikes in Libya than the threat of conventional war with Russia. The American military, once the guardian of the free world and the bulwark against Soviet aggression, is now more prepared to take on ragtag terrorists than Russian tanks. Even if NATO politicians wake up to the military threat that Russia poses, it will take years to refocus its budgets, procurement, training, and strategic preparedness on Russia and to bring NATO militaries up to speed.

NATO'S ABDICATION

NATO has done little to deter Russia in Ukraine. President Obama infamously responded to Ukraine's request for aid against Russia with Meals Ready to Eat, or MREs, the preprepared food rations issued to US troops.[12] Ukraine had asked for arms, ammunition, and intelligence support. Instead they got chicken fajitas, and Putin ate Crimea for dinner. The Western European countries have scarcely been more helpful, fretting over the implications that providing military support to Ukraine might have on commercial and energy relationships between Moscow and Paris, Berlin, or Amsterdam. Put simply, Western Europeans have found it easier to ignore the war Russia has started in Ukraine than to confront the chilling reality of Russian territorial expansion in Europe. As a direct result of this inaction, more Ukrainians die, and Russia is emboldened to continue its conquest of Eastern Europe.

Not every NATO member has turned a blind eye to Ukraine's desperate need for military assistance. Lithuania has agreed to supply Ukraine with lethal military equipment.[13] Similarly, Poland has approved plans for a joint Polish-Lithuanian-Ukrainian brigade of 4,500 troops, further enhancing the ability of these militaries to cooperate and sending a clear signal to the Kremlin.[14] This is exactly the sort of confidence-building solidarity with Ukraine that the United States and major NATO powers should be showing. Instead, America, Canada, and the United Kingdom have sent "instructors" to help "train" Ukrainian troops.[15] Without the proper equipment and weapons necessary to counter Russian capabilities, no amount of training will give the Ukrainian military a fighting chance. The Obama administration has claimed that nonlethal aid to Ukraine has helped, but as Democratic senator Robert Menendez puts it, "Providing nonlethal equipment like night vision goggles is all well and good, but giving the Ukrainians the ability to see Russians coming but not the weapons to stop them is not the answer."[16]

Indeed, it is shameful that the United States, once heralded as the arsenal of democracy, has not provided Ukraine with the weapons it needs to defend itself. Defense Secretary Ash Carter has said that he is "very much inclined" to provide Ukraine with lethal aid, but Obama has yet to follow the advice of America's top defense official.[17] Ben Rhodes, Obama's deputy national security advisor, went so far as to say that "we don't think the answer to the crisis in Ukraine is simply to inject more weapons."[18] Perhaps Obama would do better to heed the advice of former chairman of the Joint Chiefs of Staff General Martin Dempsey, who thinks that "we should absolutely consider lethal aid and it ought to be in the context of NATO allies because Putin's ultimate objective is to fracture NATO."[19] A spokesman for former House speaker John Boehner was just as unequivocal, suggesting that "the Ukrainians are begging for help, and the Congress is begging the administration to provide the defensive lethal assistance we authorized in December. Our allies deserve better."[20]

We are witnessing a partial unraveling of the European security order, driven by America's abdication of its obligation to protect Europe and a failed rebalancing of responsibilities within NATO, both taking place during a period of overt Russian military aggression and territorial expansion. Whether this partial unraveling becomes a full-blown breakdown depends on whether Western leaders wake up and address the Russian threat. So far, the response has been anemic.

Part of the problem is that America cannot turn the tide against Russia on its own. NATO's European members, having failed to meet their defense spending obligations, seem helpless against a massive and constantly growing Russian military budget. Western Europe has been lulled into complacency by decades of peace, forgetting that the peace it has enjoyed was accomplished by trillions of dollars of American defense spending. More recently, its leaders have been blinded by political correctness. Diplomacy and political outreach are all well and good, but when it comes to protecting a country, there is no substitute for lots of troops, tanks, jets, missiles, guns, and other military equipment that might make an aggressor think twice. Western Europeans, insulated from an increasingly violent world by American defense guarantees, seem to have forgotten this truism. Putin has not. Russia's defense budget is shattering records, and its nuclear forces are expanding so rapidly that experts are warning of a new arms race.[21] America and Western Europe, by contrast, cut defense spending last year.[22]

NATO recommends that each member state spend 2 percent of its annual gross domestic product on defense.[23] This is a fair, commonsense arrangement that asks each country to contribute to common defense according to its means, even though what this involves, in real terms, is that large economies like the United States, the UK, and Germany shoulder most of the spending burden. Historically, America has far exceeded this 2 percent target, and despite defense cuts and sequestration, the United States is on track to spend 3.6 percent of GDP on defense in 2015. And only four other NATO states even will spend enough to meet the 2 percent target: Greece, Poland, the UK, and Estonia.[24] Some countries, including Italy, Belgium, and Spain, are only spending half of what they should be.[25] Even worse, countries like France and Germany, already well below the 2 percent target, are cutting their defense budgets.[26] Because these are two of the largest economies in NATO, these cuts will have a real impact on the ability of NATO to fund its operations and respond to Russian aggression. But Berlin and Paris are, apparently, unconcerned with the military consequences of these budget cuts.

Since Western European countries are refusing to do their fair share to pay for NATO defense spending, Eastern European states have had to increase their defense budgets drastically. Lithuania is boosting defense spending by 29.8 percent, Poland by 21.7 percent, and Latvia by 13.4 percent.[27] NATO is meant to be about mutual defense, and that means its member states have obligations to one another, including the obligation to kick in part of what it costs to defend the whole organization. The leaders of Western European countries appear to have made a determination that since they are not yet under direct threat from the Russian military, they will not pay for the defense of Eastern Europeans, for whom that threat is very real. This approach will lead to the collapse of NATO as we know it. NATO defense spending simply must reflect an equal obligation from all its members, or else the organization and its security guarantees will become a sham, along with its actual military capacity.

THE GROWING IMBALANCE OF POWER

While Western Europeans are busy slashing budgets, the Russians are spending more than ever: $81 billion in 2015 alone[28]—a 25.6 percent increase from 2014.[29] This massive budgetary increase has led to major improvements in Russian military capabilities. As Igor Sutyagin of the Royal United Services Institute notes, "While uniformed manpower has declined in every Western nation since 2011, the number of Russian personnel increased by 25 percent to 850,000 between 2011 and mid-2014."[30] Global Firepower, which aggregates publically available information on the world's military forces, ranks Russia second on its military power index, just behind the United States.[31] And while American military power is spread across the world, and must be ready to deal with crises from the Middle East to East Asia to Africa, Putin is able to concentrate his military power on core strategic goals, namely Europe. Classified exercises conducted by the Pentagon over the summer of 2015 revealed severe shortcomings in America's ability to confront the Russian military. As one defense official put it, "Could we probably beat the Russians today [in a sustained battle]? Sure, but it would take everything we had."[32] That assessment ought to raise alarms in Washington and in every European capital.

Our weakness in Europe is not some unhappy accident. America, sidetracked by the wars in Iraq and Afghanistan and distracted by the halfhearted "pivot to Asia," has let its presence and capabilities in Europe decline considerably. Underfunding and understaffing have seriously compromised key portions of the American military, with only 76 percent of army forces and 69 percent of the marines ready for the field, according to the Heritage Foundation's "Index of U.S. Military Strength."[33] Michèle Flournoy, Obama's former undersecretary of defense for policy, enumerates the mounting challenges facing America's military: "Budget cuts and sequestration are undermining the department's ability to maintain a robust and ready force, to retain the best and brightest people, and to invest in the capabilities that are going to be necessary to keep our technological edge and our military superiority in a more challenging future."[34]

Compounding these systemic problems is the Obama administration's unfathomable decision to close European bases and reduce the number of American troops stationed in Europe. The administration plans to close fifteen bases across Europe, including a strategic air base north of London that houses tanker, reconnaissance, and special operations aircraft.[35] At a time when the British are being buzzed by Russian bombers for the first time since the Cold War,[36] America has decided to reduce its military personnel stationed in the United Kingdom by 3,200 people.[37] America's only combat aviation brigade stationed in Europe, the Twelfth CAB, based out of Katterbach Kaserne in Germany, will be reduced from 150 aircraft to a mere 90.[38] This includes moving twenty-four Apache attack helicopters, key assets for turning back Russian tanks, from Germany to Alaska.[39] We, the authors, are firmly in favor of a robust American presence in the Arctic, but not at the cost of leaving Europe defenseless. These self-inflicted mistakes hand effortless victories to the Kremlin and make Putin more likely to use military force where he believes it is superior to American and NATO capabilities.

America's naval power has also dropped to historic lows, endangering our interests around the world and leaving us especially vulnerable to growing Russian naval strength. Today, the United States Navy has 273 ships, the fewest since 1916.[40] This unacceptably low number has been condemned by Republicans and Democrats alike. In 2014, a bipartisan panel recommended that the navy increase its fleet by at least fifty ships, if not more, to meet America's strategic needs.[41] So far, the Obama administration has dismissed legitimate concerns about the navy's strength as warmongering and needless alarmism. But as Jim Talent notes, "In total, we have at least two former Secretaries of Defense, the current Secretary of the navy, the former Chief of Naval Operations, and a unanimous bipartisan panel of defense experts all stating for the record that the navy is far too small."[42] Yet the consensus from defense experts and military leadership has not been enough to spur action from the administration. America's navy continues its decline.

While the American navy deteriorates, Russia's navy has grown steadily. A recently released Russian naval doctrine declares Moscow's intention to "guarantee a permanent naval presence in the Mediterranean and boost its strength in the Atlantic and Arctic."[43] The document specifically references NATO's "unacceptable plans to move military infrastructure towards the Russian Federation's borders and attempts to assume global functions"[44] as the reasons for Russian naval expansion, and Russian deputy prime minister Dmitry Rogozin openly states that the new naval doctrine is intended to address "changes in the international political situation and the objective strengthening of Russia as a great naval power."[45] Rogozin adds that "the main emphasis is in two directions—the Arctic and Atlantic."[46] Indeed, Russia's strength in the Arctic is unparalleled. In early 2015, the Russian military conducted an Arctic military exercise with eighty thousand troops, 220 aircraft, forty-one ships, and fifteen submarines that served as a clear signal to Arctic NATO allies Canada, Iceland, Denmark, and Norway.[47] Indeed, America even lacks the necessary vessels to keep up with Russia in frozen Arctic waters, with only two operational icebreakers—the ships that smash up sea ice and allow other vessels to pass—to Russia's forty.[48] The day may soon come when America is unable to guarantee safe passage for NATO-flagged ships in the Arctic, Atlantic, or Mediterranean.

Russia's conventional military forces are formidable, but the nuclear arsenal at Putin's disposal is even more imposing. Putin has announced plans to build forty new intercontinental ballistic missiles, adding to Russia's existing stockpile of approximately 4,500 nuclear warheads.[49] Russian deputy defense minister Anatoly Antonov tried to blame this nuclear buildup on the West, claiming that "the feeling is that our colleagues from NATO countries are pushing us into an arms race."[50] This is bald-faced propaganda. NATO secretary general Jens Stoltenberg decried Russia's "nuclear sabre-rattling" to be "unjustified . . . destabilising and . . . dangerous."[51] Russian officials have already suggested that they will put nuclear weapons in the territory of illegally annexed

Crimea, effectively daring the West to risk a confrontation if it tries to restore Crimea to Ukrainian sovereignty.[52] As a Center for Strategic and International Studies report explains, "The United States is not well postured for this type of nuclear employment scenario" and "needs to develop and deploy more employable nuclear weapons, ones that enable the United States to respond directly and proportionately to an adversary's employment of a nuclear weapon."[53] As we noted in the introduction, a recent American intelligence assessment suggests that Russia plans to double the number of strategic warheads on its missiles.[54] NATO remains vulnerable to Russian nuclear attack.

A FAILURE OF LEADERSHIP

These military shortcomings are daunting, and one is inclined to wonder why NATO's failure to address the Russian threat has been so complete. To be sure, much of the blame lies with feckless Western leaders, cowardly accommodation of Russia's outrageous behavior, and flat-out denial of the fact that millions of Europeans are living under the daily threat of Russian aggression. But there is more at play in NATO's inability to respond to Putin's aggression. Russian diplomatic machinations within NATO, and Moscow's penetration of certain NATO member states, have called into question the ability of NATO's consensus-based decision-making process to yield decisive policy and set clear limits on Russian conduct. In short, NATO is failing because some compromised member states *actually want it to fail.*

It is important to be clear on this point. We do not suspect the militaries of NATO allies are double dealing, nor are we suggesting some wide-ranging McCarthyite conspiracy to undermine NATO from within. The simple truth is that some NATO members that were hostile to the Soviet Union are not necessarily as hostile toward Putin's Russia, and indeed some have friendlier relationships with Moscow than they do with Washington, London, or Brussels. Greece and Hungary are at the top of this list, with both having been denounced as a "Trojan horse" for Putin within NATO.[55]

There is also cause for concern over whether NATO members Bulgaria, Slovakia, and Turkey might take a more explicitly pro-Putin stance. We therefore need to be realistic about how far these countries are willing to go when it comes to taking direct action to counter Russian aggression. Since NATO makes all decisions based on consensus, if any one country winds up beholden to the Kremlin—either through coercion, elite corruption, or some perverse miscalculation about its own self-interest—it would fully compromise NATO's ability to respond effectively to Russia.

This is no easy problem to solve. Putin is using every tool at his disposal to win over populists and Euro-skeptics in NATO states, on both the left and the right.[56] Many factors beyond the direct control of Western leaders—from economic stagnation, to Orthodox Christianity, to old ties between Moscow and Europe's Left—are being exploited by the Kremlin to build political alliances in Europe. But when NATO fails to perform its core functions, like protecting the territorial integrity of member states or meeting defense spending targets, it makes the Kremlin's case more persuasive and undercuts the diligent work of advocates for increased NATO cooperation. Putin would like nothing more than for current trends to continue, and for NATO to make clumsy excuses for its ineptitude, while member states threatened by Russia make independent arrangements for their own security. That, Putin knows, is the beginning of the end of the NATO alliance.

Indeed, Putin and his Rasputins in the Kremlin don't believe that NATO's guarantees to its members are reliable. A senior non-NATO European diplomat indicated in a private interview that it is "unclear how seriously the Russians take NATO's Article 5 commitment to the Baltic States," referencing the article of the North Atlantic Treaty that would obligate a collective response by NATO to an attack on any of its member states.[57] The Kremlin has gotten away with starting wars before, so why should the Baltic States be different? "Aren't they like Georgia or Ukraine?" the European diplomat asked.[58] It is tempting to dismiss this concern: the Baltics are full NATO member states with the implied protection of every Western power, including America. But as the Kremlin sees it, there is doubt as to whether Washington or London will really send young people from Boston or Bristol to fight and die for Estonia.

It doesn't help that Putin has called Obama's bluff on a "guarantee" before. Obama's failure to enforce his infamous "red line" on chemical weapons in Syria discredited him in the eyes of the world. It suggested to America's allies that we don't keep our promises and suggested to our enemies that testing our rhetorical commitments with military assertiveness pays off. If a Putin-backed Assad can walk all over Obama in Syria, then why can't Putin himself do the same in Ukraine, or the Baltics, or anywhere else he chooses, Article 5 notwithstanding? Indeed, the same non-NATO diplomat confirmed that his sources in the Kremlin identified Obama's failure to enforce the red line in Syria as a turning point in the Russian calculus over using military force in Ukraine.

Interviews that we conducted in Estonia's capital of Tallinn during August 2015 uncovered widespread skepticism that NATO would ride to the country's rescue in the event of a Russian invasion. Indeed, Estonians have all but written off the Western Europeans, and they know that help from Poland or Lithuania wouldn't stop Russia. The fate of their country rests with American willpower and commitment to Europe—in other words, our willingness to enforce Article 5. But the defense guarantee has gone from a treaty-based obligation—basically a certainty—to a policy choice subject to decision in Washington. This must change, and it must be made crystal clear to both our NATO allies and Putin that Article 5 is not a dead letter but a real consequence for military aggression against *any* NATO country.

Why should America risk a devastating war with Russia over Estonia? some will ask. The answer is that making and keeping clear promises to retaliate is the most likely way to deter and *avoid* any new Russian aggression. Russia will not attack Estonia, or any other NATO country, if it knows that America will respond. If America continues to vacillate on its commitment to Article 5, and the Kremlin decides an attack is worth the risk, then we may well wind up with a war between NATO and Russia.

We have made it clear just how uncertain the outcome of a direct military confrontation between NATO and Russia in Europe would be. Russia has gained considerable ground on NATO militaries, reversing two decades of military decline since the collapse of the Soviet Union. NATO military spending is slowing, with American military capabilities dangerously out of sync with current realities and focused on threats other than Russia—most prominently counterterror and counterinsurgency operations. So it is hard to say who would win in a limited or even a more expansive conflict in Europe.

Our mission, and NATO's mission, must be never to find out if NATO militaries, in their current weakened positions, would lose a war to Russia. Increasing military budgets across all NATO states, rebuilding America's military footprint in Europe, and reversing the decline of American military capabilities are all urgent necessities for discouraging Russian military adventurism. A strong and vocal commitment to Article 5 is the only way to convince Putin that any attack on any NATO member would not be worth the cost. NATO must guarantee, and Putin must fully understand, that aggression against a NATO member will have devastating military consequences for Russia—including but not limited to retaliatory strikes on Russian forces, as well as naval blockades against every Russian port. This is not warmongering, and it is not an overreaction. The best way to keep America and Europe safe, and to prevent Putin from starting even more wars, is to let him know in the simplest, most straightforward terms exactly what we would do to Russia if he decides to test the waters.

THE STAKES

War between Russia and America, the stuff of nightmares since the dawn of the atomic age, is closer to reality now than at any point since the end of the Cold War. Putin bears primary responsibility for this, and the blood of thousands is already on his hands. But NATO was supposed to guard against Russian aggression through a combination of coercive diplomacy and insurmountable military strength. It has failed on both counts, and Putin has gleefully taken advantage of those failures. Western Europe has failed to meet its NATO obligation to provide for the common defense, and America has staggered under the burden of protecting all of Europe on its own. Eastern Europeans, particularly the Baltic States, have ramped up their own defense efforts in a desperate attempt to compensate. But Russia's massive military and ballooning defense budget dwarfs what a country such as Poland or Lithuania can do on its own. Without a clear signal from Washington that America will step in to defend every NATO state, the Russians continue to plot their next moves, while countries unfortunate enough to sit in their sights have little choice but to tremble and wait.

Putin regularly tests the waters with provocations and border or airspace violations. Time and again, he lets NATO countries know that he can reach them with the long arm of Russian bombers, or with the boots of special operations forces, or with submarines that slip silently into their harbors—and NATO fails to respond. These provocations are meant as a less-than-subtle prelude to the real thing: a strategic strike from above, first-echelon forces smashing across a border, or a nuclear-tipped cruise missile coming from the sea. Russian forces have been caught playing this deadly game in the Arctic, the Black and Baltic seas, the Estonian forests, over the English Channel, and off of America's Pacific coast. If there is no pushback from NATO, the Kremlin will keep pushing—all the way to Article 5.

There are two possible outcomes if the Russians get that far: war between NATO and Russia, or capitulation by the West and the collapse of the NATO alliance. The stakes couldn't be higher.

Despite the threat of such consequences, NATO and its member states continue to fail to address the Russian threat, endangering the lives of every European and American, and the millions of others who would inevitably be drawn into a military confrontation. NATO must revive its central mission and founding purpose: to stop Russian aggression and defend human rights, liberal democracy, and free markets in Europe. Since NATO's incompetence has allowed Russia to make territorial gains in Ukraine and political gains elsewhere, its mission must also include rolling back Putin's successful conquest of Crimea and the Donbas, and dismantling the Kremlin's network of influence in Europe.

This is what NATO was built for. The end of the Cold War caused a full-blown identity crisis within the alliance, leading to its involvement in the Balkans, Afghanistan, and Libya. The wisdom of NATO's role in these conflicts is rightly the subject of keen debate, but the consequences are clear: NATO is critically underprepared to fulfill its core purpose of defending Europe from Russian military aggression, at precisely the moment when Russia has begun to wage wars of conquest against its neighbors.

As it stands, NATO is a failure, both in Europe and in America. Our militaries are dilapidated and shrinking and our response to the Russian invasion of Ukraine has been pathetic. While NATO stumbles, Russia has devised an entirely new way to wage war—one that we are completely unprepared to counter. NATO must change now—and America must lead the charge.

CHAPTER 4

The New Warfare

Russia's Arsenal of Aggression

Could we probably beat the Russians today [in a sustained battle]?
Sure, but it would take everything we had. What we are saying is
that we are not as ready as we want to be.

—AMERICAN DEFENSE OFFICIAL[1]

Putin's larger goal appears to be to change the nature of the international system, particularly with respect to Europe. If he's successful it
will have exposed the hollowness of the Western model approach
to international affairs.

—KIM R. HOLMES, *FOREIGN POLICY*[2]

"If I wanted, in two days I could have Russian troops not only in Kiev,
but also in Riga, Vilnius, Tallinn, Warsaw and Bucharest," Vladimir
Putin said in September 2014, according to Ukrainian president
Petro Poroshenko.[3] The threat shocked European observers, but not those
who understand the way Putin thinks—those who have been paying
attention over the last half-decade or so, as the Russian leader has taken
one aggressive step after another in Eastern Europe, continually escalating tensions and testing the resolve of NATO, the European Union, and
the United States.

"In 2014 alone," writes Stephen J. Blank, a longtime Soviet and
Russian Federation expert, "Moscow repeatedly threatened the Baltic
and Nordic states and civilian airliners, heightened intelligence penetration, deployed unprecedented military forces against those states,
intensified overflights and submarine reconnaissance, mobilized nuclear
forces and threats, deployed nuclear-capable forces in Kaliningrad,

menaced Moldova, and openly violated the Intermediate-Range Nuclear Forces Treaty of 1987."[4]

Indeed, as that litany indicates, Putin isn't just sitting around waiting for the NATO alliance to collapse so that Russia can strengthen its hand in Eastern and Western Europe. Russia is actively shaping events that are destabilizing NATO at the same time as they put Moscow on stronger footing in any potential future conflict. Over the last half-decade especially, Putin has developed a range of tools that facilitate and help achieve his goals. Call it Russia's arsenal of aggression—one for which the West has yet to formulate an effective response.

Russia is developing terrifying new weapons and military capabilities and deploying them against targeted countries, including Ukraine and the Baltics. Moscow has developed new tanks, fighter planes, and nuclear weapons that experts agree are at least as good, and quite often better, than American or NATO equipment. The Russian military, once dilapidated and discouraged after the fall of the Soviet Union, has come roaring back as a modern, well-equipped, and highly skilled fighting force that is a match for any Western army, navy, or air force. Marine Corps general Joseph Dunford, the chairman of the Joint Chiefs of Staff and the highest-ranking American military officer, says that "Russia presents the greatest threat to our national security" and "could pose an existential threat to the United States."[5] Putin's willingness to flaunt his newly empowered military has dragged NATO to the brink of all-out war in Europe.

But Putin's arsenal includes more than the traditional array of military hardware. By employing hybrid warfare, which combines conventional military forces with unconventional forces, information warfare, subterfuge, and propaganda, Russia has pioneered a new and dangerously effective method of conquest—as the world saw when Russia annexed Crimea. And Russia is waging aggressive economic combat against the West and any country it deems too friendly to the West—especially those, like the Baltic nations or other nearby neighbors, that are trying to break out from under Moscow's political and economic dominance. Worst of all, the United States and NATO, which have spent more than a decade fighting counterinsurgencies and terrorists, so far have lacked the vision and resolve to neutralize Russia's new weapons, counter Putin's asymmetrical warfare, or mitigate the impact of Russia's hardball economics.

What Putin is waging can be thought of as war without war—with all the means and goals of warfare but none of the costs and the traditional forms of battle. So long as the West remains acquiescent, confused, and timid, he will continue to notch victory after victory.

PUTIN'S MILITARY BUILDUP

"We should not tempt anybody with our weakness," Putin wrote in 2012.[6] In his long years in power in Russia, that principle has governed his actions—and his spending.

In 2015, the Russian defense budget reached a record high of $81 billion ($84 billion by some estimates), a $20 billion increase from 2014.[7] Only the United States and China spend more on defense; since first taking the helm of Russian leadership in 2000, Putin has boosted defense spending, in ruble terms, twenty-fold.[8] Russian defense spending is 4.5 percent of GDP, compared with 3.5 percent—and falling—for the United States.[9]

A good portion of Russian defense spending is also being conducted off-budget. "Putin is allocating unprecedented amounts of secret funds to accelerate Russia's largest military buildup since the Cold War," Bloomberg writes. "The part of the federal budget that is so-called black—authorized but not itemized—has doubled since 2010 to 21 percent and now totals 3.2 trillion rubles ($60 billion)."[10]

Russia has big defense plans for the future, despite its economic struggles and the burden of Western economic sanctions for its actions in Ukraine. Some analysts see military spending as Putin's economic-development plan. Whatever the motivations, the particulars are sobering.

Over the next decade, Putin plans to acquire and develop four hundred new intercontinental ballistic missiles (ICBMs); more than two thousand next-generation tanks; six hundred modernized combat aircraft; eight nuclear ballistic submarines; fifty warships; and "a whole new inventory of artillery, air defense systems, and about 17,000 new military vehicles," according to Fred Weir, a Moscow-based journalist and Russia specialist.[11] What Russia seeks, in the view of Stephen J. Blank, is nothing less than strategic and operational parity—if not even superiority—with the United States, in both conventional and nonconventional warfare, as well as the ability to "conduct operations in space, under the ocean, in the air, on the sea and the ground, and in cyberspace."[12]

A crucial element to the Putin defense buildup is manpower. Every Western nation has seen its troop sizes decrease over the last five years, but Russia increased its soldiers by 25 percent from 2011 to 2014, during which time it added 850,000 personnel—still short of the one-million target that Putin had set. Putin's goal by 2020 is to have one million combat-ready, active-duty troops, structured around easily deployable, mobile brigades, about 70 percent of whom would be equipped with next-generation weaponry and equipment.[13] He's ready to spend upward of $800 billion over the next decade to make this happen. The Russian manpower plans also include a crucial reserve component. Currently, Russia has 2.5 million active reservists.[14] In the years to come, Russia plans to train them intensively and regularly with the goal of having them ready at a moment's notice to take their place in a unit and fight.[15]

In several cases, the Russians are developing new weaponry that simply out-strips current American capabilities.

One of the most disturbing aspects of Putin's defense buildup is the tank superiority he seems to be developing. In 2015, at its annual Victory Day Parade in May commemorating Russian triumph in World War II, the military unveiled "possibly the most ambitious ground vehicle program since the end of the Cold War":[16] the T-14 Armata battle tank, which employs a radical, new design and is considered by some analysts to be Russia's "secret weapon." The Armata is said to boast superior firepower and greater speed and maneuverability, and to be more durable against attacks than anything the West has right now. Its weaponry is state of the art; its outer armor explodes on impact to vaporize incoming shells, thus protecting the crew inside.[17] The Russians say that the tank is protected by sensors that detect incoming rounds and automatically fire off countermeasures. And, alone among tanks, the Armata has the capability to become completely automated, guided by remote control—making it the world's first "robot" tank. In British and American tank designs, these defensive systems are barely in the planning stage. No wonder the Russians claim that the Armata puts them twenty years ahead of the West in tank warfare.[18]

That's not the only area of hardware in which the Russians may have gained an edge. Russia's newest stealth fighter, the PAK FA fighter jet, also known as the T-50, may be even better than American jets. The first model is expected to appear in late 2016. The Russians boast that the plane is essentially a "flying robot," where the pilot "is actually one of the constituent parts of the flying apparatus," according to an official from Rostech.[19]

It's easy to dismiss as bluster Russian boasts that operating the T-50 puts them ahead of any other military in the world. But listen to what the Americans say.

"The analysis that I have seen on the PAK-FA indicates a pretty sophisticated design that is at least equal to, and some have said even superior to U.S. fifth-generation aircraft," according to US Air Force intelligence chief, former lieutenant general Dave Deptula. "It certainly has greater agility with its combination of thrust vectoring, all moving tail surfaces, and excellent aerodynamic design, than does the [American] F-35."[20]

The Russian military buildup also includes a deeply troubling nuclear component—in a country that already possesses the world's largest nuclear arsenal.[21] For years now, Putin has sent disturbing signals about his nuclear aims, even saying on Russian TV in March 2015 that Russia is ready to put its nuclear forces on alert during the crisis in Crimea. "We were ready to do it," he said.[22] In May 2015, Putin sent two Russian nuclear bombers into American airspace over Alaska. These provocations are part of a broader effort to strengthen Russia's nuclear posture—across land, sea, and air—even as his American counterpart, President Obama, has set out to dismantle the US nuclear deterrent.

The nuclear component of the Russian defense buildup will be front and center until at least 2025, as Russia sees these weapons as "the great equalizer and intimidator of Europe and other potential adversaries," Stephen Blank writes. In fact, Moscow is "signifying its belief that future nuclear, biological, or chemical warfare scenarios are likely" and equipping and training regiments for "offensive and defensive capability in this style of war."[23] Russia added thirty-eight nuclear missiles in 2014 and another forty in 2015.[24] The new ICBMs, Putin boasted at an arms show in June 2015, would be "capable of penetrating any, even the most technologically advanced missile defense systems."[25] Russia is also building out its submarine-launched ballistic missile (SLBM) capacities.

A centerpiece of the nuclear plans is completing the RS-28 Sarmat, a new hundred-ton, heavy-liquid-fueled ICBM that will be tested in late

2017. The Sarmat, which will be able to fly over the North and South poles and be fitted with "maneuvering warheads," is seen by many as Russia's response to Prompt Global Strike, an effort by the US military to develop a precision-guided conventional (nonnuclear) warstrike capable of reaching anywhere in the world within one hour. Russia claims that the Sarmat would be capable of overcoming virtually any missile-defense system. American military experts see no analogue to the Sarmat in our current arsenal.[26]

The Russian navy is getting more aggressive, too, both in its missions and deployments and in its future plans and investments. "As for missions of Russian naval ships, there will be 50 percent more of them than in 2013," said General Valery Gerasimov, chief of staff of the armed forces in Russia, in December of 2014.[27] The Russian defense minister, Sergei Shoigu, has called for a naval modernization plan to "improve the operational readiness of Russian naval forces in locations providing the greatest strategic threat."[28] And the Russians plan to get there by building out the fleet. A few years ago, the Russian shipbuilding budget was less than 10 percent of that of the United States; it is now about half.[29]

The Russian naval presence in the Black Sea has expanded dramatically in response to NATO's heightened naval presence due to the crisis in Ukraine. Russia's Black Sea naval commander promised Putin that the Russians would deploy *eighty* new warships and complete a second naval base in the region by 2020. "The Black Sea Fleet will have 206 ships and vessels by 2020," the commander told Putin.[30]

And the Russian navy is flexing its muscles in quieter spots, too—like the Arctic, where the Russians are cleaning our clocks in the race to secure the rich resources of the region and establishing military, naval, and other footholds. It's "a rivalry some already call a new Cold War," says the *New York Times*.[31] If so, it's a one-sided battle so far.

The Arctic is stocked with valuable natural resources—oil, gas, minerals, and fishery reserves. Within the region's seabed, the United States estimates, lies 15 percent of the world's remaining oil reserves, 30 percent of the world's natural-gas deposits, and 20 percent of the world's liquefied natural gas. The Russians are going after the resources hard, playing to their natural geographic advantages—but also to American complacency and poor planning. Only recently have Russian activities started getting the West's attention—such as when Putin deployed air defenses in the far north, including surface-to-air missiles. Russia is also opening up bases it had closed after the collapse of the Soviet Union. In March 2015, Russia ran an unannounced military exercise in the far north involving forty-thousand troops, and also including, according to the *New York Times*, "dozens of ships and submarines, including those in its strategic nuclear arsenal, from the Northern Fleet, based in Murmansk."[32]

Meanwhile, the United States lags behind, not mounting a serious effort in the region—beyond President Obama's visit to the Arctic to warn about climate change. "The United States really isn't even in this game," says Admiral Paul F. Zukunft, the Coast Guard commandant. "We're not even in the same league as Russia right now."[33]

The United States and NATO have air power and missile defenses in the Arctic, but at least until recently, America was considering drawing down. The American navy has *zero* ice-capable warships and has publically acknowledged that it lacks experience operating in the Arctic (though American submarines have a long history of experience in these waters). And of Russia's forty icebreakers, six are nuclear-powered.[34]

As in so many other instances, the American attitude seems complacent.

"We're seeing activity in the Arctic, but it hasn't manifested in significant change at this point," says Admiral William E. Gortney, head of the Pentagon's Northern Command and North American Aerospace Defense Command.[35] Gortney acknowledges that Russia is bolstering its capabilities in the region but feels that it doesn't suggest a present-day threat.

In this attitude might be glimpsed the symptom that plagues so much of the American approach to foreign policy today, and particularly as regards Vladimir Putin: an inability to look ahead and recognize materializing threats, even if they don't seem terribly formidable today. Fortunately, not all American officials are so shortsighted.

"We have been for some time clamoring about our nation's lack of capacity to sustain any meaningful presence in the Arctic," said Zukunft in 2015. "When Russia put Sputnik in outer space, did we sit with our hands in pocket with great fascination and say, 'Good for Mother Russia'?"[36]

"Good for Mother Russia" might be a phrase that rings in Putin's mind when he thinks about Kaliningrad, the Russian exclave on the Black Sea between Poland and Lithuania. For it is in Kaliningrad that we glimpse another crucial aspect of Putin's mounting arsenal of aggression. For years now, Putin has been funneling troops and weaponry—which may include Iskander missiles capable of carrying conventional and nuclear warheads—into Kaliningrad, making the region, by some estimates, one of the most militarized zones in Europe.[37]

The Russians have used the region as the basis for making threats for years. In 2007, General Vladimir Zaritsky, chief of artillery and rocketry for Russia's ground forces, suggested moving Iskander missile platforms armed with nuclear weapons into Kaliningrad in response to American plans to build a missile shield over Poland and the Czech Republic. "Any action meets a counter-action," Zaritsky said then, "and this is the case with elements of the U.S. missile defence in Poland and the Czech Republic."[38] But President Obama wound up scrapping that missile-defense plan.

In August 2015, tensions in the region continued to mount, raising alarms in Lithuania and Poland, and promoting speculation that Kaliningrad might become the next battleground in Putin's war with the West. Aleksandras Matonis of Lithuanian National Radio and Television described the Russian military presence as follows:

> Reportedly, there are 30,000–35,000 troops, two mechanized brigades, armoured vehicles in the hundreds rather than dozens. They hold regular exercises at sea, usually to coincide with NATO exercises. There's also intelligence work, they monitor NATO squadrons. Moreover, Kaliningrad hosts huge air defence forces. . . . Their range is rather extensive, over 400 kilometres. That covers not just the entire territory of Lithuania, but also most of Latvia and Poland. Besides, the units are highly mobile, they are mounted on vehicles and can be easily redeployed to any site, which increases their coverage.[39]

The Kaliningrad situation has crucial relevance to the Baltics, from which Putin leveled a nuclear threat against the United States and NATO in early 2015, warning the Western allies about their expanding military presence in Estonia, Latvia, and Lithuania. Russia sees these states, even though they have joined NATO, as similar to Ukraine, with a minority Russian population that Moscow claims is being mistreated. "The same conditions that existed in Ukraine and caused Russia to take action there" are present in the Baltics, said Russian envoys in a diplomatic cable to their Western counterparts early in 2015.[40] Thus it's not surprising that the Baltic countries have been feeling increased pressure from Putin.

"They're making quite big military exercises in the Kaliningrad district [which is] very, very close to our neighborhood," said Andrius Kubilius, the former Lithuanian prime minister. "So of course we are worried about such military developments very close to our borders."[41] Lithuania's foreign minister, Linas Linkevičius, went further. Pointing out that Lithuania was already suffering cyberattacks and an information offensive by Moscow designed to win the loyalty of the country's Russian minority, he claimed that Putin was already waging a brand of war against his country—a "hybrid war" designed to destabilize the only nation that has openly admitted to providing lethal aid to Ukraine.[42]

Indeed, for all of its growing conventional military might, it is Russia's skillful use of hybrid war—or nonlinear or asymmetrical war—that has taken Putin's offensive to new levels of complexity, giving him a reach beyond what he could gain with traditional means.

RUSSIA'S HYBRID WARFARE

It was during the Ukraine crisis of early 2014 that the world first saw the Little Green Men: armed men in Crimea who looked like Russian military members—they carried Russian arms, wore Russian-style uniforms, and spoke with Russian accents—but bore no identifying insignia. They were Russians, the Ukrainians said. No, Vladimir Putin insisted; they were "self-defence groups" organized by locals.[43] Whoever they were, they were effective: they manned roadblocks and held strategic positions in support of Moscow.[44]

A few months later, Putin admitted to a Russian audience that the Little Green Men were in fact Russian troops. They were part of a whole complex of tactics—information warfare, cyberattacks, propaganda, military saber rattling—that Putin has used in Ukraine and elsewhere to gain and maintain an upper hand. In April 2015, Anders Fogh Rasmussen, the former NATO secretary general, issued an explicit and chilling warning: Russia was engaging in a "hybrid war" with Europe, he said, working to undermine states from within.

"Russia has adopted this approach and it is a mix of very well-known conventional warfare and new, more sophisticated propaganda and disinformation campaigns including Russian efforts to influence public opinion through financial links with political parties within Nato and engagement in NGOs," Rasmussen said. Rasmussen went on to say that its current posture and tactics actually made Russia more dangerous than the Soviet Union had been during the Cold War. "Even during the Soviet time they were hesitant to talk about nuclear conflict," he said. "Now we see an open debate. In that respect the Russia of today is more dangerous than the Soviet Union. The USSR was more predictable."[45]

The lack of predictability is a hallmark of the vision of twenty-first-century war that Putin has developed along with his staff, including Valery Gerasimov, chief of staff of the Russian armed forces. In a January 2013 speech, Gerasimov called for the Russian military to practice what he called a "new kind of war," which would be waged with "nonmilitary methods to achieve political and strategic goals." These methods, Gerasimov said, would include fomenting popular protests, using special ops troops (the Little Green Men), and furnishing pretexts—like peacekeeping—for their presence.[46]

Hybrid war also places a premium on propaganda and disinformation, and on winning the battle not only in the streets but also in the television studios, the newspapers, and the hearts of the people. Putin accused the United States and NATO of the very thing he is in fact doing—trying to take over a sovereign nation—thereby diverting the focus from Russia's own engagement in this practice. Similarly, Gerasimov pointed out that the United States had practiced hybrid war tactics for years.

"In this hybrid war," the *Washington Post* editorialized,

a civilian airliner was shot down by surface-to-air missiles, but the triggerman or supplier of the missile was never identified; artillery shells are fired but no one can say from where; Russian military material and equipment appears suddenly in the villages and fields of eastern Ukraine. While people are being killed, as in any war, and while Ukraine has mustered its forces admirably to push back, this hybrid war features an aggressor whose moves are shrouded in deception.[47]

Hybrid war has been central to Russia's keeping the upper hand in Ukraine—a conflict that Putin increasingly seems to have won. And if hybrid war is an asymmetric version of conventional war, Putin's aims in Ukraine can also be seen as an asymmetric version of his conflict with the West. He clearly sees it as a testing ground, even a proxy war. As he sees it, the United States and its Western Europeans sought to destabilize Russia by pulling Ukraine into the Western embrace—offering it a chance to enter the European Union and even NATO. To Putin, these were provocations, as was Western support for the coup in Kiev against Viktor Yanukovych and his replacement by Western-friendly Petro Poroshenko. Ukraine is where Putin draws the line against the West. It's all part of an evening of the odds. Russia still lacks military superiority compared with the United States, but hybrid war—especially when combined with the audacity of the man waging it—evens things up pretty effectively.

Hybrid war is adaptive and iterative. Putin and his pro-Russian allies in Ukraine constantly update their tactics—military, diplomatic, economic, political—to push their interests and their agenda. At many points since the outset of the Crimean crisis, the West has seemed completely off balance, and not at all aware of what Putin will do next.[48]

Hybrid war is so flexible, in fact, that it can put conventional weapons—the instruments of warfare, as it is more straightforwardly understood—to unconventional uses. Consider how Putin has used the S-300 missile to menace Georgia and other neighbors. Airspace incursions mark yet another dimension of hybrid war, and the S-300 is the tool Russia uses for that tactic.

Putin has either positioned or has the capacity to position S-300s in Abkhazia and South Ossetia, the two Russian-occupied breakaway regions in Georgia. Those kinds of assets mean that Russia has de facto control over Georgian airspace, even if that control is exercised without a military demonstration. (The capabilities of the S-300 also demonstrate why the West should be so concerned about Moscow's sale of the missiles to Iran.) Putin can also potentially menace the airspace of the Baltic nations, none of which have fighter jets or effective air defenses. In Kaliningrad, just south of the Baltic region, Putin has stationed S-400 missiles, a more advanced version of the S-300.

What matters most about hybrid war is less what specific tactics Putin uses than how they fit within Russia's broader strategic vision.

Putin has made it clear that he doesn't think that the United States or NATO is willing to confront him. Consider the airspace violations that Putin has already pulled off in Georgia. What if he were able to replicate these inside a NATO country—and without having to invade? Even though Article 5 of the North Atlantic Treaty guarantees that an attack on one NATO member is an attack on all, it says nothing about "air sovereignty." If Putin established air dominance over a NATO nation, would his action trigger Article 5—or would NATO members find a way to reason themselves out of it? If the latter, it would mark the practical end of the alliance. These are the kinds of questions that Putin is forcing the West to ask itself.[49]

Similarly, what if the Little Green Men were to show up in the Baltic states of Estonia or Latvia, both of which have sizable ethnic Russian populations? We've already seen how Putin has used the complaint that ethnic Russians were being mistreated to work his will in Crimea. What if the Little Green Men seized assets on the ground, under the guise of protecting ethnic Russians? The same question applies here as to the airspace violations: How would NATO regard these actions, and how would the alliance respond? NATO may well have to answer these questions soon.[50]

RUSSIA'S ECONOMIC WARFARE

Another weapon in Putin's arsenal is economic warfare, which Moscow has been waging in Eastern Europe for years, threatening the region with everything from gas cutoffs to import bans. Russia targets countries like Moldova that are pursuing EU integration and sanctions key export products that are dependent on the Russian market, like agriculture. Russia has pulled out all the stops in its economic warfare against Ukraine, where the annexation of Crimea alone cost Ukraine over $1 trillion. Putin has also banned food and agricultural products from the United States, the EU, and other targeted countries in retaliation for their sanctions. Moscow has bulldozed and burned hundreds of tons of imports.

The Russians most avidly want to punish former Soviet republics that are forging closer links with the European Union, even when they aren't being offered membership. The EU's Eastern Partnership includes Ukraine, Belarus, Moldova, Azerbaijan, Armenia, and Georgia, with which the union is forging closer ties, including possible trade deals.

For Moscow, of course, these countries lie within what it has historically been seen as its sphere of influence. Putin has created the Eurasian Customs Union, part of his Eurasian Economic Union, as an exclusive alternative to the EU that he has urged these nations to join. In particular, he leaned hard on Armenia, and when Armenia showed signs of wanting to sign up with the Europeans instead, Putin threatened to step up arms shipments to its foe, Azerbaijan— with which Armenia is entangled in a "frozen" conflict. That did the trick; the Armenians backed down and joined the Customs Union. The Russians also have tried to squeeze Moldova, which remains heavily dependent on Russian gas.[51]

"Energy supplies are important in the run-up to winter. I hope you won't freeze," Russian envoy Dmitry Rogozin told Moldovans in 2013.[52] But the Moldovans have hung tough so far, even as Moscow's economic pressure continues to hit the poor nation's economy.

"I see they have been threatening Moldova with a cut-off in gas supplies as well as a cut-off in wine exports," said Swedish foreign minister Carl Bildt in 2015. "This is economic warfare they are threatening against these countries." The EU, Bildt suggested, needs a strategy to deal with Moscow's economic intimidation. "What we have seen during the past few weeks is brutal Russian pressure against the partnership countries of a sort that we haven't seen in Europe for a very long time," he said.[53]

Indeed, Putin has punished Moldova for its ratification of an association agreement with the European Union. Georgia and Ukraine have also signed association agreements, but Moldova, the poorest country in Europe, with an economy still largely agricultural, was the first to move theirs forward. So, Putin slapped an import embargo on Moldovan fruits. For some farmers, the Russian market represented 99 percent of their market.[54] And Russia contemplated a new ban on importing wines from Georgia when that nation joined the economic sanctions against Russia over the war in Ukraine.

Putin is also employing the Russian armed forces when he feels that his economic interests are at stake. This was the situation in Lithuania, a Baltic state and former Soviet republic that was long dependent on Russian gas and electricity, until recently. This arrangement ended when Lithuania started acquiring liquefied natural gas from Norway, and began laying electric cables under the Baltic Sea that would run 250 miles to the Swedish city of Nybro, and connect Lithuania to the Swedish energy grid.

That's when the Russian navy showed up.

"The Russian Navy is back," said the captain of the *Emanuel*, a trawler helping to lay electric lines in April 2015, after unexpectedly spotting a Russian warship in the area.[55] The Lithuanians sent a warship of their own. No incident occurred, but Russian ships have been conducting constant naval exercises in the Baltic Sea, and Russian warplanes have regularly penetrated Baltic airspace.

"They keep up constant pressure just to show they have influence," said Lithuanian energy minister Rokas Masiulis. "It is all part of the general atmosphere of provocation and rising tensions in the region."[56]

At stake, as Moscow sees it, is economic leverage over Lithuania. If the Lithuanians succeed in weaning themselves from dependence on Russian gas, as they seem poised to do with the liquefied natural gas from Norway, and if they complete the electric-cable project to Sweden, they will become essentially energy independent—or at least, energy independent of Moscow. And that will change the political and economic dynamic between the two countries. For Putin, that is a high price to pay; one of Moscow's central missions under his rule has been maintaining a tight grip on the economic leverage—principally the energy leverage—that Russia holds over its neighbors. This applies even to Lithuania, a relatively small market for Russian gas or electricity. The point is that energy independence would set a precedent for Lithuania's neighbors.

"We are a good example for others to follow," said Masiulis.[57] He's right. The question is what the price will be for Lithuania and others that stand up to Moscow's attempted economic intimidation. We know what has happened to other countries that are losing their fight against Putin: an invasion in Ukraine, dismemberment in Moldova, and economic domination in Armenia.

CONCLUSION

Taken together, Putin's military, economic, and "asymmetrical," or "hybrid," warfare initiatives have combined to present a formidable challenge to Western democracies. At every step of the game over the last five years, Putin has taken actions that the West wholly did not anticipate and for which it could formulate no effective responses. The result is a Russia emboldened by Western weakness and inaction, and in a much stronger position than it was five years ago. Even with its economic woes, Russia has strengthened its hand through Putin's strategic leadership and Western weakness. At the heart of his successes are a few fundamental insights and principles.

First, underlying all that Putin does is his deep-seated conviction that the United States and Western Europe simply don't want open conflict with Russia—not a small skirmish, not a "hybrid" showdown, and certainly not a full-scale war—and that leaders in Washington and in the European capitals are willing to go to extraordinary lengths to avoid it. The evidence of the last several years suggests that Putin is correct to feel confident about this. Armed with the knowledge that the West will shrink from open confrontation, the Russian leader *doesn't need a war to achieve his objectives*—all he needs is the consistent application of pressure, confrontation, and high-stakes moves that will intimidate Washington and Europe into backing down. Time and again, he has been successful. This dynamic helps explain the effectiveness of Putin's hybrid war model. He can use the threat of war and warlike tactics—from cyberwarfare to espionage, from counterinsurgency to energy politics—to keep his neighbors on their heels and their supposed protectors, the United States and the EU, off balance.

At the same time, Putin knows that he cannot level all these threats without building up his own conventional military capability. And he has been busy doing so for nearly a decade. While analysts disagree on how effective the buildup has been, it has unquestionably moved the Russian military forward since its low point, when Putin first took office. Putin's newfound confidence in his conventional capabilities can be glimpsed in the threats he has been increasingly willing to make—especially as regards Eastern Europe.

In June 2015, Russia sent a clear signal that it would regard any military move by the United States into Eastern Europe to fortify the defenses of those former Soviet republics that are now NATO members as "the most aggressive step since the Cold War," in the words of Russian army general Yury Yakubov.[58] Moscow would respond, Yakubov suggested, by rushing more troops, planes, tanks, and missile systems to Russia's western border. His words came as speculation increased about whether the Pentagon would send heavy weaponry to the Baltics, which, if it had come to pass, would mark the first time in history that the United States had sent such arms to former Soviet states. Russia was making it clear to the West how it would regard such an action.

Russia's firmness came in the context of another related insight: Putin's awareness that America and the West, at least up to the present, simply aren't committed to the values and principles that they profess. In recent years, Putin has been outspoken in dismissing Western values such as open political systems, freedom of speech, gay rights, and the like. The West professes to believe deeply in these things—and in the institutions of democracy that it has always suggested are superior to other systems. But an ever-widening gulf exists between what the West says and what it is ready to do, and Putin knows it. Putin has made a mockery of Western expressions of tolerance, peace, and conflict mediation—all the values that the West believes grew out of its painful experiences in the twentieth century. In his view, one shared by many antidemocrats, democracy and its institutions are a smokescreen to cover American and Western interventionism. Putin himself does not genuinely believe in these values, though he pretends that Russia is a democratic country with democratic institutions.

At the core, Putin believes that democracy is incapable of defending itself. So far, the responses of America and the Western alliance haven't dissuaded him from this conviction. Time and again, Western leaders have shown themselves unwilling to defend their values. "Putin's larger goal," writes Kim R. Holmes in *Foreign Policy*,

> appears to be to change the nature of the international system, particularly with respect to Europe. If he's successful it will have exposed the hollowness of the Western model approach to international affairs. . . . How far Putin will press matters is anyone's guess, but after all the dust settles the European order will not be the same. The European Union's vaunted faith in the sanctity of transnational rules and democracy will be diminished. Their confidence in America's commitment will be weaker.[59]

Indeed, for all the specific types of warfare we have laid out in this chapter—the troop buildup, the fancy new tanks and sleek new aircraft, the sophisticated asymmetrical warfare, the bare-fisted economic warfare—what matters most in Putin's arsenal of aggression is a fundamental imbalance of conviction. He believes in what he is doing; the West does not, or, if it does, it lacks the courage of its convictions, which is operationally the same thing. The United States and the Western democracies face many challenges ahead in checking Putin's moves, not the least of which is a wholesale reevaluation of our own hybrid-war capabilities. But underlying it all is the sober fact that we cannot hope to put a stop to Russian aggression until we become fully invested philosophically, politically, and even morally in what is at stake.

CHAPTER 5

Shadowboxing the Kremlin
Spies, Propaganda, and Cyberwarfare

The threat from Russia is increasing almost every day. We are back in the bad old days of the Cold War.
—BRITISH INTELLIGENCE SOURCE[1]

We will say what others are silent about. The world is tired of one country thinking of itself as exceptional. Our country—Russia—needs our love. A hostile attitude . . . can be left to private media.
—DMITRY KISELYOV, HEAD OF ROSSIYA SEGODNYA[2]

Vladimir Putin has a secret army. It's an army of thousands of "trolls," TV anchors and others who work day and night spreading anti-American propaganda on the Internet, airwaves and newspapers throughout Russia and the world.
—CONGRESSMAN ED ROYCE[3]

This is an entirely new way of waging war. It is like the invention of planes or submarines. Suddenly you can attack the enemy from a completely new and unexpected direction.
—FORMER KGB GENERAL[4]

Russia has never been shy about using tanks and bombers to get its way, or cutting off energy supplies to neighboring countries until their leaders capitulate and bow to Vladimir Putin's will. But some of the Kremlin's most destabilizing capabilities are also its most subtle, shrouded in the mysterious world of espionage; the twisted distortions of a vast propaganda machine; and the technical intricacies of relentless cyberwarfare against Western governments, companies, and individuals. Putin deploys these nonconventional weapons alongside conventional ones, launching online assaults that come on the heels of tanks, or deploying spy rings that feed him information on NATO's latest moves. Putin is, after all, a former KGB agent trained in the dark arts of Soviet spying and communist propaganda. He is also a thoroughly twenty-first-century adversary who leverages the Internet and global media to achieve his goals. From old-fashioned spies, to online troll farms, to cyberattacks against the Pentagon, Putin uses a full arsenal of subterfuge to gather intelligence on, confuse, and disrupt the West. He thrives in the shadows, where his spies, propagandists, and hackers diligently work to subvert Western governments and actively target citizens, businesses, and government officials.

As American military personnel have recently admitted before Congress, Washington has fallen well behind in its ability to anticipate and track Russian plans and movements in Europe and Asia. These blind spots help account for how off balance the Obama administration was when Putin made his move into Crimea. But the threat extends beyond the intelligence and counterintelligence failures of the United States—we're also facing an ever-increasing presence of Russian spies, both in the United States and in Western capitals. They haven't scored any major coups yet, but they are reaching critical mass—including in the Russian diplomatic corps—and their presence indicates the seriousness with which Putin is waging his contest with the West.

Another indicator of the level of seriousness is the increasingly sophisticated and effective manner in which the Kremlin spreads pro-Russian propaganda through its media assets while manufacturing support online. With an annual budget of $300 million, the Kremlin directly operates television network RT (formerly Russia Today), which "works to discredit critics of the Russian government and justify Moscow's actions." There's also Sputnik, a "global propaganda effort" with a Web site and radio stations broadcasting in thirty languages from "hubs" in major cities such as London, Paris, Washington, Rio de Janeiro, Berlin, Buenos Aires, Kabul, and New Delhi. Russian propagandists on RT and paid trolls online shape pro-Putin narratives and spread disinformation about the West, Ukraine, and any other Kremlin target—sometimes fabricating news stories out of whole cloth, like the account of Ukrainian forces crucifying a child. The outreach plays on cultural and religious sympathies as far west as the United States, where some religious conservatives have felt drawn to Putin's appeals to traditionalism and his persecution of homosexuals, while some on the left have been drawn by his appeals to "antiimperialism."[5] These extensive efforts make it clear that the Kremlin has big plans to shape opinion abroad.

Russian cyberhackers read President Obama's e-mails, tap into State Department and Pentagon systems, concoct hoaxes about terrorist attacks via social media, steal billions of dollars and millions of identities, and disappear into the mists of the Internet. It's widely believed that Russian-trained operatives were behind the infamous hack against Sony Pictures in 2014. And Russia has already wielded its formidable cyberwar capabilities against its neighbors. The question for the United States is not whether Russia will bring these tactics to bear against us but whether we can get ready in time.

Up until now, the United States and its Western allies have seemed wholly unprepared for the sophisticated, multipronged threat that Putin's nonconventional capabilities pose. Part of the reason is an imbalance of priorities and obligations: Russia is able to focus its attention on the West, while Western counterintelligence, media, and cybersecurity operations are pulled in a dozen different directions. But another cause is simple Western negligence. Through strategic ineptitude and moral and political blindness, we have not taken the Russia challenge seriously until very recently—and even now, we are temporizing, seemingly content with half measures and rationalizations. The hour is growing late, however: rebuilding our intelligence capabilities, developing an effective, modernized response to Russian propaganda, and getting serious about cybersecurity are absolute necessities if we are to counter Putin's mounting strategic and operational advantages.

SPIES

The United States has known that Russia is actively spying on us since the infamous 2010 breakup of a spy ring, the Illegals Project, which was dedicated to obtaining secrets about American nuclear weapons, CIA leadership, and congressional politics, among other subjects. The Russian spies used fake civilian identities and a combination of tactics, including old-fashioned espionage, forged passports, and stolen identities, and high-tech devices.[6] In a coded message, one Russian couple had the purpose of their trip disclosed to them: "You were sent to USA for long-term service trip.... Your education, bank accounts, car, house etc.—all these serve one goal: fulfill your main mission, i.e. to search and develop ties in policymaking circles and send intels [intelligence reports] to C[enter]."[7]

In addition, federal agents arrested eleven Russian spies in New York and Washington in June 2010, shocking the neighbors of the accused spies on hearing of the arrests. As one of the neighbors put it, "They couldn't have been spies. Look what she did with the hydrangeas." Another neighbor referred to one of the couples as "suburbia personified."[8] American officials noted that the operation, surprising as it was, hadn't had much success and in fact seemed comical in some respects, such as the spies' use of invisible ink.

"What a feckless operation," says Mark Lowenthal, a former senior CIA official. "So many of the things they seemed to be after you can find out by listening to the right radio station or reading the right newspaper. . . . It doesn't say a lot about the smarts of the SVR," referring to Russia's foreign intelligence service, a successor to the old KGB.[9]

But we know now that the illegals program was only the tip of the iceberg. In 2015, the FBI broke up another Russian spy ring in New York that collected intelligence on a wide range of American topics, including developments at the New York Stock Exchange. The ring centered on Evgeny Buryakov, who arrived in the United States in 2010 with a civilian cover story: he said he was a deputy representative for a Manhattan-based, Russian-owned bank. In reality, he was an agent of the Foreign Intelligence Service of the Russian Federation, or SVR. Buryakov regularly met with two Russian operatives in an office in the Bronx; the two operatives, in turn, met at an office in Manhattan, which, unknown to them, was bugged by the FBI. The federal agents picked up conversations regarding UN sanctions against Russia and American efforts to develop alternative energy sources.

"This case is especially egregious," said an FBI counterintelligence official observing Buryakov, "as it demonstrates the actions of a foreign intelligence service to integrate a covert intelligence agent into American society under the cover of an employee in the financial sector."[10] The United States also alleges that the SVR agents tried to recruit Americans working for major companies.

Russia is turning its spying capabilities not just against America but also against American allies in Europe. MI6, the UK's intelligence service, has warned staff that they and their families are being targeted by Russian spies. A leaked memo from agency officials to staff and operatives warned that British agents, both active and retired, are "high priority targets" of Russian agents, who may seek to turn them into double agents.[11] The MI6 set up an emergency hotline for staff to call if they should get approached by a Russian spy. The Russians use a variety of methods, from cash payouts to "honey traps"—where seductive female spies get information from targets after sexual encounters. The head of MI5, Britain's domestic security service, says that more Russian agents are working in the UK today than at any time since the Cold War.

"The threat from Russia is increasing almost every day," says a British intelligence source. "We are back in the bad old days of the Cold War."[12]

Germany's counterintelligence agency, the BfV, now believes that up to a third of Russian diplomats in Berlin are actually spies who target German government workers and employees of major companies for sensitive information.[13] Even NATO's headquarters in Brussels has been infiltrated; it recently had to expel dozens of suspected Russian spies, who were determined to make up approximately half of Russia's nonmember delegation. This news came on the heels of another move by NATO reminiscent of the Cold War: the reinstatement of hotlines between NATO officials and the Russian general staff to avoid misunderstandings that might lead to military confrontation—a suddenly relevant issue, as NATO jets have been intercepting more and more Russian planes flying over the Black Sea, as well as over the Baltic and Norwegian seas.

"It's important to have contacts military to military in a normal situation so that if something not normal happens, you're able to clarify misunderstandings, to avoid situations out of control," said NATO secretary general Jens Stoltenberg, trying to play down the move.[14] We need to consider that it's been more than two decades since Western leaders worried about such things. The conflict in Syria and Iraq—in which Russian, American, and Turkish jets operate in close proximity and have had a series of ominous run-ins—foreshadows a future where global politics once again play out in the air.

Meanwhile, Moscow continues to play host to Edward Snowden, the most notorious American defector in a generation. "The [Russian intelligence service] FSB are now his hosts, and they are taking care of him," says former KGB major general Oleg Kalugin. "These days, the Russians are very pleased with the gifts Edward Snowden has given them. He's busy doing something. He is not just idling his way through life."[15] Kalugin believes that Snowden has shared major American intelligence secrets with the Russians through his trove of documents—what he sees as one of Russia's biggest intelligence coups since the Cold War. Snowden's files have provided information, for example, on the National Intelligence Agency's close ties with Google and the agency's attempts to turn Facebook into a surveillance tool.[16] The London *Sunday Times*, in an a disputed report, has suggested that both Russia and China have access to Snowden's documents, and that the intelligence haul has led Britain's MI6 "to pull agents out of live operations in hostile countries."[17]

The ongoing Snowden fiasco serves to magnify American failings more broadly in the crucial area of intelligence. If the Snowden episode were merely an isolated-if-sensational case, then its effects might be mitigated. But the fact is that American intelligence has been playing catch-up. General Philip Breedlove, the supreme allied commander Europe, admitted that when it comes to Russia, "there are critical gaps in our [intelligence] collection and analysis."[18] Speaking before the Senate Armed Services Committee in spring 2015, Breedlove told the senators that gaps in US intelligence gathering in Eastern Europe had prevented the Americans from discerning Russian plans.

"Some Russian military exercises have caught us by surprise," he admitted, "and our textured feel for Russia's involvement on the ground in Ukraine has been quite limited." In one case, the Americans were reduced to *learning through social media* about a large Russian military exercise. The pool of experts on Russia has "shrunk considerably" since the end of the Cold War, Breedlove said, with our focus shifting over the last decade and a half to the Middle East.[19]

These are remarkably frank admissions to make in a public hearing, and several senators expressed frustration with American intelligence failures. But Breedlove's candor is commendable, and his call for more intelligence, surveillance, and reconnaissance (ISR) assets is overdue. The United States must rebuild its intelligence apparatus as regards Russia and Eastern Europe. We are being robbed blind of critical intelligence in our own country, and outhustled, outthought, and outspied abroad.

PROPAGANDA

On September 11, 2014, a provocative news story broke on Twitter: "A powerful explosion heard miles away happened at a chemical plant in Centerville, Louisiana #ColumbianChemicals."[20] The story was apparently a major news development, as other tweets linked to Web screen shots showing CNN coverage of the story, and another tweet linked to a YouTube video in which ISIS already appeared to be claiming responsibility, suggesting that the explosion was a terrorist act.

But ISIS wasn't behind it, because there was no such explosion in Louisiana. It was an Internet hoax, though one of peculiar sophistication. It took two hours for the chemical company to convince the public that nothing had happened.

With all the worries about ISIS, and the group's sophisticated usage of the Internet and social media, it wouldn't have been surprising to learn that the terrorist group had perpetrated the hoax to spread fear and sow confusion. But as it turned out, the hoax was the work of a secretive Russian group, the Internet Research Agency, run by a close associate of Vladimir Putin. The plot, as later reported by Adrian Chen in the *New York Times*[21] and summarized by L. Gordon Crovitz in the *Wall Street Journal*,[22] required elaborate, months-long preparation involving the creation of dozens of fake Twitter accounts in phony American names, the creation of phony Web sites to resemble Louisiana television stations and newspapers, and simulated photos and reporting. The Internet Research Agency employed as many as four hundred Internet "trolls" to perform these tasks.

The trolls' duties aren't confined to such dramatic, cloak-and-dagger Internet operations. More commonly, their work takes the form of a slow-and-steady grinding out of Web comments in the reader comment sections of stories on American and other Web news sites, where the trolls leave statements either taking pro-Russian stands or misrepresenting typical American viewpoints. In Germany, in particular, many of the most frequent "professional" commenters of online stories are Russian emigrés pushing the pro-Putin line. (Not all of these trolls are directly coordinated by Putin, by any means; many pro-Putin Russian emigrés are private citizens who live happily in the West, but have fallen for Putin's appeal to Russian chauvinism and are acting independently to push a pro-Russian viewpoint.) German journalists also get letters on a nearly daily basis from writers claiming to have "explosive information about the Ukraine crisis" and the supposedly quasi-fascistic Kiev government. The journalists believe that, though the letters are written in German, the writers themselves are native Russian speakers.[23] The Kremlin's propagandists have even begun illegally publishing Russian translations of foreign authors, like of the work of British journalist Edward Lucas of the Center for European Policy Analysis, in order to "portray Russia as a besieged fortress surrounded by malevolent outsiders."[24]

It's clear that, for Putin, who once called the Internet a "CIA project," turnabout is fair play. Time will tell whether more hoaxes like the one in Louisiana (and another involving a false Ebola scare) are in the offing—whether the chemical plant story was the dress rehearsal for a more ambitious information operation in the future.[25]

The Louisiana deception is just one strand in a larger web of Russian propaganda and information warfare that has become a staple of Putin's arsenal of aggression. Using these assets, Putin is waging "the most amazing information warfare blitzkrieg we have ever seen," says NATO commander Breedlove.[26] The Kremlin actively "weaponizes information" and "exploits the idea of freedom of information to inject disinformation into society . . . to sow confusion via conspiracy theories and proliferate falsehoods," according to the *Interpreter*, the online magazine of the Institute of Modern Russia, a prodemocracy, New York–based nonprofit.[27]

At its most overt, the Russian propaganda strategy revolves around traditional broadcast media—specifically, RT, formerly known as Russia Today, which Putin started in 2005 and which has expanded substantially since its original English-language-only focus. RT now broadcasts in French, German, Arabic, and Spanish; it has dedicated stations in the United States and England; and it has styled itself as an alternative news source to Western media. The Kremlin invests $136 million a year in promoting Russian media abroad, with considerable success: RT has close to 1.2 billion views on YouTube, second only to the BBC. RT's video arm, Ruptly, looks to compete with Reuters and the Associated Press. And now Putin has upped the communications ante further.

Late in 2014, Russia announced Sputnik, a new communications effort focusing on radio and the Internet to supplement RT. Sputnik, part of the new Russian news conglomerate Rossiya Segodnya, will broadcast in thirty languages from locations around the world. Its focus?

Countering Western "propaganda" and the "unipolarity" promoted by Western allies.

"We are against the aggressive propaganda that everybody is fed with and that imposes a unipolar model of the world," says Dmitry Kiselyov, who heads Rossiya Segodnya. "We will say what others are silent about. The world is tired of one country thinking of itself as exceptional"—a not-very-subtle dig at the United States. "Our country—Russia—needs our love . . . a hostile attitude . . . can be left to private media."[28]

Putin's communications apparatus has been particularly effective in shaping the news narrative and influencing opinions on Ukraine. It is all part of Putin's effort to shape what Margarita Simonyan, editor in chief of RT, calls "an alternative discourse" to the West's version of events—and RT, with its reach, looks to bring that alternative discourse within Western countries themselves. Simonyan says that when Putin founded RT, he told her that her mission was to "break the monopoly of the Anglo-Saxon mass media." And some of Simonyan's RT colleagues say proudly: "We're something along the lines of Russia's Information Defense Ministry."[29]

Indeed, "we're in the middle of a relentless propaganda war," as Andrew Weiss, vice president of studies at the Carnegie Endowment for International Peace, puts it.[30] Russian-language media remains influential throughout Eastern Europe and the former Soviet Union, and Senator John McCain has called attention to the "inundation today in the Baltic, in Moldova, in Romania, and Poland even of Russian constant, incessant sophisticated messages that we have to counter."[31] Russia's propaganda campaign in the Baltics is estimated to cost $350 million. "They are in all those spaces, from print, to Internet, to TV, and they're in those spaces in a dedicated, capable way," says General Breedlove.[32] In these countries, Moscow seeks to rally Russian-speaking minorities against the West, NATO, and the EU, fomenting opposition to their own ruling governments and sowing the seeds of instability. Most Russian minorities in these countries already get their news from Russian sources.

What to do? Russia's information barrage, especially in concert with its "hybrid" war capabilities, has finally gotten the attention of at least some American officials in Washington. Calls have gone up in Congress for the United States to revive its antipropaganda efforts, which, at the height of the Cold War, were sophisticated and effective. But that was a long time ago. One of the voices calling for a revival of these efforts is Republican congressman Ed Royce, chairman of the House Foreign Affairs Committee. Russia's "secret army" of propaganda warriors, he has written, "may be more dangerous than any military, because no artillery can stop their lies from spreading and undermining U.S. security interests in Europe."[33] His warnings have been echoed by Congressman Eliot Engel, and the State Department itself has appealed to companies like Sony Pictures to help out in countering Russian propaganda.[34]

The main problem for the United States is that our flagship international communications tools from the Cold War—the Voice of America, Radio Free Europe, and the like—haven't really adapted themselves for today's ideological combat. (And they barely reach the Russian audience at all.) Some in Congress, like Royce and Engel, want to see the VOA overhauled and reoutfitted for the new propaganda demands—that is, they'd like to see it make explicit statements in support of US policies abroad. Others resist that effort, seeing it as a corruption of VOA's mission that would simply confirm, for many, Moscow's assertion that there is no objective news, just competing propaganda sources.

And herein lies a good deal of the Western dilemma when it comes to the new propaganda age, in which Putin is the undisputed maestro: to win at such a battle, we have to be willing to hear such criticisms and persevere. During the Cold War, for the most part, American resolve was not lacking. Today, it's different; after more than a generation of post-Vietnam erosion of confidence in Western governments, waging a new postmodern propaganda offensive requires a level of self-confidence that, in the West, just isn't there anymore.

"People focus on communication, how to get our message across. But they don't notice we have a problem with our message," says Kadri Liik of the European Council on Foreign Relations in London. "We are not really necessarily living the model we are preaching," she suggests, referring to Western failings on everything from human rights to political corruption. "I think we don't really understand the way our political model comes across, how people who live in different societies interpret our reality through their own experience."[35]

Any way you look at it, Western efforts to counter the Russian propaganda offensive have a long way to go.

CYBERWARFARE

Chinese hackers dominate the headlines, but the "threat from China is overinflated, while the threat from Russia is underestimated," says Web-security consultant Jeffrey Carr, author of *Inside Cyber Warfare*. "The Russians are the most technically proficient. For instance, we believe that Russian hackers-for-hire were responsible for the Sony attack."[36]

Carr is referring to one of the most dramatic cyberhacks in recent history: the December 2014 hack of confidential data belonging to Sony Pictures Entertainment, including employee information and e-mail correspondence among high-level personnel. The hackers demanded that Sony Pictures withdraw a new film satirizing North Korean leader Kim Jon-un—and Sony caved, in part because leading cinema chains were withdrawing the film from their distribution.[37] The United States alleged that the attacks were sourced from North Korea, though this fact remains in dispute. Carr and others believe that wherever the attacks originated, Russian personnel were involved.

Carr is right to highlight the Russians' cyberwarfare capabilities, and United States officials are starting to recognize the threat. Speaking about the findings of the 2015 *Worldwide Threat Assessment* report, editor and political analyst Franz-Stefan Gady suggests that Russia and China rank as the "most sophisticated nation-state actors" in cyberwarfare overall, with Russian hackers serving as the leaders in overall sophistication, programming power, and inventiveness.[38]

Consider that in recent years, Russian hackers have successfully compromised the State Department, the Pentagon, and the White House, even gaining access to some of President Obama's e-mails. A Kremlin-sponsored hacking group called the Dukes has been carrying out organized cyberattacks on Western government and political targets, including American defense contractors, NATO, and European government and security organizations, for at least the last seven years. These targets include "Georgia's Defense Ministry, the foreign ministries of Turkey, Ukraine, and Poland, and other government institutions and political think tanks in the United States, Europe, and Central Asia," says Radio Free Europe in reference to a report by F-Secure, a data-security firm based in Finland.[39] The Dukes specialize in using malware to infect computer networks and gain access to confidential information. "All the signs point back to Russian state sponsorship," says Artturi Lehtiö of F-Secure,[40] which believes that the Dukes are run by professional software developers working for Moscow.

So far, Russia is the only country that has deployed cyberwar as part of more conventional offensive warfare measures. While Russia was in the process of annexing Crimea, "ground assaults were accompanied by a deluge of mostly low-tech cyberassaults on over a hundred government and industrial organizations in Poland and Ukraine, as well as attacks on the European Parliament and the European Commission," Owen Matthews writes in *Newsweek*.[41] Data-security specialists warn that smaller countries in Eastern Europe and the Caucasus are especially vulnerable to Russian intimidation, as Moscow can use cyberwar to shift the balance of power or affect government decision making in these countries.[42]

The Russian cyberwar threat is also a direct threat on the US mainland. The Russians have been hacking into sensitive American government systems for years. In 2015, they perpetrated one stunning hack after another. Throughout 2014 and into 2015, Russian hackers—whether the Dukes or some other group of sophisticated operatives—broke into the State Department's servers, despite multiple efforts by State Department IT personnel to keep them out. One frustrated official told CNN that the Russians "owned" the State Department system for months.[43] Insiders investigating the breach called it the "worst ever" cyberattack against a federal agency.[44] The Russians used their access within the State Department system to crack into the White House computer system, where they gained access to a trove of sensitive information, through e-mail and other sources. White House spokesmen stressed that the breached systems contained only unclassified information, but as a CNN article makes clear, "That description belies the seriousness of the intrusion. The hackers had access to sensitive information such as real-time non-public details of the president's schedule. While such information is not classified, it is still highly sensitive and prized by foreign intelligence agencies."[45] The information can also include correspondence with diplomats and discussions about policy and personnel.[46]

Russian cyberwarriors haven't just bedeviled the State Department and the White House; they've also broken into the unclassified e-mail system of the Pentagon's Joint Chiefs of Staff, gaining access to the correspondence of some four thousand employees. This attack may have been the Russians' most sophisticated yet, as the operatives coordinated their moves via encrypted social media accounts and used an apparently automated tool that could extract and distribute information within one minute. The attack, unnamed American officials say, "was clearly the work of a state actor."[47] And, like the White House and the State Department, they assured anxious Americans that no classified information had been seized. But it's difficult to feel much reassurance when the Defense Department itself is being hacked. Additionally the Pentagon thought enough of the attack to shut down the e-mail system for several weeks.[48]

Russian cyberwarriors don't just target Western governments but Western companies and private citizens as well, such as the bank-fraud ring that cost J. C. Penney, JetBlue, and French retailer Carrefour $300 million from 2010 to 2013, or the one that stole 1.2 billion Internet logins and passwords and more than five hundred million e-mail addresses in 2014. Another cyberattack that targeted banks in Japan, the United States, and Europe in 2013 and 2014 could wind up costing nearly a billion dollars for these countries.

But perhaps the most frightening of all scenarios involves cyberattacks on infrastructure systems. Already, some dry runs have taken place—as when unknown hackers nearly seized control of US electrical, water, and fuel distribution systems in 2014. National Security Agency director admiral Michael Rogers warns of "truly significant, almost catastrophic failures if we don't take action."[49] A major cyberattack on infrastructure systems could take us into a new age of high tech war and civilian terror.

"This is an entirely new way of waging war," says a former KGB general. "It is like the invention of planes or submarines. Suddenly you can attack the enemy from a completely new and unexpected direction.... This is the essence of warfare: constant surprise."[50] The increasingly digital networked systems that run our transportation infrastructure, electrical grid, urban water systems, and financial markets are highly vulnerable. Eugene Kaspersky, creator of many security products for his firm, Kaspersky Labs, says that there has been a huge increase in attacks against such networks worldwide. The increasing reliance on digital networks, a great advancement in efficiency and performance, also paradoxically creates enormous new vulnerabilities.

In spring 2015, a fleet of Boeing 737s was grounded when the pilots' "electronic flight bag"—the information used for safety checks preflight, previously stored on top of thirteen pounds of paper manuals—crashed. The United States worries about "unauthorized remote access to aircraft avionics systems" from hackers. "What has security officials worried," writes Owen Matthews in *Newsweek*, "is the new and dangerous world of cyber-to-physical infrastructure attacks."[51] The most dramatic warning of this danger was made in 2012 by then defense secretary Leon Panetta, speaking to an audience in Manhattan.

"A cyber attack perpetrated by nation states or violent extremist groups could be as destructive as the terrorist attack of 9/11," Panetta said. "Such a destructive cyber terrorist attack could paralyze the nation."[52] Broad-based infrastructure attacks, he warned, "would cause physical destruction and loss of life, paralyze and shock the nation, and create a profound new sense of vulnerability." He suggested that sophisticated computer hackers could bring down portions of the nation's infrastructure. "An aggressor nation or extremist group could ... gain control of critical switches," Panetta said. "They could derail passenger trains, or even more dangerous, derail passenger trains loaded with lethal chemicals. They could contaminate the water supply in major cities, or shut down the power grid across large parts of the country."[53]

Panetta's warning is even more relevant today than it was in 2012. As they have done in spying, intelligence gathering, and propaganda, the Russians wage cyberwar with no holds barred. If we expect them to set limits on what they're willing to do or curtail their activities voluntarily, we haven't been paying attention.

CONCLUSION

In the areas detailed in this chapter—spies and intelligence, propaganda, and cyberwarfare—Russia has eagerly and effectively seized the offensive, often catching the United States and other Western governments unawares and forcing us and our neighbors to adapt to new circumstances and respond to unanticipated tactics and capabilities. The narrative of recent years has all too often involved the concept of surprise: in the aggressive Russian moves, especially in Ukraine, that the West apparently didn't see coming; in the spy rings and intelligence theft right under America's nose; in the cyberattacks on the most sacrosanct institutions of the United States government; and in the propaganda offensives that go unanswered.

Since the end of the Cold War, as by now should be clear, Russia has rebuilt its intelligence services and extended its international capabilities. That's a key lesson of the spy rings that the United States rolled up in 2015 and 2010. The naïve might point successful identification of these rings by the United States and make snide comments or author ironic op-eds, half jokingly comparing the episodes to an old Cold War spy movie. The more politically astute will see these incidents as preludes for more advanced, ambitious operations in the future. If we have learned anything about Putin, it's that he doesn't do anything halfway. His spy offensive is likely to intensify, especially with Russia and the United States estranged and with Moscow laboring under the economic sanctions that America and its Western allies slapped on Russian businesses. The stakes are higher now than they were a few years ago; we should expect more attempts to steal state secrets, gain access to corporate and financial information, and use diplomats as cover for international espionage.

Likewise, the increasingly effective Putin propaganda offensive shows no sign of letting up. In fact, with the rollout of Sputnik, it's clear that Moscow intends to create a multichannel effort to disseminate a 24/7 corrective to what it sees as the corrupt and duplicitous Western geopolitical narrative. Putin has two audiences in mind with his propaganda: the international community and his own people in Russia. By using state propaganda to cast himself as the nationalist defender of Russia against its many international enemies—especially those in the West—Putin has kept a strong hand at home. Clearly, he has already persuaded most Russian citizens that the Ukraine government is quasi-fascist. He has effectively used the specter of World War II and even the Holocaust to paint his adversaries in Kiev in the darkest hues. One member of the Duma called a fire in Odessa that killed thirty pro-Russia activists "a new Auschwitz," and 89 percent of listeners in a radio poll agreed with the proposition that "participants of the mass murder in Odessa should be found and executed without trial."[54] In a more ambitious venture, Putin is making serious inroads in his goal of convincing many in the international community, and especially ethnic Russian minorities in neighboring states, that his intervention in Ukraine is just and justifiable. The state-driven Russian propaganda effort has become, in barely a decade, a formidable weapon.

Finally, the Russian cyberwar effort seems destined to cause the United States more trouble in the years ahead—especially since President Obama has shown himself willing, perhaps even eager, to weaken American intelligence capabilities and to relinquish American leadership in maintaining an open Internet. As far as the cyberhoax about the explosion at the Louisiana chemical plant, our own Department of Homeland Security never identified it as the work of Russian trolls; it was journalists who broke that story. The DHS people had no data on it; they could only assume it was some kind of online prank. That's a chilling reminder of the gaps in our intelligence, but they're not surprising when you remember that under Obama, we have narrowed the abilities of US intelligence operatives to monitor digital data that identifies suspicious or dangerous actors online. And under revisions to the Patriot Act, our intelligence agencies can no longer mine anonymous phone records in search of suspicious foreign actors.

Obama has also inexplicably stood against perpetuating our country's contract with the Internet Corporation for Assigned Names and Numbers (ICANN), which works to block authoritarian regimes from gaining control of naming conventions for Internet URLs.[55] If the United States gives up its role as international steward of the Internet, who will step up to take on that responsibility? We can think of at least one ambitious candidate for the job—he works in Moscow.

CHAPTER 6

Sowing Disorder

Russia, Rogue Regimes, and Terror

We must leave all arguments and disagreements behind and make one powerful fist, a single anti-terror front, which would work on the basis of international law under the aegis of the United Nations.
— **VLADIMIR PUTIN**[1]

At the political level, the White House will say we're cooperating on terrorism, but that doesn't mean anything. So if the [Russian] FSB is now sending jihadists to Syria so that they can die at the hands of the Americans rather than the Russians, should we be surprised? We're just so goddamn ignorant.

—FORMER CIA OPERATIVE[2]

"**W**e must leave all arguments and disagreements behind and make one powerful fist, a single anti-terror front, which would work on the basis of international law under the aegis of the United Nations," said Vladimir Putin, speaking gravely to the Russian federal assembly in the Kremlin in December 2015. "That means no shelter to bandits, no double standards, no contacts whatsoever with any terrorist organizations, no attempts to use them for some other goals, no criminal, bloody business with terrorists." And he lashed out at the West for creating a double standard on terrorism, creating "a zone of chaos and anarchy threatening the entire world" in the Middle East and elsewhere.[3]

Rarely has a more blackened pot cried out against the kettle.

The particular focus of Putin's ire in the speech, in addition to the United States and its Western allies, was Turkey, which, only a few weeks earlier, had shot down a Russian jet near the Syrian border, an action that Putin decried as "a treacherous war crime." The incident represented the first time in a half-century that a NATO member had downed a Russian plane, and the tensions between the two countries had escalated in its aftermath, with each blaming the other for the tragedy and the two leaders trading insults in the media. Keeping the pressure on before his Kremlin audience, Putin accused Turkey of letting ISIS sell stolen oil. With the revenues, Putin said, the terrorist group was "recruiting mercenaries, buying weapons and staging cruel terror attacks aimed against our citizens, as well as citizens of France, Lebanon, Mali and other countries." Coming back to the national outrage Russians felt about the downed jet, Putin vowed to make Turkey "feel sorry about it more than once."[4]

You wouldn't know, listening to any of this, that Vladimir Putin is playing the world's most sophisticated double game when it comes to simultaneously battling terrorism and standing up against rogue regimes. The record of his behavior indicates clearly that he is willing to use terrorism and rogue states to further his own goals. And so his protests about Turkish behavior and how ISIS has penetrated Turkey need to be taken in context. However much Putin talks about his desire to fight global terrorism, and to fight ISIS in Syria more particularly—especially in the aftermath of the terrorist group's destruction of a Russian passenger jet over Egypt in November 2015—his words belie his deeds. Or put more accurately, his unambiguous words belie his multifaceted deeds.

In many ways, ISIS represents an opportunity for Putin. The terrorist group, which also calls itself the Islamic State, spent the latter half of 2015 preying on Western cities, from Paris to San Bernardino to London. Not since the attacks of September 11, 2001, has a terrorist group been more prominent in the Western mind; not since those historic attacks have the citizens of Western democracies, very much including those in the United States, felt more existential uncertainty and dread. ISIS, more and more analysts have come to agree, represents a genuine threat to the Western future.

And Putin, to hear him tell it, sees ISIS as a threat as well. Yet ISIS also allows Putin to use the rhetoric of antiterror to justify his policy of protecting Syria's Bashar al-Assad. ISIS's ongoing fight in Syria created the refugee crisis in Europe that divides Europe and creates instability. That ISIS destroyed the Russian plane is a blow to Putin, to be sure, but it is also an opportunity for him to reinforce his positions. The incident enabled Putin to accuse Turkey, a NATO member, of tolerating ISIS, putting pressure on the whole NATO alliance. And while Putin rightly warns of a growing terrorist threat in Russia's Caucasus region, he is at the same time willing to use ISIS and rogue regimes—such as Iran, Syria, and North Korea—for his own purposes. Russia shares with all of them a commitment to anti-Westernism and anti-Americanism.

ISIS, then, is just the latest iteration of a long-running dynamic involving Putin, in which he enables and facilitates disruption of the Western-led, norms-based post–Cold War order. (The main thrust of Putin's propaganda is that the West, and especially America and Britain, have violated this order—and thus, by implication, he has the right to violate it as well.) Whether that disorder comes from North Korean nukes or ISIS driving a refugee crisis is not something Putin needs to or even wants to control. Rather, it's about fostering an international climate where rapidly escalating crises erode Western influence, test the limits of American/European capabilities and willpower, and provide openings for Putin to pursue Russian strategic aims. He's been at the game for years, sowing discord and instability around the world.

PUTIN'S PHONY WAR ON ISIS

As this book goes to press, there is much talk among analysts and commentators about the prospects of an antiterror alliance between the United States and its Western allies and Putin's Russia. After all, this line of thinking goes, whatever their differences, all the players share a common enemy in Islamist terrorists, especially those involved in ISIS. All the parties have homegrown terror problems. All of them have a desire to see some kind of stability emerge out of the roiling cauldron of the Middle East.

It is on that final point, the search for stability, however, that the equation breaks down. For it is in our differing ideas of what stability means, what its value is, and what it would constitute that the Western allies are far apart, and why they won't be able to make common cause with Putin against terrorism. Perhaps some symbolic alliance may be entered into against ISIS, but if so, its terms won't be binding, and even if they are, Putin will flout them whenever they conflict with his goals. In the end,

"Putin [is] not interested in fighting Islamism," says Russian dissident and political commentator Igor Eidman.[5]

Why? Because at the core, the Russians are obsessed with the West as their antipode and enemy. They are *not* obsessed with terrorists or Islamists. They know that they can always come to terms with these groups in one way or another—just as they did with Ramzan Kadyrov in Chechnya. They have done it for centuries. Islamism, while a problem when it thwarts Putin's initiatives or political standing at home just as often supports his own goals, which, as Eidman says, "to a large extent do not differ from the tasks of the Islamists." These goals include nothing less than "the destruction of the civilized world order,"[6] which for Putin would lead to a different kind of order—one better suited to his ends.

"The whole region is watching this," says James F. Jeffrey, a former American ambassador in Iraq and Turkey, about the Syrian situation. "Russia is trying to change the security dynamic in the Middle East and demonstrating that it supports its allies to the hilt. The White House is sitting there and worrying about de-conflicting airplanes when we should be upping our efforts against Assad."[7]

Currently, Europe faces its greatest refugee crisis since the end of the Second World War—and Vladimir Putin is a key player in exacerbating that crisis. While he continues to claim that his support for Bashar al-Assad is keeping a bad situation from getting even worse,[8] the facts tell a different story. Russian escalations in the Syrian conflict, especially from the air, have sent countless innocent Syrians into exile, where they join a diaspora that continues to grow and fan out across Europe. Those who haven't joined them on the roads—up to five million Syrians—are living in areas that relief groups find difficult to access. In central and northern Syria, Putin's September 2015 offensive on behalf of Assad—directed almost entirely against the Syrian rebels, not ISIS—has brought more chaos, bloodshed, and displacement.

The Russian airstrikes are "the major reason" for the despair and fear of the people, said a Syrian relief worker. "There is some psychological effect for people, hearing there is a superpower intervening in the war."[9]

To be clear, this is not to claim that Putin intended to create a refugee crisis or that he even desires one—only that the refugee crisis, as it is presently unfolding, is not inimical to his broader designs. Those who doubt that Putin is personally invested in fomenting chaos in the region need to explain how it is that Russia has, in effect, provided ISIS with an air force in Syria. That is another key effect of the Russian air campaign in Syria. To be sure, the primary mission of Russian aerial efforts is to strengthen its ally, Assad. But look at how ISIS benefits as well.

The United States has long understood that Assad, though an enemy of ISIS, has willingly empowered the terrorist group when it clashes with the Syrian rebels who want to overthrow his regime. In 2014, Washington accused Assad of making air strikes against the rebels on behalf of ISIS. "We have long seen that the regime avoids [ISIS] lines," said the US Embassy in Damascus, "in complete contradiction to the regime's claims to be fighting [ISIS]."[10]

Since then, Russia has picked up the slack for Assad. After ISIS blew up the Russian airliner in Egypt in November 2015, Putin vowed a huge offensive against the terrorists—including in Syria. It was this event, and the Paris terror attacks soon after, that led some in the West to believe that an anti-ISIS alliance with Putin might be in the cards. But despite all his rhetoric against ISIS, Putin has concentrated Russian efforts in the skies over Syria overwhelmingly against the anti-Assad rebels. And in doing so, he is serving as a de facto air force for the caliphate.

Russian air strikes have destroyed artillery and armored personnel carriers belonging to the Free Syrian Army. A local commander of Liwa Suquor al-Jabal, a brigade of the Free Syrian Army, says in a recently posted YouTube video, "The Russian airplanes are targeting Suqour al-Jabal's weapon depots in Aleppo and ISIS attacked the bases with explosives at the same time."[11] It has all been part of a Russian aerial offensive directed overwhelmingly against the rebels, not ISIS. State Department estimates at the end of November 2015 show that less than 10 percent of Russian air strikes were directed against the Islamic State.

"What is a consensus view among analysts is that ISIS clearly is not Putin's quarry in Syria, at least not yet, because he's too busy killing the anti-Assad rebels supported and armed by the Central Intelligence Agency," writes Michael Weiss in the *Daily Beast*. "U.S. officials have acknowledged as much."[12] While ISIS may well threaten Assad's rule eventually, for the moment, it is the Syrian rebels who pose the most serious threat to the strongman's rule—and this is where Putin has focused his efforts. And ultimately, of course, if it comes down to ISIS versus Assad, this too plays into Putin's calculus—he is confident that most Syrians will choose the dictator and his brand of "stability" over the apocalyptic vision of the Islamic State.

Putin's intrigues on behalf of ISIS go well beyond what even most interested observers understand. For example, according to former Defense Intelligence Agency official Jeffrey White, Putin's federal security service—the successor organization to the KGB—is actively helping jihadists in Dagestan immigrate to Syria to join the Islamic State. Doing so serves two purposes for Putin: First, it thins out the ranks of jihadis in Russia's backyard. Some reports indicate that with thousands of bloody-minded Islamists now removed from the Caucasus, terrorist violence in the region has been cut in half.[13] Of course, there is some danger here for Russia, too, because at some point the jihadis will likely try to return. But the FSB, Russia's internal security service, has confidence in its border security and carefully tracks suspected terrorists who leave the country. Second, it gives fresh recruits to the Islamic State in its battle against the American-backed Syrian rebels. Recent estimates indicate that Russia is the world's third-biggest supplier of foreign fighters to ISIS or other Islamist groups fighting in Syria and Iraq, behind only Tunisia and Saudi Arabia.[14]

White compares the Russian effort here with the Red Army's advance westward in 1944. Although moving on Berlin, the Russians allowed the Germans to crush a Polish rebellion, pacifying the insurgency and saving Moscow the trouble. Then the Russians forced the Germans out of Poland on their way to Berlin and war's end.[15]

The analogy assumes, however, that once ISIS has triumphed over the Syrian rebels, Russia will move against the caliphate. Yet that scenario seems unlikely. The bottom line is that ISIS and radical Islam are to Putin akin to the enemies whom, in the famous *Godfather* formulation, one must keep even closer than one's friends.

"It's perfectly conceivable that the FSB would take their most violent types and say, 'Yeah, you want your caliphate? Go set it up in Raqqa,'" says a former CIA operative who spoke to Weiss for his major exposé in the *Daily Beast*. "The Saudis did this in the '80s with the Afghans. It's sort of tried and true. We could do the same thing. Of course, we're not."[16]

Weiss also cites Glen Howard, a Central Asia and Caucasus specialist, who explains Putin's thinking: "What's the most significant policy decision we made to bring down the Soviet Union? Us sending foreign fighters into Afghanistan. This [Putin sending jihadis into Syria] is the perfect form of payback. Create a quagmire in Syria, get us bogged down—all the while, offer your cooperation in helping to root out terrorism."[17]

And it goes deeper. Even the jihadis who remain in the Caucasus serve Putin's interests by justifying strong-arm national security and surveillance tactics, deprivation of individual liberties, and a displacement of blame for the jihadist insurgency. Having ISIS around means that Putin can look to the terrorist group as an explanation for Islamist behavior in his backyard—as he particularly did when the Caucasus Emirate, Russia's leading Islamist insurgency, declared allegiance to ISIS in summer 2015. It's all ISIS's doing, Putin says—and he goes further still.

ISIS, the Russian president suggests, is a Western creation—specifically, a creation of the United States, which, after all, housed the group's leader, Abu Bakr al-Baghdadi, as a POW in Iraq. The Russians have helped foster this conspiracy theory among many Iraqis, which doesn't make the American project in that beleaguered country any easier.

The truth about ISIS is far different, as Putin—and Bashar al-Assad—well know. Assad funded ISIS's predecessor organization, al-Qaeda in Iraq, for nearly a decade, as it fought against American forces there. And Assad has a Putin-like understanding of how an enemy that is near can serve as a shield against one nearer still: When the uprising against him began in 2009, the Syrian dictator released countless jihadis from his jails, knowing that they would either fight the moderate Syrian opposition or help radicalize it. A little of both has happened since— and Assad's efforts, like Putin's, have been overwhelmingly directed against the moderate rebels, not the jihadists of ISIS or other terrorist groups. And remember those ISIS oil sales that Putin blamed on the Turks? Guess who one of ISIS's main oil buyers is? You got it—Bashar al-Assad.

"Assad is both a duplicitous and failed counterterrorist," writes James Miller.[18]

So is Vladimir Putin.

Ultimately, what we have is a situation in which Putin nominally wants to control terrorism—and ISIS—but only so much, and only in the areas in which tamping down terror will serve his broader aims. No coalition against ISIS that has Putin as a member will be worth the paper it is written on. The broader question—and the answer is not likely to be reassuring—is whether, strategically, our policy makers in Washington truly grasp Putin's multilayered approach.

"At the political level, the White House will say we're cooperating on terrorism, but that doesn't mean anything," says the former CIA operative whom Weiss spoke with for the *Daily Beast*. "So if the FSB is now sending jihadists to Syria so that they can die at the hands of the Americans rather than the Russians, should we be surprised? We're just so goddamn ignorant."[19]

THE MOSCOW-TEHRAN ALLIANCE

We have seen how Putin takes what seem to be contradictory positions on international terrorism—fighting ISIS while also seemingly enabling it. In his posture toward a nation with which the old Soviet Union had poisonous relations—the Islamic Republic of Iran—Putin has shown again that he is willing and able to make common cause with a premier sponsor of international terrorism. In fact, Iran is regarded as the world's leading nation-state sponsor of terrorist organizations, especially of Hezbollah in Lebanon; it is a staunch ally of the Assad regime in Syria; and it oppresses and even kills its own people when they attempt political expression.

But Russia and Iran are hardly natural allies, even now. They compete for natural gas markets and jockey for the upper hand in Central Asia. And they were bitter adversaries during the long decades of the Cold War. What unites Russia and Iran today, though, are three common concerns: first, a shared goal of protecting Bashar al-Assad's regime in Syria, a mission that places them firmly against the United States and its Western allies; second, a common general interest in opposing radical Sunni Islamist movements, today exemplified by ISIS (though, as we have seen, Putin also finds uses for ISIS); and third, a common interest in smashing internal dissent in their own countries and quelling secessionist movements—whether from the Chechens in Russia or from the Kurds in Iran.[20]

Undergirding it all, however, is a common foe: the United States. And Russia and Iran have long seen the Obama administration as a weak opponent—one which they have been fortunate to have at this time in history. In fact, according to Middle East specialist Amir Taheri, the Russians have a phrase, "*Fortochka* Obama," that means the "Obama window of opportunity." It refers to the sense among many that the time is now—while the dilatory Barack Obama remains president of the United States—to make aggressive moves internationally. That view is particularly taken by Moscow and Tehran. "By the time the 'fortochka Obama' is closed," Taheri writes, "Moscow and Tehran hope to have consolidated a firewall spanning a vast territory from the Baltics to the Persian Gulf, shielding them against what Putin and Iranian 'Supreme Guide' Ali Khamenei designate as 'American schemes.'"[21]

A perfect example of how Moscow and Tehran play off the weakness of Obama's leadership came a few months after the landmark nuclear deal that the Obama administration closed with Iran in summer 2015, in which long-standing sanctions on Iran were lifted in exchange for tempo- rary limits on Iran's nuclear program. American critics of the deal worried about the ease with which Tehran would violate it, and also about the possibility that the lifting of sanctions would restart talks between Iran and Russia on the sale of Russian-made S-300 missile systems to Tehran. The two countries had originally signed a deal for Iran to purchase the missiles in 2007, but Russia suspended the agreement in 2010. At that time, Moscow was involved in its short-lived "reset" with the United States, which soon foundered.

Now, with the nuclear deal bringing Iran back into the good graces of the international community, Russia has wasted little time reviving the S-300 deal, and in November 2015 the announcement was made: Russia would begin delivering S-300 systems to Iran by the end of 2016. In announcing the deal, Sergey Chemesov, chief executive of the Russian defense-contracting firm Rostec, said that the Obama administration's deal with Iran, in which sanctions were lifted, had been crucial in mak- ing the decision.

"Due to the changed situation today," he said, "we are developing contacts and co-operation with Iran."[22]

How important is the deal? As with most such developments, inter- pretations vary, but it's worth remembering that Israeli prime minister Benjamin Netanyahu journeyed to Moscow in 2013 to plead with Putin to kill the agreement. The Israelis worry that the S-300 will make it difficult for their air force to operate with impunity over Syria or Iran. And Michael Eisenstadt and Brenda Shaffer of the Washington Institute for Near East Policy consider Iran's acquisition of the S-300 system "a potential game-changer, since Iran's current air defenses are relatively weak and plagued by coverage and capability gaps."[23] The system would force an enemy aircraft into a much more defensive position, diverting it away from its ostensible goal—say, striking a nuclear facility. And the system would give Iran the capability of intercepting cruise missiles such as the American Tomahawk as well as medium-range ballistic missiles.[24] In short, it's a huge upgrade.

Coming so soon after Tehran formalized the nuclear deal with the United States, the S-300 purchase suggests that Iran is emboldened by the arrangements it has made with Washington, while also preparing itself defensively for any consequences of breaching the agreement. Indeed, the S-300 sale raises the possibility that the Iranians could use the Russian-made systems to protect the country's nuclear sites from air strikes should Tehran violate the terms of the nuclear deal with the United States. Many observers assume that those violations are not a matter of if but of when. By making the S-300 system available, Putin has made it easier for Tehran to cheat.

The S-300 sale is just the latest effort by Putin to shore up Iranian nuclear ambitions. During the long years when the Tehran regime negotiated with the Obama administration on the nuclear deal, Putin helped Tehran get closer to its goal of reaching "breakout" nuclear capacity by helping the Iranians build more nuclear facilities. In 2014, Moscow announced that it would build two more nuclear reactors in Bushehr—possibly to be followed by the construction of six more.[25]

In recent years, the most high-profile stage of the Moscow-Tehran partnership has been Syria, where both countries have played an essential role in the survival of the Assad regime. The Iranian Revolutionary Guard Corps (IRGC) is fighting on behalf of Assad's army in Syria, joined by forces of Hezbollah.[26] Putin has been flooding Syria with resources—including tanks, air-defense systems, and armored personnel carriers—for years, and he is building at least two military bases in the country.[27] He has also deployed thousands of Russian troops in the country.[28] Russia is building an additional weapons depot and military facility north of the city of Latakia, Assad's stronghold—clearly laying the groundwork for escalating its involvement.[29] And Putin's plan to ship out Islamists from the Caucasus has led to the development of a "green corridor" by which Russian jihadis can reach Syria and join up with ISIS.[30]

But, as one must always bear in mind where Putin is concerned, the Russian leader is adept at playing both sides. No one in Tehran is pleased with Putin's de facto ISIS recruitment, but that operation is only one piece of Putin's Syria puzzle. Another is his close collaboration with Shi'a Iran and its terrorist client, Hezbollah.

One way to understand the Moscow-Tehran nexus and how it works in Syria is through the person of Qassem Soleimani, leader of Iran's elite Quds Force of its Revolutionary Guards corps. Some call Soleimani the most powerful operative in the Middle East today. Others, like Middle East analyst Michael Pregent, a former intelligence advisor to General David Petraeus in Iraq, call Soleimani "a uniformed Osama bin Laden."[31] Soleimani is widely seen as the bankroller and mastermind behind Hezbollah and Hamas, both of which do Iran's bidding. And Soleimani supplied Iranian weapons to the insurgency in Iraq that killed American soldiers.

In July 2015, Soleimani paid a high-profile visit to Moscow, and two months later, Russia began air strikes in Syria on behalf of Assad. During the fall of 2015, Soleimani stepped up his force levels in Syria. Several thousand Iranian or Iranian-backed fighters were in the country, joined by thousands more from Hezbollah. And the Iranians shared intelligence with Putin and Assad.[32]

More recently, US officials said that elite fighters from the Iranian Revolutionary Guard were retreating from the Syrian military campaign after some bloody setbacks. Whether that pullback proves temporary or more permanent—in what might suggest encouraging progress for the United States and its allies in the Syrian conflict—remains to be seen. Yet even if the Iran-Hezbollah-Russia alliance fails to get its way in Syria, it has already turned its attention to other projects.

One of these is Yemen, where a brutal civil war is raging. Another client of Soleimani's, the Houthi rebels in South Yemen, has taken a higher profile of late in its struggle against forces supporting Yemen's president, Abd Rabbuh Mansur Hadi, whom the Houthis forced to flee power early in the year. Hadi, an ally of the United States, is trying to reclaim power with the help of a Saudi-led coalition. Fighting alongside the Houthis are Hezbollah operatives, with strong support from Tehran—and Moscow, which is providing weapons to the rebels.

Asked to confirm that the Russians were working with Iran and Hezbollah, a senior official from the terrorist group tells the *International*

Business Times, "Of course they are."[33] Thus the Iran-Hezbollah-Russia alliance in Yemen mimics the one in Syria.

In Yemen, Putin has strategic interests both broad ranging and narrowly self-interested. Yemen is another battleground in Russia's effort to thwart American power and displace Washington (and its Saudi ally) as the dominant power player in the Middle East. More narrowly, Putin sees in Yemen an opportunity to reclaim an old client for Russian arms sales: in the Soviet days, before it united with the North, South Yemen used Moscow as a key weapons provider. Thus the Houthi rebels, should they prevail, offer Putin a prospective new client. That would be especially welcome, since Yemen is exporting much of its oil to China, cutting in on Putin's efforts to become a larger oil supplier to Beijing.[34]

Although close Moscow observers think that Putin won't sell weapons to the Houthis until they become the official government of Yemen, the Hezbollah official who spoke to the *International Business Times* claims that the Russians have already supplied the rebels Tochka missiles, one of which was used to kill dozens of pro-Hadi forces in the deadliest attack against the coalition of the conflict so far. The Hezbollah official says that the Tochkas are being smuggled into Yemen from Russia "one by one."[35] And most believe that the Houthis lack the operational expertise to operate the missiles without guidance from Russian operatives.

All of this brings us back to the Iran deal, which, by lifting sanctions on Tehran and unfreezing assets, will only make Iranian (and Russian) support for the Houthis easier. "Everybody is concerned that the money that is being released is going to enable Iran in a large part, or even a small part, to give more money to Houthi rebels in Yemen, the Assad regime in Syria, Hezbollah, Hamas, etc.," says Matthew Levitt, a former FBI and Treasury department analyst.[36]

NORTH KOREA

Of all the world's rogue regimes, North Korea remains a pariah with few peers, a dictatorship exceeding by far the "normal" standards of autocratic repression. The Pyongyang regime of Kim Jong-un is less autocratic than psychopathic, a dystopia out of a novelist's nightmares. The horrors that North Koreans endure are magnified by the regime's possession of nuclear weapons, which are used to menace its neighbors and the United

States and create an ongoing climate of tension. While the United States has tried to isolate and neutralize North Korea, China, its traditional benefactor, has mostly propped up the communist regime, standing as its main friend and protector in the world. More recently, however, Beijing has pushed back on Kim, taking him to task for his refusal to pursue economic reforms and especially for his nuclear provocations. North Korea test launched a submarine-based ballistic missile in 2015, showing that its capabilities were more advanced than previously suspected. Chinese nuclear experts even met with American nuclear experts in April 2015 to warn them that they were underestimating North Korea's nuclear capabilities. The Chinese believe that the North Koreans could double their count of twenty warheads within a year, and Washington is already worried about Pyongyang's capacity to put a nuclear warhead on an intercontinental ballistic missile, or ICBM, that could reach the West Coast of the United States.

To be sure, Chinese cautions need to be taken with skepticism, since the Chinese, like Putin, are adept at playing the double game. But some longtime observers have speculated about some new distance opening up between Beijing and Pyongyang.

That's where Putin comes in. Sensing an opportunity, Russia announced a "year of friendship" with North Korea for 2015, in which the two countries would commemorate "Korea's liberation and the victory in the great Patriotic War in Russia" while deepening their political and economic ties. In November 2015, a Russian military delegation arrived in Pyongyang to sign an agreement formalizing protocols for the conducting of military exercises between the two countries to avoid misunderstandings. More substantively, Moscow has announced plans to cancel the $10 billion in debt owed by Pyongyang, develop the North Korean Rason port for export of Russian coal to the country, and invest $25 billion in infrastructure in North Korea, including railways. The communist backwater badly needs those investments. And, though the terms haven't been formalized, the two countries are working on a deal in which Russia would sell a state-of-the-art fighter aircraft to North Korea.[37]

None of these developments is necessarily earthshaking, and the Russia-North Korea partnership is clearly not a major factor as of yet. But what commentators call a "pariah alliance" certainly contains the potential to wreak havoc internationally. At minimum, moving closer to

Moscow allows Pyongyang more leverage against American attempts to isolate and punish the regime.[38] As for Putin, having North Korea in his pocket gives him yet another destabilizing chip to play in his long game.

LATIN AMERICA

"The People's Republic of China and Russia know the world's problems much better than the United States," wrote former Cuban leader Fidel Castro in December 2015, "because they were obliged to endure the terrible wars imposed on them by fascism's blind egoism. I do not doubt that, given their historical traditions and their own revolutionary experience, they will make the greatest effort to avoid a war and contribute to the peaceful development of Venezuela, Latin America, Asia and Africa."[39]

Castro's letter, a rare public utterance for the aging and ailing leader, who handed power to his brother Raúl in 2008, is addressed to Venezuelan president Nicolás Maduro, whom Fidel praises for recognizing the parliamentary elections in Venezuela in which his party lost its majority. It is no secret that Castro and Maduro, along with other Latin American leaders, have grown increasingly close to Russia in recent years. In Latin America, America's traditional sphere of influence, Russia has announced plans to pursue rights to military facilities in Cuba, Venezuela, and Nicaragua. These will not be military bases per se (the only current Russian base outside the old Soviet Union's borders is in Syria). But they will represent a heightened Russian military presence in America's backyard.

"The talks are under way," says Russian defense minister Sergei Shoigu of the plans for the Latin American bases, "and we are close to signing the relevant documents. We need bases for refueling near the equator, and in other places."[40]

Putin has been working his intrigues in Latin America for years. He enjoyed particularly close relations with Venezuelan strongman—and terrorist supporter—Hugo Chavez, whom he eulogized on his passing in 2013 as "an uncommon and strong man who looked into the future and always set the highest target for himself."[41] Since then, Putin has done his best to keep the momentum going with Chavez's successor, Nicolás Maduro. Russia has stood with Maduro against what it considers

American efforts to destabilize the country through support for democratic movements.

In Cuba, Putin has worked hard to rebuild the once rock-solid Russian-Cuban relationship, which waned after the fall of the Soviet Union. Putin has maintained a growing military relationship with the communist regime, a bitter foe of Washington for half a century, despite the recent normalization of relations. In 2014, Putin sent a Russian spy vessel to dock in Havana Harbor, which arrived just as the foreign ministry announced Russia's plans to deepen Latin American ties.

And perhaps even more worryingly, there is the developing relationship between Putin and Nicaraguan president Daniel Ortega, who called Putin "a brother president" and asked him in a letter to "defend the peace that the world needs so dearly."[42] Ortega recently announced an agreement in which Russian ships and aircraft will visit Nicaragua for training exercises. While all of this may be preliminary for now, Putin's efforts to put down roots in Latin America has many in Washington concerned—especially since an increased Russian presence in the region will only heighten the chances for a confrontation with the United States.

CONCLUSION

For years now, Vladimir Putin, often in alliance with his friend in Beijing Xi Jinping, has facilitated the interests of North Korea, Iran, and other rogue nations—especially Bashar al-Assad's Syrian regime—and, reaching into America's backyard, the interests of Venezuela, Cuba, and Nicaragua. More recently, Putin has been benefitting from the rise of ISIS, even as he takes steps to fight the terrorist group (but only on his terms).

Putin has been a champion of the principle of "noninterference": a doctrine holding that states should not interfere with the internal affairs of other states. The two nations that benefit most from this seemingly high-minded doctrine are North Korea and Iran, two of the world's most notorious autocracies. By working closely with Iran and seeking closer relations with North Korea, Putin has reaped the whirlwind. It is beyond dispute that Hezbollah has gotten weapons from Iran—often Russian-made weapons. North Korea almost certainly sent to Syria the technology used to build the nuclear plant that Israel destroyed in 2007. Moscow's noninterference doctrine has made it much easier for traffic in arms and military technology to flourish between these regimes.

In short, whether around the world or closer to home, Russia has done the bidding of forces inimical to US interests, democratic values, and international stability. Putin supports rogue regimes and dangerous terrorist groups by providing them with economic, political, diplomatic, and military support. Although Putin's strategies are often complex and even sometimes seemingly contradictory, they are made coherent by his prevailing mission to weaken the fundamentals of Western strength by unleashing violent and unpredictable historical forces around the world. Through years of double dealing, fearless instigation of regional conflicts, and facilitation and support of terrorism, Putin has continually destabilized the post–Cold War order and fomented crises that challenge Western power.

CHAPTER 7

Black-Gold Bully
Russia's Oil and Gas

The Russians are looking for ways to break the unity of Europe, and they are targeting the weaker states. Hungary and Bulgaria have energy needs. Greece has financial needs. It is all part of the Russian design.

—SENIOR WESTERN DIPLOMAT[1]

Russia is one of the world's predominant energy powers, with vast oil and gas resources that it pumps out of the Russian heartland into factories, gas tanks, and power stations around the world. These enormous energy supplies give Putin a tool that he has never hesitated to use to punish his enemies, reward his friends, and influence business and politics around the world. Europe does have encouraging present and future plans for energy diversification, along with a growing spot market for natural gas; nonetheless, for the time being, the continent relies strongly on Russian oil and gas. Putin could dramatically disrupt the continent's economy at a moment's notice, sending German factories, Dutch ports, and Italian gas stations scrambling to keep the lights on. The prospect of Putin again switching off the heat to entire countries in the dead of winter, and leaving millions to freeze in the cold, chills even the most anti-Putin Swede, Dane, or Estonian.

But it's not just Europe that's vulnerable to Putin's manipulation of energy markets: the entire global economy would feel the pain if Putin stopped the gas flow to Europe for just a few days. And to make matters worse, Putin has cut a landmark $400 billion gas deal with the Chinese. The full impact of that agreement will likely take many years to determine, but it was a big win for Putin and his energy strategy. Japan and India are next on his list.

Putin repeatedly uses this control over European energy and global markets to bully and threaten countries into submission, as he has by shutting off gas to Ukraine, and by suggesting that harsh sanctions or a military response to Russian aggression would cause Russian-supplied pipelines throughout Europe to run dry. European businesspeople concerned with their bottom lines and politicians beholden to their constituents can't stomach the prospect of a Russian oil or gas shutoff, so they accommodate and appease Putin instead of calling his bluff.

But Putin always wants more power and control. That's why he's making bold and aggressive moves to seize even more of the world's energy supplies—forging alliances with friendly, energy-rich countries while targeting rivals with military and diplomatic force. Putin is already working to build an energy axis with Iran, a task he has pursued vigorously since President Obama's nuclear deal lifted sanctions. At the same time, Russia and Iran have encircled leading oil exporter Saudi Arabia by seizing control over Shiite-controlled regimes in Iraq and Syria, sending a clear message to Riyadh that leaves Russia's aims in the region unambiguous. Putin is also moving to lay claim to vast energy reserves in the Arctic, deploying troops and ships, and thereby bringing Russia into conflict with its Arctic neighbors. Putin has been most successful in Central Asia, where Russian pipelines feed oil and gas to China and fill the Kremlin's coffers.

Stopping or even slowing down Putin's energy push will be a stiff challenge for America and its European allies. In recent years, we've seen some encouraging moves—like the EU's Third Energy Package and American efforts to halt deals like South Stream—but overall, our strategy remains inadequate. Day by day, as the United States and its Western allies look on, Putin grows Russia's access to the global supply of oil and gas, creeping closer to inordinate control over the world's energy markets.

RUSSIAN RESERVES, EUROPEAN DEPENDENCE

Fossil fuels—petroleum, natural gas, and coal—account for 80 percent of the world's energy supply, and Russia produces more fossil fuels than any nation in the world except for Saudi Arabia.[2] For years, Western commentators have been predicting that Russia's energy power was on the wane. Over the last decade or so, we often heard that Russia had reached "peak oil" and would soon start to decline as one of the world's leading producers and suppliers. As it turns out, these hopeful predictions are simply wrong, whether on oil or on gas. In both areas, Russia is poised to remain a world leader in energy production—and will continue to use its strength in this crucial area to intimidate and manipulate its neighbors.

Putin has effectively weaponized Russia's energy reserves and leveraged them as a foreign policy tool, with his strategic vision trumping markets, contracts, and economic stability. Moscow continues to derive significant strength from its energy resources. Russia has the world's largest natural gas reserves,[3] second-largest coal reserves[4]—with a 455-year supply[5]—and sixth-largest global reserves.[6] The country's oil and gas reserves are growing rapidly as producers make new discoveries, with ten billion barrels of additional oil reserves discovered in Russia between 2013 and 2015—more than anywhere else in the world.[7] In 2015, Russian oil output broke post-Soviet output records four times. This despite a global collapse in oil prices due to oversupply. Favorable tax policies for Russian oil firms allow the government to take most of the hit for price drops. The companies can keep producing, putting them in strong position when prices recover.[8]

Russia is extracting and exporting these huge reserves at a staggering rate: Moscow is currently the world's largest gas exporter and the second-largest oil exporter, giving it enormous influence in global energy markets.[9]

All of this energy might is vital particularly in regard to Europe, the largest energy importer in the world, which relies on outside sources for more than half the energy it consumes. The EU gets one-third of its natural gas and 35 percent of its crude oil from Russia.[10] Far from declining, the Russian hand in energy on the continent is only strengthening: between 2010 and 2014, Russia extended its share of total European gas imports by one-third, from 48 percent to 64 percent. "The EU is set to be dependent on Russian gas for some time and that's the reality," says Maria van der Hoeven, executive director of the International Energy Association.[11] Six EU countries import *all* of their gas from Gazprom,

the state-owned Russian energy firm. And at least 15 percent of the gas
that the EU imports runs through Ukrainian pipelines—magnifying the
importance of that country's vulnerability to Russian aggression.[12]

For years, the world has seen how Putin is willing to use Russia's dominance of global energy markets to advance his political goals. In 2009,
Russia shut off gas supplies to Ukraine in a move designed to undermine
then president Viktor Yushchenko. Putin isn't afraid of collateral damage
or losing customers due to his punitive energy policies. During the 2009
Ukraine shutoff, Putin also cut supplies to Bulgaria, Greece, Macedonia,
Romania, Croatia, and Turkey. But all of these countries had no choice
but to remain Russian energy customers. The move sent Europe into an
energy crisis "within hours."[13]

Russian weaponization of energy works in two ways: Whereas Putin
is willing to punish adversaries, he is also eager to reward like-minded
countries and allies with a favorable energy supply and transit deals.
Putin's use of "petrocarrots" and "petrosticks," as some analysts call them,
was on display in Putin's 2015 attempt to replace Ukrainian transit routes
taking Russian gas to Europe with routes through Turkey. The move was
criticized for making "no economic sense," but from Russia's perspective,
the move wasn't about economics—it was about politics.

"We are diversifying and eliminating the risks of unreliable countries
that caused problems in past years, including for European consumers,"
says Russian energy minister Alexander Novak, making a clear reference to Ukraine.[14] It was a bold effort to punish Ukraine further, though
financial snags caused Russia to abandon the project.

Putin also makes sure that allies like Armenia and Belarus can buy
Russian gas at cheaper prices (and without supply interruptions) than his
enemies Georgia, Ukraine, and the Baltic States, all of which have faced
price gouging and the constant threat of cutoffs. He uses cheap energy
to prop up Russian-backed leaders in unrecognized Abkhazia, South
Ossetia, and Transnistria—all economically impoverished regions in
Russia's "near abroad" that couldn't survive without Moscow's political
and economic sponsorship.[15] Putin has supplied subsidized gas to South
Ossetia and Abkhazia, and Gazprom has spent generous sums building
infrastructure in South Ossetia.[16]

Though Putin deals primarily in oil and natural gas, he has also used
other energy resources to build Russian influence and foster dependence

on Moscow. Perhaps the most dramatic recent example is a Russian-built nuclear power plant in Hungary, which will supply a third of that country's electricity. For those doubting that Putin is playing a long game, the Hungary nuclear plant is instructive.

"You cannot afford in this part of the world not to have a pragmatic cooperation with Russia," says Hungary's foreign minister, Péter Szijjártó.[17] Having already imported nearly 80 percent of its natural gas from Russia, the Eastern European nation has now become even more entwined with Russia as an energy provider. Putin has offered Budapest what has been described as a "sweetheart deal" on a nuclear power plant that would generate one-third of Hungary's electricity by 2025. The plant would be primarily built and paid for by Russian state-owned companies—two of which were sanctioned by Western governments for their involvement in the Ukraine crisis. The gesture was a clear effort on Putin's part to keep Hungary—an influential EU member—on the side of Russia and deepen Hungarian dependence on Russian energy.

Did it work? Well, just consider that not long after the nuclear plant agreement was reached, Hungary stopped reselling Russian gas to Ukraine, putting even more pressure on the beleaguered government in Kiev.[18]

In the words of one Western diplomat: "The Russians are looking for ways to break the unity of Europe, and they are targeting the weaker states. Hungary and Bulgaria have energy needs. Greece has financial needs. It is all part of the Russian design."[19] Putin sees a natural ally in Hungarian prime minister Viktor Orbán, a former dissident. Orbán has left his youthful idealism behind and now seeks to emulate Putin in building what he frankly calls an "illiberal democracy" in Hungary.[20] By keeping Orbán close in his orbit, Putin has an influential ally within the European Union. And the entire effort is underpinned by Russian energy supplies.

None of this should surprise those who have studied Putin's career. Two decades ago, before he became the Russian president and prime minister, Putin authored a dissertation at the St. Petersburg Mining Institute. The subject: the strategic importance of Russia's energy reserves. In his dissertation (though some allege that he wrote only a few pages of it), Putin argues strongly for state oversight of energy-industry priorities.

Russia's energy supplies, he asserts, are a key guarantor of the country's national security and future economic prosperity. This outlook is clearly reflected in Putin's current policies, which continue to meet with success—especially due to Europe's energy dependence.

Every major European power is significantly dependent on Russian energy imports, with Russian energy accounting for 30 percent of energy imports to Germany, 28 percent of imports to Italy, 17 percent of imports to France, and 13 percent of imports to the UK. A disruption in supplies to any of these countries would have serious global consequences.[21] Less powerful European countries are even more dependent on Russian energy, with Russian energy accounting for 46 percent of energy imports to Sweden, 40 percent of imports to Greece, and 34 percent of imports to the Netherlands, home to Europe's busiest and most important port, Rotterdam.[22] For now, despite ongoing efforts to diversify their sources and free themselves from Russian energy dependency, Estonia, Latvia, and Lithuania remain at the mercy of Putin—as does Finland. Poland, Bulgaria, and the Czech Republic are almost as vulnerable.[23]

Putin uses European dependence on Russian energy to keep America's EU and NATO allies off balance, with the implied threat of a partial or total energy shutoff a specter constantly looming over European business and political elites. The EU is, after all, among the world's largest economies, accounting for 24 percent of global GDP. Putin knows that if he pulls the plug on European energy supplies, the world economy will take a hit. Russia holds an energy trump card over Europe and, by extension, on all of global trade.

"Europe would collapse," says Russian political expert Paul Craig Roberts, if Putin were to shut off its gas supplies for any serious period of time. "Without Russian gas they can't survive the winter, their industries can't run and that would be the end of it."[24]

By "the end of it," Roberts is referring to a potential situation that has already threatened to occur. The Ukraine crisis, in 2014, led leaders in Europe to explore sanctions against Russian energy companies. But the Eurozone backed down when the implications of such actions became clear: Putin could turn the gas-shutoff weapon against Europe in retaliation, and the Europeans would pay the price.[25]

RUSSIA'S EXPANDING CONTROL

Just as Putin uses energy to exert political control abroad, he also uses Russia's political might to exert control over the energy supplies themselves—always with the goal of expanding Russian access to and ownership of the world's oil and gas.

Not content with his clout on the European continent, Putin is positioning Russia to be the preeminent energy supplier to Asia, with a focus on supplying liquefied natural gas (LNG) to China, India, and Japan. Putin has signed a massive contract for a new West Siberian oil pipeline that will supply $400 billion worth of gas to China and a follow-up deal that will make China the primary customer for Russian gas.[26] These developing accords will extend Russia's reach while cultivating energy-based relationships with rising and established Asian powers.

Russia's political alliance with Iran, another globally important oil and gas producer, is turning into a "Russia-Iran energy axis" that offers Moscow considerable leverage over energy supplies in the Middle East, Central Asia, and Eastern Europe. America's nuclear deal with Iran and the lifting of international sanctions against Tehran have cleared the way for Russia and Iran to begin formal energy cooperation. The two nations have set up gas and oil swap deals, while discussing potential pipelines and LNG transport agreements. Russia and Iran are also targeting Saudi Arabia, the ringleader of OPEC and the only country that exports more oil than Russia, by encircling it with a Putin-orchestrated alliance of Iraq, Syria, and Iran—backed by Russian military and diplomatic support.

Indeed, those puzzling over Putin's motives in intervening in Syria on behalf of his ally, Bashar al-Assad, have offered many explanations—from distracting others from the Ukraine crisis to weakening NATO—but have paid comparatively little attention to how Putin's Syrian intervention supports one of his overarching goals: to become the key player in charge of the global oil supply.[27] How would he do this? By using his new alliances to outflank the Saudis, who have been flooding the world market with cheap oil (in part to work against the new competition from shale sources coming from the United States). Cheap energy prices have wrought havoc on the Russian economy, and Putin wants to change the dynamic. He wants to do for Russian oil what he has already done for Russian gas—make it the resource that holds the European market hostage. To do that, he must displace the Saudis as the oil market's kingpins, and, by combining forces with Iran, Iraq, and Syria, Putin has a chance to do just that.

By some analyses, these motives explain entirely what Putin is up to in Syria, where he has already deployed Russian special forces, and where he might be preparing to unleash as many as 150,000 Russian ground troops. While Putin is ostensibly fighting ISIS in these regions, the Russian offensive, at least until November 2015, had been heavily directed against the Syrian rebels trying to overthrow Assad. In the wake of ISIS's bombing of a Russian airliner and its murderous attacks in Paris in November 2015, Putin suggested that he was genuinely determined to battle the terrorist group. But it soon became apparent that Putin's aims remained the same: to put down the rebels, save Assad, and position the Syrian dictator as the viable alternative to ISIS. And he has now essentially achieved these aims, as his announcement of a Russian troop drawdown in March 2016 made clear. With his allies in place, Putin might yet dictate terms to the Saudis regarding oil supplies and prices.[28]

Time will tell how far Putin is willing to go. It is not out of the question that the Russian-Iranian-Syrian alliance could lead to a war, as the Saudis move to protect their global energy preeminence—not to mention their oil fields.[29] Those fields are under threat from the Yemen-based Houthi rebels, who just happen to be trained and funded by Iran.

And yet, it is that very threat, among others, that Putin is leveraging to hold out an alternative scenario to the Saudis: one of cooperation in a mutual goal of achieving higher oil prices. This is a goal that not only the Russians and Saudis but also the Iranians share. Thus Putin met with Deputy Crown Prince Salman, the Saudi Arabian defense minister, to discuss an oil agreement. Even as he exerts pressure on Riyadh, Putin recognizes that Russia and Saudi Arabia might yet come to an accommodation. "The thing to look out for," says Larry Jeddeloh, the editor of the *Institutional Strategist*,

is a deal in which Iran will stop backing the Houthi and, in return, Saudi Arabia stops pumping 10.3 million barrels a day and reduces output.

The Russians broker the deal because they can benefit dramatically from a Saudi shift in oil policy. You get a more formal relationship developing between Russia and Saudi Arabia, which together have 21 million barrels a day in production. And they regain control of the pricing mechanism in the next six months.[30]

As Jeddeloh sees it, the Saudis will stop pumping so much oil once they're confident that their oil fields are secure from threats. Then they'll reduce output and global prices will rise again, benefiting Moscow, Riyadh, and Tehran.

The power of Putin's energy vision lies not only in its strategic sophistication and his tenacity in pursuing it but in the scope of its goals. Witness the Russian effort to secure energy resources in the Arctic, where Putin has moved swiftly to exert Russian control, claiming over 463,000 square miles of the Artic seabed, which could contain up to a quarter of the world's untapped global oil and gas reserves.[31] Russia is backing up its Arctic claims with military force, including six thousand troops[32] and a fleet of forty ice-breakers, including nuclear icebreakers—compared with America's two.[33] Russian aggressiveness has already led to confrontations with Norway over exploration rights and century-old border treaties, with tensions reaching "potentially dangerous levels" that will continue to escalate as Putin claims more of the Arctic and its energy reserves for Russia.[34]

It should come as no surprise that, in the Arctic as elsewhere, Russia is outhustling and outthinking the United States. Washington "has failed consistently to demonstrate it has the political will and agency know-how to allow Arctic offshore oil-exploration to move forward," writes retired navy admiral Gary Roughead, who warns that American "dithering must end soon." He points to a recent report from the National Petroleum Council, which finds that unless the United States ramps up exploration of Arctic energy resources now, it "risks a renewed reliance on imported oil and jeopardizes America's global competitiveness, leadership and influence in the Arctic."[35] In our absence, Russia (along with China, which is also moving in aggressively) will have free rein.

Finally, in Central Asia, home to considerable oil and gas fields, Russian state oil giant Rosneft has locked Kazakhstan—the region's leading hydrocarbon producer—into Moscow's energy orbit, with Russian-built pipelines delivering seven million tons of Kazakh oil to

China annually.[36] The deal helps all three players: the Chinese get oil, the Kazaks get a foundational economic relationship with both Moscow and Beijing, and the Russians get an important Central Asian partner in Kazakhstan, President Nursultan Nazarbayev. And, of course, the Russia-Kazakhstan-China oil pipeline also brings more straightforward economic benefits: hundreds of billions of petrodollars flowing to Russia.[37]

OUTFLANKING PUTIN

The Russian-energy power play resembles Russian offensives in other areas—military, economic, diplomatic—in being serious and formidable while also containing the seeds of its own demise should a concerted, determined Western effort be brought to bear against it. Up to now, this is precisely what we have lacked in the West. Yet the avenues for trumping Putin's energy hand are clear.

One piece of the puzzle involves European efforts to form an energy union that would both increase coordination between member nations' economies and reduce dependence on Russian energy. The union is an idea whose time has come, though making it a reality will involve surmounting member nations' objections to ceding some sovereignty over national energy policy.[38] The French are heavily nuclear dependent, for example, while the Germans generally enjoy favorable gas prices from the Russians. Via Nord Stream, a pipeline running under the Baltic Sea, Russia delivers natural gas to Germany. Other nations already enjoy relatively good pricing on Russian gas and won't want to risk those arrangements by joining such a union. Poland, meanwhile, is less dependent on Russian gas and more reliant on coal—an energy source high in carbon emissions and thus frowned upon by many EU member states, like Germany, that are working hard to reduce emissions and increase energy production through renewable sources. But the Poles put energy security first, environmental sustainability second.[39]

These competing and conflicting aims will have to be resolved, but a unified EU on energy issues, resources, and policies would present a formidable obstacle to Russian attempts at economic intimidation and blackmail.[40] And by becoming one large customer for Russian gas, a European energy union would become more powerful and better able to negotiate favorable prices for its members than those members are currently able to do individually (with some exceptions, as noted). Only such an entity would have the clout to stand up to Gazprom in price negotiations. And the more secure Europe becomes in its position with Russia on gas, the better able EU states will be to diversify their energy marketplaces and foster more economic competition and innovation.[41]

The crucial underlying theme in an American and Western counter-offensive on energy is Russian vulnerability. Russia's economy is *wholly dependent* on its vast reserves of oil and natural gas—a critical weakness that has nevertheless not prevented Putin, at least up to now, from influencing global markets, punishing specific countries, and building relationships of dependency that limit the ability of Russia's energy customers to act against Kremlin interests. The last thing Europe's anemic economy needs is the shock of Kremlin-ordered oil and gas shutoffs. Powerful corporate interests lobby hard against any move that could endanger cheap, hassle-free energy. State-owned Russian energy firms have no qualms about buying the business of European politicians by structuring deals and megaprojects to reward pro-Russian parties and leaders, leading to Soviet-style corruption within many European institutions.

Substituting Russian oil and gas suppliers with American and indigenous European sources is the only way out of this vicious cycle of dependence and corruption. All the more reason for a comprehensive, unified effort—one that must include European initiatives to create a competitive energy marketplace. Europe should import more natural gas from the United States and start producing more of its own oil and natural gas—both of which it possesses in abundant quantities. Studies show that Europe has enough gas reserves to last at least a generation; Sweden might have enough to last 250 years. Other countries also have rich deposits. The problem? It would require hydraulic fracking to extract them.[42]

The Europeans—except for Poland and Britain—have so far been unmoved by America's fracking revolution, which has made the United States the world's leading natural gas producer in a matter of half a decade or so. Rigid environmentalist policies and NIMBYism in Europe have blocked fracking on the continent, despite the evidence not only of its benefits in America but also of Russian funding for antifracking activity. Moscow is clearly motivated, says NATO secretary general Anders Fogh

Rasmussen, by the desire "to maintain European dependence on import-ed Russian gas."[43] It's past time for Europe to embrace fracking, which will reduce energy prices, cut carbon emissions—since natural gas is cleaner than coal—and, above all, make the continent more energy independent. Shale gas is a crucial hedge against Russian energy exploitation.[44]

Momentum is building in Europe to make such changes. In a 2014 report, the International Energy Agency warns that Europe needs to diversify its supplies, especially of liquefied natural gas (LNG)—though so far, the Asian market has been snapping up much of the American LNG supply.[45] The IEA urged Europe to take a long look at shale gas and learn from the experience in America, where more information about the environmental impact of fracking is becoming available. In short, the IEA says, the EU "cannot afford to reduce its energy options; nuclear, coal and unconventional gas and oil will need to be part of the mix."[46]

The United States has a critical role to play as well in outflanking Putin. Most importantly, we need to commit ourselves to a major effort and presence in the Arctic. Russia has already flooded resources into the region as it tries to secure vast energy stores. A US geological survey estimates that the Arctic Circle possesses nearly a third of the world's undiscovered natural gas and 13 percent of its undiscovered oil,[47] and Putin is going after it all. America is way behind here, and we don't have a moment to lose. The Obama administration has been worse than inattentive—it has been actively opposed to developing these resources, closing off regions of Alaska to energy exploration, including the Arctic National Wildlife Refuge (ANWR) and a vast portion of the Alaska Outer Continental Shelf.[48]

"Opening these regions," writes retired US army colonel David Hunt,

> could help counter Russia's military advancement in the Arctic while creating thousands of jobs for Americans and further improving U.S. national and energy security. It would also force Russia to spend even more hard-to-find rubles on its military, a scarce commodity in an economic recession. The administration's order to prohibit energy pro-duction in millions of acres in and around Alaska impedes our ability to learn valuable maritime information, grow our navigation and border security capabilities and expand our energy infrastructure, the latter of which keeps us somewhat reliant on rival nations for oil.[49]

Making a serious move into the Arctic will serve US energy, economic, and national security interests—while also reducing Putin's energy leverage. It's almost a crime that the Obama administration refuses to pursue it.

Alas, such indifference hasn't been confined to the United States. Europe, too, must wean itself from dependence on Russian energy. America can help itself and its allies with a more robust energy policy, but unless Europe gets on board, Putin is likely to keep holding the energy cards—and to keep playing them.

CHAPTER 8

Putin's Proxies

How Russia Influences Europe

I share at least a part of Vladimir Putin's economic vision. That's for sure, but it didn't start yesterday. The Front Nationale has never changed its position on this subject. We welcomed the arrival of a government that did not serve the 'apparatchiks', and which developed a patriotic economy...I admire his cool head...I admire that he has managed to restore pride and contentment to a great nation that had been humiliated and persecuted for 70 years. Simple as that. I think that there are things you have to look on with a positive eye, or at least with an impartial eye.

—**MARINE LE PEN**[1]

Putin is a cunning man who has mastered the art of influencing and impacting events far beyond Russia's borders. When Russia's military might, economic weight, or diplomatic muscle can't get the job done, Putin has an army of proxies at his disposal who are tethered to the Kremlin through complex networks of money, loyalty, and political comradery. Putin has updated the old KGB playbook for the twenty-first century, combining Soviet-style support for opposition political parties throughout Europe with private-sector scheming facilitated through Kremlin-dependent oligarchs and state-owned megafirms. Unlike the Soviet Union's subversive support for communist and socialist parties in the West, today Russia's proxies are ideologically diverse, from the far left in Greece to the far right in France. Unhindered by Soviet-era economic dogmatism, Putin has happily taken advantage of capitalism and globalized markets to advance Russian interests, and hasn't been shy about enriching himself and his cronies in the process. Taken together, Putin's network of political lackeys and private sector servants form a dangerous, subversive web of Russian proxies throughout Europe.

Putin's political proxies are a mixed bag of opportunists, ideologues, and nationalists who are united only by their acceptance of Moscow's patronage. Some of them are explicitly pro-Russian parties in former Soviet countries where there is a sizable or influential Russian minority, including the Baltics, Ukraine, and Moldova. Others are far-right nationalist parties that admire Putin's muscular, boldly chauvinistic leadership style, such has Marine Le Pen's National Front in France or Jobbik in Hungary. And some are far-left radical parties that share Putin's antipathy toward the economic and political institutions of the West, such as Greece's infamous SYRIZA or the newly ascendant Podemos in Spain. In some countries, including Greece, France, and Germany, Putin has allies on both the left and the right who compete fiercely, but what's important to him is that both answer the phone when Moscow calls. Putin has wormed Russia into the very fabric of European democracy, filling the political organs of the EU government with Russophiles, anti-NATO activists, and paid spies. With his finger ever on the pulse of the European body politic, Putin has shrewdly cultivated proxy parties with sharply populist appeal, riding the wave of antiestablishment passion sweeping the West and positioning his European allies to grow in influence. Preventing these parties from gaining any more power than they already have is critical to maintaining the functionality of NATO and the EU, and of preventing Putin from establishing a zone of influence deep inside Europe.

In the private sector, Putin's stable of regime-dependent oligarchs have bought up assets across Europe, from British soccer clubs to Austrian construction firms, creating a web of companies that are indirectly beholden to the Kremlin and can be utilized to achieve its aims. Putin's oligarchs park their money in Western financial institutions, particularly British and Swiss banks, creating perverse political incentives against any action or policy that could destabilize Russia's economy. This has proven especially problematic for the EU's sanctions regime against Russia, which the financial sector resisted even as Russian-backed separatists shot EU-flagged airliners out of the sky. Russian-state megafirms such as Gazprom and Rosneft, which take their orders directly from the Kremlin, spend billions to supplement the efforts of the oligarchs and weave Russian capital inextricably into the fabric of the European economy. Only by targeting the assets of Russian state firms and Kremlin-dependent oligarchs, and punishing inappropriate commercial relations with them, can the West free itself from Putin's extended network of economic control and influence. Otherwise, Putin will be in a position to pull the rug out from underneath the European economy, constituting an effective kill switch for global markets and a powerful deterrent against America and NATO.

PRO-RUSSIAN POLITICAL PROXIES

In countries neighboring Russia, Putin has built or co-opted parties that explicitly promote the interests of ethnic Russian minorities and take their marching orders from the Kremlin. Often, these parties have legitimate political foundations in the very real divisions that exist between minority Russians and the majority population, but Putin exploits these rifts to promote instability, undermine democracy, and foment a fifth column of citizens more loyal to the Kremlin than to their own government.

Latvia

In Latvia, where Russia has clear ambitions and Russians make up 26 percent of the population,[2] Putin backs two political parties, the Latvian Russian Union (LRU) and the social democratic party Harmony. The LRU and Harmony were both founded as ethnic Russian parties and lean left, emerging from the old leadership of the Latvian branch of the Communist Party of the Soviet Union. Several of the founders worked actively to prevent Latvian independence when the Soviet Union collapsed.[3] Tatjana Ždanoka, cochairperson of the LRU and former member of the Supreme Soviet of the Latvian Soviet Socialist Republic (SSR), currently represents Latvia in the European Parliament. At Russia's invitation, Ždanoka "observed" the sham Crimean referendum and is now under investigation by Latvia's security authorities for being a Russian agent of influence.[4]

Indeed, the LRU has signed a cooperation agreement with the Russian Unity Party in Crimea, which has illegally governed that territory since its annexation by Putin.[5] A statement from the LRU says that the aim of the agreement is to "strengthen the unity of the Russian world."[6] At home, the LRU has tried to alter the law governing Latvian nationality, attempting to subvert Latvian democracy by making hundreds of thousands of nonresidents voting citizens without their knowledge.[7] The LRU has also pushed to make Russian an official language of the country (along with Latvian), despite the brutal suppression of the Latvian language during Soviet and Tsarist times.[8]

While Harmony is not as overtly anti-Latvian as the LRU, it is even more dangerous as the single-largest party in Latvia's parliament, leading the opposition and exerting partial control of Latvia's capital, Riga. Intrepid investigative journalists have discovered that Russia's foreign intelligence agency, the SVR, secretly financed the 2009 election of Harmony leader Nils Ušakovs as mayor of Riga.[9] In Latvia's 2014 elections, where Putin's bought-and-paid-for stooge Ušakovs was Harmony's candidate for prime minister, Harmony received more votes than any other party. Fortunately, a center-right coalition of patriotic Latvians has repeatedly prevented either the LRU or Harmony from winning the government, but as Europe continues to deteriorate economically and the Left sharpens its pocketbook argument, the chances rise that Putin's handpicked proxies could soon find themselves in control of Latvia, a NATO and EU member.

Estonia

Estonia is in a similar position to Latvia, with ethnic Russians making up a 25 percent minority and the Putin-backed Estonian Centre Party claiming to represent their interests while actively working to destabilize the country.

In 2004, the Estonian Centre Party signed a cooperation agreement with Putin's United Russia party to bring the two parties closer together, and to establish interparty commissions bringing the parties into alignment on everything from cultural to economic policy.[10] At the time the pact was signed, Valery Bogomolov, the first deputy head of United Russia, said: "The Center Party . . . has a rather constructive position on all issues of interest to us," especially "our interest in the continuation of an open dialogue for the settlement of problems of the Russian-speaking minority, as well as of Russian territories adjacent to Estonia."[11] At least Bogomolov is upfront with his Estonian partners about having his eyes on their land.

Edgar Savisaar, the leader of the Estonian Centre Party and mayor of Estonia's capital, Tallinn, has consistently been described as authoritarian and corrupt, although one comes to expect no less from Putin's partners. Savisaar has been the only leader of the Estonian Centre Party in its entire twenty-four-year history, and is currently suspended from the mayor's office due to an ongoing corruption investigation.[12] Savisaar accepted 1.5 million in euros from a Russian NGO, the Andrei Pervozvanny Fund, claiming that the funds were for the building of a church, when they appear to have made their way to the coffers of the Estonian Centre Party. Savisaar is listed as a Russian "agent of influence" by Estonia's intelligence agency.[13]

Like Latvia, Estonia remains vulnerable to Russian land grabs and direct military assault, and the presence of Kremlin agents like Savisaar within the political ecosystem is highly concerning and extremely dangerous should Putin ever make a more aggressive play for influence and control in the country. It is clear that Savisaar would happily throw open the gates of Tallinn to Kremlin forces rather than fulfill his duty to defend his constituents.

Ukraine

Putin has long maintained control over Ukraine's Party of Regions, the party of former Ukrainian president Viktor Yanukovych. When Yanukovych was president, his capitulation to Putin's wishes for Ukraine not to become part of the European Union prompted the Maidan uprising as well as Yanukovych's own overthrow and the ongoing conflict in eastern Ukraine.

Even after the ousting of the president with the Ukrainian revolution in 2014, and despite being discredited by many Ukrainians, the Party of Regions still demonstrates considerable loyalty to the Kremlin. On September 14, 2014, while the war in Donbass was raging and Ukrainian soldiers were dying at the hands of Russian-backed separatists, twenty-four people's deputies of Ukraine from both the Party of Regions and the pro-Russian Communist Party of Ukraine met with the chair of the Russian state duma, Sergei Naryshkin.[14] As a result, the Central Investigation Administration of Ukraine's Ministry of Internal Affairs opened an investigation and a criminal case against those who attended, rightly claiming that they were aiding the infringement of Ukraine's territorial integrity. But shame doesn't come easily to the Party of Regions, whose members still liaise with Russian officials even as Putin's troops continue to occupy their country.

Some former members of the Party of Regions, desperate to salvage their political careers, have joined the ambiguously named Opposition Bloc, a union of small parties that holds pro-Russian views. As of 2016, the bloc has forty-three seats in the Verkhovna Rada of Ukraine, Ukraine's parliament. It advocates for Russian to be made an official regional language, and for a nonaligned status for Ukraine, which effectively means a return to Russian domination of the Ukrainian economy and Kremlin control over its internal politics. The bloc claims to want a negotiated end to the war in eastern Ukraine, but only with "maximum decentralization"[15] for the region, which would cripple Ukraine's federal government and give Russia a proxy veto over its foreign policy. In short, the so-called Opposition Bloc is opposed to everything that is good for Ukraine, and supports what is good for Russia.

While the Opposition Bloc is flagrantly pro-Russian, it persistently attempts to distance itself from that label by claiming that it desires the return of Crimea to Ukraine. However, this is little more than distractive rhetoric, as the bloc has not presented any real plan for how Crimea should be won back, and has, more or less, avoided foreign affairs entirely, instead choosing to focus on domestic affairs where they remain an obstacle to any real reform. Nestor Shufrych, a member of the Opposition Bloc, has stated publically, that it will "be in opposition to any pro-government political force, including [President Petro] Poroshenko, [Prime Minister Arseniy] Yatsenyuk and [pro-European political party] Batkivshchyna."[16]

Yet the Opposition Bloc has the support of Ukrainian businesspeople and oligarchs, who stand to lose large amounts of money due to deteriorating relations with Russia. This group includes Rinat Akhmetov, Ukraine's richest man.[17] With considerable funding and powerful backers, the Opposition Bloc are able to continue to stymie reform and perpetuate Ukraine's economic and political death spiral, hoping that if it can discredit reformers and pro-Westerners in the eyes of voters, it will be rewarded at the ballot box. In the meantime, the bloc represents Putin's best ally in Ukrainian politics, save the outright traitors in the Party of Regions.

Moldova

Moldova, by many measures the poorest country in Europe,[18] has a relatively small Russian minority, making up only 6 percent of the population.[19] But Transnistria, an unrecognized separatist slice of Moldova, independent since 1990, is home to nearly 170,000 ethnic Russians and a contingent of Russian army "peace keepers," giving Putin considerable control over this little country's politics.

The Party of Communists of the Republic of Moldova (PCRM) has always been pro-Russian and nostalgic for Soviet times. The more recently ascendant Party of Socialists of the Republic of Moldova (PSRM), which split from the PCRM, is also extremely pro-Putin. Together, these two parties control a third of parliament, with repeated political crises preventing the decisive selection of a prime minister and keeping Moldova weak.

The recently elected government has been racked by major scandals, such as the theft of approximately $1 billion from state-controlled banks[20] and the discovery that the former prime minister falsified his school documents.[21] But this hasn't stopped pro-Putin forces from gaining steam: Renato Usatii, a pro-Russian businessman, won the mayoral election for Moldova's second largest city, Bălți, while Ilan Shor, a pro-Russian businessman and the main suspect in the $1 billion bank theft[22] won an election for mayor in the eastern town of Orhei.[23]

Putin's proxies in Moldova want to join Russia's Eurasian Union, a neo-Soviet imperial project, at the cost of Moldova's European future and any chance at political independence.[24] The EU has failed to offer Moldova a viable alternative, or to adequately support and encourage Moldova's pro-European parties. The end result is that Putin's lackeys in the PSRM and PCRM appear poised to dictate the country's future.

RIGHT-WING POLITICAL PROXIES

Most countries in Europe do not have a significant Russian-minority population, but that doesn't stop Putin from meddling in their internal politics. A bevy of right-wing populist and nationalist European parties, with a hint (sometimes a dollop) of neofascism, are aligned with Russia and more than a few have been found to receive money directly from

Kremlin coffers. In addition to financial support, Putin offers these parties diplomatic cover, high-level meetings, and opportunities for international recognition. Because these right-wing groups are markedly radical, they often struggle for sympathetic press coverage and frequently find themselves isolated in their domestic political environment, making the legitimacy that Putin can offer highly attractive and valuable. In return, these right-wing parties support Putin at home and in the European Parliament, help Russia legitimize contested election results such as the Crimean referendum, and provide a justificatory narrative for Putin's aggression and destabilizing activities.

France

In France, the populist-nationalist National Front (whose French acronym is FN) has wormed its way back to political relevance after a generation of being known as the party of anti-Semites and post-Vichy fascists. Its leader, Marine Le Pen, daughter of FN founder Jean-Marie Le Pen, rails against Muslim immigration, the supposed erosion of French values, and encroaching EU bureaucratic power. As the most prominent French opponent of European integration and the transatlantic alliance, the FN is a natural ally for Putin. Indeed, Jean-Marie Le Pen confirmed that the party had accepted a loan of €9.4 million from the First Czech Russian Bank in Moscow.[25] Separately, Le Pen revealed that on April 18, 2014, his FN-linked company, Cotelec, borrowed another €2 million from Cyprus-based Vernonsia Holdings Ltd., a company allegedly owned by a former member of the KGB.[26] Shortly after these loans were made, Marine Le Pen publically recognized the results of Putin's sham referendum on Russia's annexation of Crimea.

Because of its not-quite-mainstream reputation and socially controversial policies, the FN is often shunned for funding by French and other European banks. Opportunities for Russian lending are a boon, and providing the FN with hard cash has bought Putin a reliable ally. Let's hear it in Marine Le Pen's own words:

> I share at least a part of Vladimir Putin's economic vision. That's for sure, but it didn't start yesterday. The Front Nationale has never changed its position on this subject. We welcomed the arrival of a government that did not serve the 'apparatchiks'; and which developed a patriotic

economy.... I admire his cool head. Because there is a cold war being waged against him by the EU at the behest of United States, which is defending its own interests. I admire that he has managed to restore pride and contentment to a great nation that had been humiliated and persecuted for 70 years. Simple as that. I think that there are things you have to look on with a positive eye, or at least with an impartial eye.[27]

Positive and impartial, indeed. The FN's ruble-stuffed bank account belies its commitment to France's "best interests." For Putin, the relationship wins him a high-profile advocate in a core EU and NATO country, and if Le Pen can ever prevail in a presidential election, Putin could get a powerful, nuclear-armed ally in the heart of Europe. Putin and Le Pen have forged a mutually beneficial partnership based on a shared view of the EU as "a meddlesome, US-controlled enemy of national sovereignty and destroyer of traditional religious and family values."[28] Le Pen's animosity toward the EU is real, and she understands that Russian leadership in Europe provides an alternative to the EU with an explicit goal of neutering or dissolving the Union. In the wake of the November 2015 terrorist attacks in Paris, Le Pen has hailed Putin as a leader in the fight against ISIS and the only true defender of European values. Putin, of course, welcomes the joint effort and exults in having an ally so deeply embedded in a key European power.

Hungary

Putin's capture of Europe's far right has yielded the most fruit in Hungary, where Russia has effective control over not only the far-right nationalist Jobbik party but the mainstream center-right Fidesz party as well. Fidesz leader Viktor Orbán currently serves as prime minister, and has made Hungary into the tip of Putin's spear to pierce the heart of Europe.

Orbán even fancies himself a quasi-authoritarian national hero, a mini-Putin on the Danube. He openly echoes Putin's governing philosophy, declaring that

[the] Hungarian nation is not a simple sum of individuals, but a community that needs to be organized, strengthened and developed, and in this sense, the new state that we are building is an illiberal state, a

non-liberal state. It does not deny foundational values of liberalism, as freedom, et cetera, but it does not make this ideology a central element of state organization, but applies a specific, national, particular approach in its stead.[29]

This "specific, national, particular approach" apparently refers to welcoming Putin to Budapest in February 2015, Putin's first visit to an EU nation after Russian-armed rebels shot down the MH17,[30] and violating a UN ban on bilateral visits with Russia.[31] During this visit, Orbán and Putin extended Hungary's sweetheart gas deal and committed a successor to the South Stream project, a gas pipeline that would have pumped Russian gas under the Black Sea to Southern Europe but that Moscow abandoned in the face of objections from Brussels.[32] Already, approximately 80 percent of Hungary's natural gas comes from Russia.[33] Orbán would have that number go up, and facilitate even more Russian gas flooding the European market.

Putin is happy to reward his puppet for such loyal advocacy. In March 2015, shortly after Putin's illicit visit to Budapest, the Kremlin offered Budapest "a nuclear power plant largely financed, built and supplied by Russian state companies," along with a €10 billion loan.[34] Hungarian officials expect the plant to generate one-third of the nation's electricity by 2025. Péter Szijjártó, Orbán's foreign minister, has framed the cooperation as a calculation of convenience, claiming that "you cannot afford in this part of the world not to have a pragmatic cooperation with Russia."[35] But any casual observer can see that Orbán's relationship with his puppeteer Putin is more than pragmatic; it is strategic, and explicitly designed to weaken the EU, NATO, and indeed the very bedrock of liberal democracy in Europe.

The far-right Jobbik party makes no pretensions to pragmatism or neutrality. Jobbik party leader Gábor Vona has denounced the United States as "the deformed offspring of Europe,"[36] and analysts have observed that Jobbik has two primary foreign policy objectives: first, for Hungary to turn its back on the EU and join Putin's Eurasian Union, and second, to maintain the status quo of EU dependence on Russian gas.[37] Indeed, Jobbik's foreign policy chair Béla Kovács is an outright Russian agent who publically declared Putin's annexation of Crimea to be legitimate, despite his being a member of European Parliament.[38] The Prosecutor's Office in Hungary went so far as to request that the European Parliament waive Kovác's legal immunity amid allegations he was spying on the EU for Russia.[39]

While the far-right Jobbik party competes with the more mainstream Fidesz party in domestic elections, when it comes to Putin both parties are in lockstep march with the Kremlin. So long as Viktor Orbán remains in power, Putin has an ally in Hungary, which is both an EU and NATO member with full access to the inner workings of both institutions.

Greece

Greece's infamous, neo-Nazi Golden Dawn party has deep connections with and receives considerable support from Russia's right-wing activists, who operate only with Putin's approval and implicit imprimatur. Golden Dawn's leader, Nikos Michaloliakos, even received a letter in prison from Putin adviser and Kremlin insider Alexander Dugin, one of the ideological architects of Putin's Eurasianist ideology, expressing support for Golden Dawn's geopolitical positions and requesting a line of communication between Golden Dawn and Dugin's Kremlin-linked think tank in Moscow.[40] Today, Golden Dawn itself boasts that Michaloliakos "has spoken out clearly in favor of an alliance and cooperation with Russia, and away from the 'naval forces' of the 'Atlantic.'"[41] While Golden Dawn has been kept from any real power by Greece's voters, it remains one of the most prominent and virulent right-wing nationalist parties in Europe, and it looks to Moscow for leadership and the party line.

Germany

In Germany, the Alternative for Germany (AfD) party advocates a set of policies similar to those of France's National Front: It is against Islamic immigration, against the EU, and against America. In July 2015, the AfD elected Frauke Petry as its leader based on "promises to make every effort to convince Berlin to strengthen ties with Russia."[42] The AfD is currently a relatively minor player in German politics but stands to rise on the basis of growing discontent with Chancellor Angela Merkel's Syrian refugee policies. Putin senses the opportunity to build a pro-Russia party in Germany to complement his FN lackeys in France and further secure his influence in Europe's largest and most important economy. As a part of its antieuro strategy, the AfD has begun fundraising by selling gold,[43] and there are already rumors that the Kremlin could facilitate a loan to the AfD, similar to the multimillion FN loan deal, in which Russia agreed to gift the party gold bars that could be sold for hard cash.[44] Plunking down a sack of gold on a German potentate's desk in order to win favors may seem positively medieval, but Putin only cares about buying himself another proxy, and the AfD cares about filling its coffers and deepening its relationship with Moscow. It seems that both will get what they want and Putin will add another European party to his collection of loyal political puppets.

Bulgaria

Bulgaria is a country in which a considerable portion of the population is already sympathetic to Russia and Putin due to cultural closeness, historical linkages, and political realities. In a 2015 Alpha Research poll, fully 22 percent of Bulgarians say they would vote to join Putin's Eurasian Union, while only 40 percent support continued EU membership.[45] Putin's closest ally in Bulgaria is the ATAKA party, whose leader, Volen Siderov, has repeatedly called for Bulgaria to veto EU economic sanctions for Russia and vowed (fortunately unsuccessfully) to topple the Bulgarian government if it backed sanctions.[46] ATAKA's parliamentary group has "insisted that Bulgaria should recognize the results from the referendum for Crimea's joining to the Russian Federation," and the party openly professes allegiance to Moscow.[47] Putin understands just how pro-Russian certain elements of Bulgarian society are and is cultivating ATAKA as a reliable fifth column within Bulgarian politics that will advocate for Russian interests, rail against America and the EU, and continue to disrupt Western efforts to sanction and punish Russia.

LEFT-WING POLITICAL PROXIES

Putin also has friends and allies on the European left, especially parties and politicians angry at German-enforced austerity and the mismanagement of the euro and the EU economy. These antiestablishment leftist leaders receive the recognition and legitimacy from Putin that is denied to them domestically, and while few mistake Putin for a leftist, working with him fulfills a need to demonstrate cross ideological partnerships and further antagonizes the political mainstream. These populist parties court Putin to spite the EU, thumb their noses at political elites, and signal their fundamental opposition to the free market institutions of the West. Many of today's leading European Leftists were active in Soviet-linked socialist or communist parties during the Cold War, and have sentimental or personal attachments to Russia that compel them to continue coopera-tion with Moscow. More than a few were educated or spent time in the Soviet Union. Today, they continue to attack Europe's institutions from the left, but with support coming from a very different Russia with a very different vision of Europe's future.

Greece

When Greece's ruling pro-Russian leftist SYRIZA party won the 2015 Greek elections, the *Moscow Times* announced the victory with the headline "Greek Election Wins Putin a Friend in Europe."[48] SYRIZA is "an amalgamation of communist, socialist and other leftist forces,"[49] many with ties to Russia going back to the Soviet era. The party with which SYRIZA has formed a coalition, the right-wing Independent Greeks, also supports Russia and calls for conservative social policies in line with Orthodox Christian teachings.[50] SYRIZA's leader and Greek prime minis-ter Alexis Tsipras was received as a highly honored guest by the Kremlin in Moscow in May 2014, using the occasion to chastise the EU's policy on Ukraine, denounce European sanctions against Moscow, and sup-port illegal and illegitimate separatist referendums in eastern Ukraine.[51] For his part, Putin remains confident "that Russia and Greece will con-tinue to develop their traditionally constructive cooperation in all areas and will work together effectively to resolve current European and global problems."[52] When Putin says he plans to "resolve" a problem he means it, and it is clear that Greece and SYRIZA are central to his plans for fracturing the EU and dismantling NATO.

Spain

Podemos, the left-wing party in Spain that surged to third place in the 2015 elections with 21 percent of the vote, is considered "broadly pro-Russian."[53] Its leader, Pablo Iglesias, has condemned the EU for a supposed "double standard" against Russia, bizarrely comparing Putin's outright invasion of Ukraine to the twisting and complicated saga of the Israeli-Palestinian conflict.[54] Iglesias decries harsh criticism of Putin and sanctions against Russia on the basis that Israel has never faced similar punishment (never mind, of course, that Israel has in fact faced far-worse economic warfare and derogatory rhetoric than Putin has).[55] This nonsensical line of argumentation is mere political smoke screen, where Podemos seeks to justify its support for Putin without being accused of having become a Russian proxy. Unfortunately, it is far too late for that, as Podemos has already thrown its lot in with the gaggle of Euro-skeptic leftist Putin boosters, who will take any alternative to the economic status quo in Europe and appreciate Putin's single-minded drive to destroy European and transatlantic institutions. To boot, Iglesias was a member of the Communist Youth Union of Spain,[56] openly admires late Venezuelan dictator and Putin puppet Hugo Chavez,[57] and actually worked as a political strategist for Chavez while he was president.[58] Today, Iglesias is one of the most influential politicians in Spain, at the forefront of the upstart European left, and well on his way to becoming a dyed-in-the-wool Putin proxy in his own right.

MOSCOW'S LONG REACH

Putin's wide-ranging web of political servants and shameless proxies covers Europe, infiltrating its major powers; subverting democratic and European institutions; and encouraging populist, antiestablishment sentiment to the detriment of European stability and the transatlantic relationship. Even in places where Putin has no direct political proxy, Russian oligarch money corrupts and corrodes European society. Private wealth from Russia continues to pour into the United Kingdom—no friend of Russia. A recent undercover investigation by two Russian journalists finds that many London real estate agents willingly gave advice on how to launder illegally obtained money through real estate. London has seen large numbers of Russian buyers with bursting ruble-denominated bank accounts enter its property market, and a foreign exchange specialist believes that a significant portion of the market is made up of "dirty money."[59] Even retired politicians who served their country honorably are not immune, as former German chancellor Gerhard Schröder, a Social Democrat who now works for the Russian energy giant Gazprom, proved when he described Putin as a "flawless democrat."[60]

By capturing pro-Russian far-right and far-left European political parties, Moscow's goal is to fracture the EU, discredit NATO and

America, and ensure that Europe remains heavily dependent on Russian gas. Moscow lends its proxy parties support, both political and financial, boosting disruptive European fascists, Russian chauvinists, and new-wave Leftists in the process. Putin has found that Europe's political system is "weak, permeable and susceptible to foreign cash,"[61] and he has not hesitated to take advantage of the chaos caused by the meltdown of the euro, the wave of Syrian refugees, or the long-simmering class and ethnic tensions. Europe's mainstream parties, bedeviled by successive and seemingly unsolvable crises, are under attack from the Far Left and the Far Right and at risk of being swept away by a wave of populist fury and discontent, as we saw in the Brexit vote. But behind both the Left and the Right stands Putin, funneling rubles to unscrupulous European politicians, who accept the money out of stark opportunism, misguided ideology, or simple greed.

Whatever their motivations might be, the end result is the same: Putin controls a network of political proxies woven deeply into the fabric of the European body politic. And that is far more dangerous than any missile, separatist, or sanction could ever be.

CHAPTER 9

The United States and Europe
How and Why We Must Fight Back

I n the face of Putin's naked aggression in Europe, the West has shown
a level of incompetence that approaches impotence. We have done
our best in this book to explicate how dangerous Putin is and to lay
out clearly the outlines of his master plan to break up the transatlantic
alliance, reestablish Russian power, and assert control over world affairs.
We have also detailed the shameful inadequacy of the Western response
to Putin, as well as the embarrassing state of American, NATO, and EU
military preparedness for renewed Russian aggression in Europe and
around the world. Putin has invaded Ukraine, mobilized in Syria, forged
strategic alliances with Iran and China, rebuilt the Russian military, infiltrated and intimidated the West, waged a propaganda war in the media
and a cyberwar online, and much more. The West has responded with
feckless sanctions and handwringing. Our leaders have proved inept as
Putin runs circles around them and advances Russian interests.

But Putin need not win in Ukraine, Syria, online, on the airwaves, or
anywhere else. The West can and must respond to Putin's warmongering
as well as his callous disregard for the innocent lives lost and ruined by
Russian aggression. If we continue to do nothing, the West will abdicate
the moral high ground on human rights, peaceful international coexis-
tence, and liberal democracy. In place of these, Putin will promote and
impose his vision of an authoritarian, belligerent, revivified Russian
Empire that makes common cause with the ayatollahs in Tehran, the
communist apparatchiks in Beijing, and a rogues' gallery of petty dicta-
tors and tyrants from Syria to Cuba to North Korea. In short, Western
inaction will guarantee the ascendance not only of Putin's Russia but
also of a dystopian world order where the most oppressive governments

have the most power and exert the most strength abroad. This would be a world where a Russian invasion of Ukraine, a Chinese seizure of the South China Sea, or an Iranian power grab in the Middle East would go uncontested by a West too busy sheltering in place and licking its wounds to stand up for its values or defend its own security.

America must do more, both unilaterally and as the leader of the West. A host of straightforward, achievable measures can turn the tide against Putin and his goon squad of fellow tyrants. These measures range from the simple and obvious, like publically naming and shaming Putin as a cancer on world affairs; to the legislatively complex, like ending the sequester and adequately funding our military; to the bold and unmistakable, like implementing billion-dollar arms deals and new American bases for Eastern Europe. The solutions we offer here come from Democrats and Republicans, military officers and university professors, Americans and Europeans, grizzled Cold Warriors and fresh-faced twenty-first-century optimists. They are diverse in their sources but united in their purpose: stop Putin, roll back his gains around the world, and defend Western values and security.

UKRAINE

The Russian invasion of Ukraine has cost thousands of lives, generated more than one million refugees and displaced persons, and sent one of the most impoverished, underdeveloped countries in Europe into an economic tailspin. By any measure, Russia has precipitated an economic, political, and humanitarian catastrophe. Patriotic Ukrainians have risen up to fight back against Putin's proxy separatists and have begun rebuilding their national economy. But they simply can't do it alone. Russia is a nuclear-armed global superpower with an enormous military and unparalleled economic power over Ukraine, thanks to its control of the country's energy supplies, and Putin seeks to cripple and destroy the Ukrainian state. Without help for Ukraine, Putin will succeed in his mission. America is treaty bound by the Budapest Memorandum to preserve Ukraine's territorial sovereignty, but we are also morally obligated to assist a free but relatively weak country in its desperate fight to remain independent.

The first step is straightforward: weapons. The Ukrainian military is run down; it tries to compensate for a shortage of modern technology with an abundance of courage and determination. Were it not for the extraordinary bravery of Ukrainian soldiers who have stared down Russian tanks, dodged Putin's artillery, and faced off against separatists toting Russian guns, Putin would have already won. The West ought to provide Ukraine's armed forces with the equipment and capabilities to match its grit in the face of invasion. As Ukrainian president Petro Poroshenko complained upon receiving a shipment of nonlethal aid, "One cannot win a war with blankets."[1] Yet President Obama and his advisors continue to insist that arming the Ukrainians will "escalate" the conflict, as though Putin's invasion and murder of innocent Ukrainian civilians wasn't escalation enough. Every day that America and its European allies refuse to arm Ukraine so that it can defend itself is a day that we consign more innocent Ukrainians to die at Putin's hands.

We also need a new Marshall Plan for Ukraine to help rebuild the industry and infrastructure destroyed by Russia and to finance the construction of an energy-supply system that is less dependent on Russian sources. Ukraine needs tens of billions of dollars to shore up its failing economy, which has been decimated by Russian sanctions. Some of that money should come in the form of favorably structured loans from the United States, but most should be financed by the IMF, World Bank, and European countries, whose economies will directly benefit from a more stable and prosperous Ukraine. While the sums involved are not small, these same institutions have proved willing to spend many times more to save profligate Greeks or bail out less-than-deserving financial firms. Unlike these beneficiaries of American and European largesse, the Ukrainians did not cause their economic crisis; it was forced on them at the barrel of Russian guns. There are few worthier causes deserving of American and European financial support than the rescue of the Ukrainian economy, and its forty-five million participants, from total ruin.

We must also think about what can be done to secure Ukraine's future within Europe and the West. It is up to the Ukrainian people whether they will choose to pursue NATO or EU membership down the road; what we in the West must do is to make it clear that the door will be open for them to receive fair and favorable consideration. Until then, there is much that Western governments can do to promote ties between Ukraine and the West, and to provide support for Ukraine's democratic and free market institutions. First and foremost, we must collaborate with Ukraine's government to develop joint economic, political, and military programs that will guarantee the country's continued independence from Russia. These might include bilateral trade agreements that build on the agreement for a Deep and Comprehensive Free Trade Area that Ukraine has already signed with the EU and special development loan programs and support for Ukrainian sectors and industries that have struggled to move past the pernicious legacy of Soviet economics. As the Ukrainian military is fully preoccupied with defeating Putin's rebel proxies, NATO should already be considering ways in which joint exercises and training could take place in the future to improve interoperability and communication between Ukrainian and Western military forces. Organizing trips to Ukraine for senior Western politicians and friendly summits with their Ukrainian counterparts would send a clear message of solidarity to the Ukrainian people.

The private sector can play a role in the country as well. One only has to look to the astonishing growth of Poland or the Baltics to understand the opportunities for foreign direct investment in Ukraine. The faster Washington assists Ukraine in driving out Russian-backed forces, the sooner investors will begin injecting capital into the country's cash-starved economy. There are also opportunities for Western universities to establish funded scholarships for Ukrainian students, and for think tanks and nonprofits to put together fellowships that will allow educated Ukrainians to build their skill sets in the West and then bring that knowledge back home with them. Pillars of Western civil society, from newspapers to unions to religious organizations, have opportunities to collaborate with their colleagues in Ukraine that should be facilitated by governments and philanthropists determined to encourage the country's own budding civil society. These efforts will yield enormous returns for the stability of Ukraine's democracy and its prospects for success, putting the country on the path to eventual EU membership—should its people desire it.

Thus, there is an enormous amount we can do for Ukraine, starting with urgent military and financial assistance and extending to wide-ranging support for Ukrainian political and social institutions. But our leaders refuse to step up to the plate. Ukraine has earned our support through the blood of its dead and wounded, and through its tireless defense of the country in the face of impossible odds and Putin's ruthlessness. These efforts ought to resonate with Americans, as our country, after all, was born in a battle against another powerful imperial overlord. We should see ourselves in the Ukrainians, and we should take the simple, inexpensive steps to help them survive and prosper. If only our leaders had the empathy or boldness to do so.

SYRIA

Putin has backed up his support of Syria's Assad regime with deeds. Putin's armed forces have aggressively intervened, working side by side with Assad's forces to preserve his regime and perpetuate Russian influence. Russian missiles have flooded into Syria, both in storage containers destined for Assad's silos and attached to the wings of Russian fighters striking rebel and ISIS positions throughout the country. Putin has also prepped facilities and bases in Syria that could host hundreds of thousands of Russian troops should he decide to redeploy a major force to the region. In short, Putin has mobilized the Russian military to protect Assad's Syria as though it were a province of Russia itself. While Putin has no special attachment to Assad personally, he is nonetheless determined to preserve Russian influence in the Eastern Mediterranean and the Levant, and to maintain Russia's sole Mediterranean naval base at the Syrian port of Tartus. Indeed, Putin considers Syria to be a lynchpin of both his Middle Eastern and European strategies; otherwise, he would have let Assad slip away long ago. And while America and its Western partners have insisted that the Syrian conflict must have a diplomatic resolution, Condoleezza Rice and Robert M. Gates astutely note that "Moscow understands that diplomacy follows the facts on the ground, not the other way around. Russia and Iran are creating favorable facts. Once this military intervention has run its course, expect a peace proposal from Moscow that reflects its interests, including securing the Russian military base at Tartus."[2] It's hard to imagine a potential settlement to the Syrian conflict that doesn't somehow codify Russia's influence.

The West's goals in Syria are twofold: Primarily, we want to bring the conflict to a favorable and rapid resolution that does not benefit either Assad or ISIS; secondarily, we seek to mitigate the violence in order to ease the pressures driving millions of refugees out of the Middle East and into Europe. These two goals are difficult to pursue simultaneously, since the most direct way to end the conflict quickly would be the deployment of an overwhelming (and politically unpalatable) military force that would only increase and exacerbate the refugee crisis. How, then, to proceed?

To achieve our goals, we must be willing to deploy our military in focused, targeted ways that immediately benefit ordinary Syrians, while setting up our allies to beat Assad and ISIS. No-fly zones that close airspace to Assad *and* to the Russians should be established. The contingent of American troops from the special operations forces should be modestly expanded to the point where they are prepared to lead local forces in securing safe zones throughout Syria for would-be refugees, which would be protected by American airpower.

The Obama administration has wrung its hands over the difficulty of finding "moderate" Syrian forces whom we can train and equip to fight against both Assad and ISIS. These hypothetical allies are difficult to find because Assad has killed most of them with Russian weapons; the ones who are left are hiding from Russian air strikes and cruise missiles. But there is one faction in Syria who remain active, successful, pro-Western, and determined to defeat both the Assad government and ISIS: the Kurds. Out of deference to our NATO ally Turkey, which has faced a decades-long Kurdish insurgency, America has always been hesitant to provide Syria's Kurds with serious military support. But in the current crisis we have nowhere else to turn in Syria, and under the leadership of Recep Tayyip Erdoğan, Turkey has done little to warrant American deference. We should be arming and supplying Syria's Kurds and coordinating the activity of our own military presence in that country with their forces. Kurdish ground forces assisted by American air power would be a formidable combination capable of defeating ISIS and Assad—and rolling back Russian influence. The Obama administration has few other options for securing an outcome that will benefit ordinary Syrians and bring the conflict to a negotiated end.

NUCLEAR WEAPONS AND MISSILE DEFENSE

Putin's nuclear saber rattling must be met with a strong NATO commitment to keeping the nuclear peace. When the Cold War ended, so did the nuclear standoff between the United States and the Soviet Union.

But while the Soviet Union has disappeared into history's dustbin, its remaining nuclear arsenal remains just as terrifyingly destructive. Putin has his finger on the same button Stalin, Brezhnev, and Gorbachev did, and he has not shied away from implying that he might push it, with Russia even threatening nuclear action against countries as strategically inconsequential as Denmark.[3] America must end senseless discussions of further reductions to our nuclear arsenal, which would only weaken our ability to deter Russian (or Iranian, or Chinese, or North Korean) nuclear activity. Instead of proposing unilateral nuclear drawdowns, our priority should be developing the next generation of nuclear warheads and missiles and keeping our arsenal a step ahead of Russian missile-defense and detection capabilities.

In the short term, we can send a clear message by deploying additional bomber-borne nuclear weapons in NATO countries that agree to host them. Since the Russians have already violated the 1987 Intermediate-Range Nuclear Forces Treaty,[4] we should scrap it and deploy land-based nuclear missiles. With approximately two hundred American nuclear weapons already based in Europe,[5] we have more than enough firepower to achieve any actual military goal should the unthinkable happen. Increasing the scope and diversity of our nuclear commitment to Europe isn't just about ensuring military superiority. It's about reassuring our allies and sending a clear message to Russia that we will not let it gain the upper hand. When Putin expands his nuclear arsenal and positions missiles closer to NATO countries, he is seeking to intimidate. He uses nuclear-oriented rhetoric to communicate Russian threats and establish dominance. When we don't push back against the language of nuclear power that Putin speaks, we accede to his claims of Russian power and concede the upper hand to him in Europe. By increasing the size of America's nuclear commitment to our European allies, we demonstrate to Putin that we intend to maintain nuclear parity and protect the existential security of NATO and of Europe.

We must also complete and expand the NATO missile shield to protect America and Europe from both Russian and Iranian threats. President Obama's ill-considered decision to downgrade the shield, leaving our NATO allies vulnerable, was made in order to appease Putin and, at least in the president's mind, to lessen tensions between Russia and the West. Since Obama's capitulation on the NATO missile shield, Putin has invaded a neighboring country and positioned nuclear weapons closer to NATO capitals than ever before. How could President Obama, not to mention secretaries of state John Kerry and Hillary Clinton, have been so naïve? Why are we providing our NATO allies with subpar protection from Russia's nuclear arsenal? It's inexcusable. We should complete the NATO missile shield as initially planned with the most sophisticated technology and capabilities possible, extended coverage and additional sites, and an accelerated schedule that accounts for Russia's rapid escalation of nuclear tensions in Europe.

NATO AND EUROPE

Putin has been especially emboldened by America's failure to rally its European and NATO allies or provide the military presence that Eastern European states are desperately requesting in the face of Russian aggression. As John Herbst, former US ambassador to Ukraine puts it, "If we made aggression really painful for Putin, he would stop—because he is not foolish. That means: deterring him in the Baltic States with major deployments, major pre-positioning of equipment in Poland and maybe in Romania too, arming Ukraine and increasing sanctions."[6] Partially because of our failure to do these things in any substantial way, Putin has not been forced to reconsider his agenda. NATO is neglecting its core mission of protecting Europe, in that Western leaders, especially Obama, are refusing to do what it takes to deter Russian aggression. Perhaps it is an ideological aversion to any use of military power, or perhaps the reluctance stems from the ghosts of the Cold War still haunting senior European diplomats and politicians. Whatever the cause, the result has been catastrophic.

There is only one real solution to Russian aggression in Eastern Europe that will guarantee that there will be no further incursions or invasions: stationing American troops at permanent bases. Obama has committed American military equipment to so-called pre-positioning in NATO's easternmost states, but that is not enough.[7] It makes sense for American forces to have rapid access to heavy equipment throughout NATO, but a warehouse of tanks will not stop Putin if there is nobody inside them. As the Council on Foreign Relations' Max Boot puts it: "The only way to restore American deterrence and credibility is by putting U.S.

troops on the frontline, as we did in Germany during the Cold War and as we are still doing in South Korea." An American base with a permanent contingent of American soldiers would be a real deterrent, as would be a permanent military presence on a foreign base. The number of troops involved does not need to be large. As Boot recommends, there needs to be "just enough to serve as a tripwire and delaying force, ensuring that any aggression will put American personnel in danger and thus require an American military response. The Obama plan will fall far short of deterring Russian aggression, [which] effectively requires arming the Ukrainians and stationing U.S. brigade combat teams in Eastern Europe and the Baltics."[8]

American fecklessness has not been the only problem in Europe. Our EU and NATO partners, addicted to Russian petrochemicals and oligarch cash, have demonstrated a spinelessness that invites comparison to the darkest days of appeasement and backroom nonaggression pacts. As we have detailed, Putin directly or indirectly controls a vast network of far-right and far-left parties throughout Europe, which are at best his lapdogs and at worst Trojan horses infiltrating NATO and the EU. But beyond this web of Russian-controlled parties, a whole slew of European politicians refuse to stand up to Putin's aggression.

Some Europeans are simply world- and war-weary, exhausted by a history of empire and a century of violence. If Ukraine were a NATO country, perhaps they would feel more urgency—but even then, would they really send British or German children to die at the gates of Donetsk? Most of Europe is generally wealthy, comfortable, and peaceful. Should we put all that at risk, they ask, over a few rundown provinces of the former Soviet Union and some little-known treaty from the 1990s? What these euro-isolationists forget is that Europe's wealth, comfort, and peace exist *because* it has taken an active interest and role in shaping world affairs, *not* in spite of those things. Wealth and peace accrue to powerful countries, and if Europe abdicates its power, it also will let slip the many benefits of that power, which will flow instead to countries like Russia that are less timid or lethargic in their global role. If Europeans wish to continue living the broadly good lives they currently enjoy, they must continue to advocate and act abroad in defense of the values and international order that has so clearly benefitted them and billions of others.

Others, primarily in well-off Western European countries like France or Italy, simply don't consider Russia or its neighbors of much importance. What difference does it make to Paris or Rome if Putin bounces around a few unfortunate Eastern countries like pinballs? Don't we have more pressing problems than protecting tiny Estonia or impoverished Ukraine? they ponder. These cynics must be reminded of the real human cost of their indifference, and further reminded that Europe's greatest and most terrible conflicts have tended to begin as dismissible land squabbles in the East. What begins in the Donbas can very quickly work its way up the Danube, and like an infection hitting the bloodstream, make its way to the heart of Europe. Putin's last war was in Georgia, on the other side of the Caucasus Mountains. His latest war is in Ukraine, considerably closer to the old capitals of Europe. Where will his next war be? Spoiler alert: he is eyeing points considerably west of Kiev.

Finally, there are those who have become addicted to the flow of rubles that the Kremlin has directed into Western companies. The City of London and the Swiss crave the ruble, and every major European city now has a mansion in its most fashionable neighborhood that is home to an oligarch whose hands are soaked in Ukrainian, Georgian, and Syrian blood. In the local retinue of these men (they are almost invariably male) are a train of lawyers, translators, administrators, bankers, facilitators, fixers, and hangers-on who spend every waking hour defending and advancing the interests of their patron, and by extension the Kremlin. These people ought to be ostracized from the circles of power, as would a North Korean diplomat or Hezbollah apologist. Putin's crimes are no less egregious, and in cases where citizens of European countries are in bed with sanctioned Russian oligarchs, their governments should consider the full breadth of legal options available for prosecution or censure.

These three classes of European obstructionists are all indicative of the same problem: a fracturing of the interests, priorities, and values that once bound America so closely to Europe. Only by recommitting ourselves to our transatlantic alliance will the West achieve the unity of purpose and intent necessary to stand up to Putin, protect the free nations of Eastern Europe, and preserve peace on the continent. Beyond the increased military cooperation that NATO must pursue, there are economic deals that should be made, especially the Transatlantic Trade and Investment Partnership (TTIP) agreement, which would transform the EU and United States into the world's largest free-trade zone. The practical benefits to this agreement are obvious, and would be a boon for struggling economies on both sides of the Atlantic as new markets get opened and capital, people, and goods flow back and forth even more freely. There are also enormous psychological benefits to agreements like the TTIP, in reminding Americans and Europeans of how close we really are. One need only remember the outpouring of American support in the wake of the November 2015 Paris terror attacks, or, further back, the Madrid train bombings, or the London subway bombings, or the European grief in the wake of 9/11 to understand how close Americans and Europeans really are. Our leaders need to translate this visceral mutual identification into constructive policies.

ASSERTING VALUES

Putin's vision for the future threatens far more than the security of Europe: He is fundamentally opposed to the Western values of liberal democracy, human rights, and market economics that won the Cold War and freed hundreds of millions from poverty and authoritarianism. Indeed, it is no accident that the global spread of Western values has coincided with the greatest period of innovation and technological progress in human history. Putin would undo all this, replacing liberal democracy with managed autocracy, human rights with the security state, and market economics with government-enforced oligarchy. He has done as much already in Russia itself. The merit, proven success, and fundamental fairness of Western values should be the ultimate motivation for resisting Putin's push for a new Dark Age.

The post–Cold War "unipolar" world order presented the United States with an opportunity unparalleled in history. Very few states had ever been hegemons in their region; no state had ever been a global hegemon before America. Whether history had "ended," as Francis Fukuyama suggests, was a matter of debate, but no one denied that America was in a position to spread freedom and democracy across the world. For a while, this is what happened. As a result, countries in Eastern Europe rapidly transitioned to market economies and democracy, though there were bumps along the way. Communist-supported regimes in Africa, Latin America, and Asia fell, and governments sympathetic to the Soviets were discredited. There were more democracies around the world than at any other point in history.

But after a brief honeymoon, unipolarity began to look more like a curse than a blessing. The Yugoslav wars, the South Asian arms race, rising tensions in East Asia, and a series of devastating wars and massacres across Africa all wound up on America's doorstep. Then, in the 2000s, 9/11 and two draining wars in Iraq and Afghanistan seemed to end all hopes of an America that could afford to devote endless resources to a global project of liberalization. Barack Obama has bungled his way through the rise of Putin's Russia, the Arab Spring, the reassertion of global Islamic jihad in the form of ISIS, Iranian expansionism, Chinese revanchism, and a host of other foreign policy catastrophes around the world. In the process, he has brought American power and influence abroad to its lowest point in the last century.

The pitiful state of the American-centered alliance system is clear evidence that the way we approach foreign relations needs to change, and soon. We must identify countries with untapped potential to be close allies, especially those that are already advocating for a closer relationship with America. In Europe, this will necessarily involve reforming and even expanding NATO in order to capture the dynamism of so-called New Europe. The politics of Europe now center on the tottering European Union and its institutions. The EU has a larger population and economy than the United States, though for how much longer either of those conditions will hold true remains uncertain, given the UK's Brexit vote to leave the EU as well as exit movements building in France and the Netherlands. What is certain is that some American policy makers seem content to let America become a minor player in Europe and to leave the Europeans to their own political devices. Not only is this strategically destructive; it also neglects those European states, especially in the East, that seek closer ties with the United States. Poland became the poster child for New Europe's cooperation with America in the 2000s, but the Poles are not the only Europeans who would prefer a more active American role on the continent. Albanians, Romanians, Czechs, and others prefer American global leadership. We should offer them a real opportunity to participate in the global democratic project. Many of these East European states are unconvinced that Western Europe will protect them from Russian aggression, a suspicion that has only been confirmed by the foot dragging about Ukraine taking place in Berlin, London, and Paris. Embracing the dynamism of New Europe means following through on missile defense, expanding military cooperation, and letting Eastern Europeans know that we don't view them as the redheaded stepchild of Brussels.

The cornerstone of American political involvement in Europe is NATO. The biggest questions about NATO's future remain unanswered. In a post–Cold War world, what do current members gain from their continued participation in the alliance? Is the mere existence of NATO antagonistic to Russia? Is more expansion wise? These questions are variations of another: are there enough shared interests and values between America and Europe for the transatlantic alliance to persist?

The answer is yes. The free nations of the world should absolutely commit to defending one another. This is also the logic under which any NATO expansion should take place. A free country with a democratic government is at liberty to enter into any alliance and agreement it pleases. If the Georgians or Ukrainians want to participate in the transatlantic security regime, Moscow does not get a say in the matter. In fact, we must make it clear that it is not Georgia or Ukraine that is being confrontational by showing interest in joining NATO—rather, it is the Russians who are initiating conflict by objecting to the freely made decisions of elected leaders.

The Russians wrongly view NATO as an American "sphere of influence," but NATO is a collective of like-minded countries and peoples agreeing to provide mutual security. Insisting on special international privileges and unchecked imperial influence, as the Russians do, is provocative. Moscow's objections to American activities in Eastern Europe should be met with intensification, not minimization, of security measures. Our European allies should never doubt that we stand with them.

When Russia throws its weight around in Eastern Europe, it should be met with new joint bases and voluntary NATO expansion. If Putin continues to funnel arms to Syria and Iran, he should not be surprised when American missiles destroy those caches. In short, America must be ready to act militarily to force the cessation and eventual reversal of Russian acts of aggression. If we refuse to do so, Putin has already won.

AFTERWORD

In January 2016, as the world rang in an uncertain new year, North Korea announced that it had tested a hydrogen bomb. Analysis casts doubt on these claims, however, and the episode seems like another instance of the rogue regime's periodic nuclear saber rattling. But even if the hydrogen bomb scare is a false alarm, it is clear that Pyongyang intends to do additional testing. For years, North Korea has made nuclear threats against the United States and Asia.

Iran is doing the same type of testing. Tehran is experimenting with long-range, precision-guided ballistic missiles that could deliver a nuclear bomb, arguably in violation of UN agreements and the terms of the Obama administration's much-trumpeted nuclear deal. Tehran also fired rockets that came within 1,500 yards of the USS Harry Truman in the Strait of Hormuz.

Central to both nations' futures and the threats they pose to the West is Vladimir Putin's Russia. Since Putin became president in 2000, Russia and China have provided North Korea with $17 billion in aid and $10 billion in debt forgiveness. The total assistance of $27 billion is two-and-a-half times the GDP ($11 billion) of the North Korean economy.[1] The Russians essentially control Iran's nuclear program, and Moscow is an integral player in the United States–Iran nuclear deal, shipping twenty-five thousand pounds of Iran's enriched uranium to Russia, as stipulated in the agreement.

Regardless of what they claim publicly, Russia and China have done nothing to shut down the North Korean nuclear program. Iran, which has made clear that it has neither formally signed nor fully accepted the nuclear deal, can at any time abrogate it. The Iranians can begin enriching uranium again whether they get their stockpiles back from Russia or not. In the best case, as Secretary of State John Kerry admitted, the nuclear deal gives the United States a one-year window to work with, and probably much less.

The United States has had no meaningful response to North Korean nuclear provocations or to Iran's brazen violations of agreements and aggressive behavior. Nor has the United States played an assertive role in other vital conflicts. While America stands idle, the Russians have been shaping the outcome in Syria for years, battling furiously to keep Bashar al-Assad in power—an effort in which they work closely with Iran and proxies such as Hamas and Hezbollah.

While America stands by, Russia is on the march. Putin's destabilization of Ukraine has turned eastern Ukraine into an economic basket case and literally wrecked Crimea. Moscow's larger purpose is to strangle the Ukrainian state economically, politically, and militarily. Ukraine is on the brink of collapse, and it is not at all clear that help is coming. The EU agreed at the end of 2015 to extend economic sanctions against Russia for another six months as punishment for Moscow's annexation of Crimea and support for Ukrainian separatists, but Europe is increasingly divided over how to address the Ukraine crisis—and especially over how much longer to punish Russia, on which it continues to rely for energy.

An even-bigger problem looming over Europe—which the Russians are encouraging—is the Syrian refugee crisis. Russia's intervention in Syria on behalf of the Assad regime has exacerbated the Syrian bloodshed and encouraged more refugees, which further destabilizes Europe and exerts greater pressure on the EU and NATO. Even now, many commentators, focused on the hopes for a negotiated agreement to the Syrian conflict in Geneva, seem not to appreciate this fully.

The fundamental issue in all these areas is that the United States is not engaged. If the history of the last century has made anything clear, it is that failing to counteract the behavior of aggressive nations will only encourage more of the same. That is what we have seen here. The United States is simply absent. It is not that we are leading from behind; we are not leading at all. You can blame other presidents for the circumstances in which we find ourselves or you can blame agreements that have been made in the past. But what is evident is that we have no clear policy, no strategy, and no plan.

In the void of US leadership, the ascendancy of antidemocratic actors, such as the Russians and their allies the Chinese, is becoming increasingly apparent around the world. At this point, the Obama administration seems to have largely conceded the Chinese their theater of operation and their investments around the globe. The Obama administration's Russian "reset" was not only a failure but also a predictable exercise in futility. In 2016, the Russians are driving the geopolitical bus, confident in their aims and willing to make any assertion, however implausible, to justify their actions. They continue to claim, for instance, that they are fighting ISIS in Syria, but in fact most of their bombing raids are against the anti-Assad opposition. And we have recently learned that Moscow has begun cooperating with the Taliban again, allegedly to undermine ISIS. Here again, Putin only pretends to be fighting ISIS; in reality, he is helping the Taliban improve its military position and consolidate control as a hedge against the US-backed Kabul government.

One need not be an advocate of an assertive American foreign policy, as the authors are, to see that this is a crisis of American national security. We are at risk of a nuclear conflict; we are at risk from the Islamic State; we have no coalition with which to work with toward stabilizing the Middle East; and we have no leadership to systematically degrade and destroy Islamist terror around the world.

At the center of all of this, operating in ways that consistently undermine American interests, is Vladimir Putin's Russia—often in tandem with its ally, China. In fact, Putin has been quite explicit about how he views the United States. In an updated version of Russia's national security plan, released publically, Putin names the United States as a direct threat to Russian interests, writing that Moscow's international goals have prompted "counteraction from the USA and its allies, which are striving to retain their dominance in global affairs."[2]

There we have it, straight from Putin, an indication of how he views the United States as a threat and obstacle to Russian plans. And his actions around the world in recent years, especially in Eastern Europe, make it clear how he has put his beliefs into practice. The new reality of an insurgent, increasingly lawless Russia opposed to American-led democratic norms must be recognized and made central to the formulation of American foreign policy. At present, in our thinking and in our policies, we are far from doing so, and prospects for change in the future—with a new presidential administration in 2017—are uncertain at best. Unless the United States awakens soon to the realities of Vladimir

Putin's leadership, his strategic goals and plans, and his unbreakable determination to achieve them, we face an imperiled future, as do Europe and other Western allies. Only vigorous assertion of US power can write a different script.

ENDNOTES

INTRODUCTION

1 Quoted in Associated Press, "Pro-Russia Gunmen Seize Government Buildings in Ukraine's Crimea," *Los Angeles Times*, February 27, 2014, http://www.latimes.com/world/worldnow/la-fg-wn-ukraine-crimea-20140227-story.html.

2 Andrew Higgins, "Grab for Power in Crimea Raises Secession Threat," *New York Times*, February 27, 2014, http://www.nytimes.com/2014/02/28/world/europe/ukraine-tensions.html?_r=0.

3 "[Putin: The Russian military acted in Crimea]," Svoboda.org, April 17, 2014, http://www.svoboda.org/content/article/25352506.html.

4 Vitaly Kadchenko, "[At 22:00 in Crimea and Sevastopol, the clock hands will be moved forward two hours—to Moscow time]," Channel One, March 29, 2014, http://www.1tv.ru/news/social/255292.

5 Thomas Grove and Warren Strobel, "Special Report: Where Ukraine's Separatists Get Their Weapons," Reuters, July 29, 2014, http://www.reuters.com/article/2014/07/29/us-ukraine-crisis-arms-specialreport-idUSKBN0FY0UA20140729.

6 Radosław Sikorski, quoted in Haroon Siddique, Tom McCarthy, and Alan Yuhas, "Crimean Parliament Seizure Inflames Russian-Ukrainian Tensions—Live," *Guardian*, February 27, 2014, http://www.theguardian.com/world/2014/feb/27/ukraine-pro-russian-gunmen-seize-crimea-parliament-live-updates?view=desktop#block-530efb46e4b0ddf5cbe7ba63.

7 "Estonia Angry at Russia 'Abduction' on Border," BBC News, November 5, 2014, http://www.bbc.com/news/world-europe-29078400.

8 Barbara Starr, "U.S., Russian Aircraft Came within 10 Feet over Black Sea," CNN Politics, last modified June 12, 2015, http://www.cnn.com/2015/06/11/politics/us-russia-aircraft-black-sea/.

9 Roland Oliphant, "Mapped: Just How Many Incursions into Nato Airspace Has Russian Military Made?," *Telegraph*, May 15, 2015, http://www.telegraph.co.uk/news/worldnews/europe/russia/11609783/Mapped-Just-how-many-incursions-into-Nato-airspace-has-Russian-military-made.html.

10 Max Fisher and Javier Zarracina, "How a Crisis in Estonia Could Lead to World War III: A Flowchart," Vox, June 29, 2015, http://www.vox.com/2015/6/29/8858909/russia-war-flowchart.

11 "Russia Examines 1991 Recognition of Baltic Independence," BBC News, June 30, 2015, http://www.bbc.com/news/world-europe-33325842.

12 Gary MacDougal, "Putin Targets Pro-Western Bulgaria: Moscow Doesn't

Always Need Tanks and Troops When Trying to Dominate Its Neighbors," *Wall Street Journal*, June 28, 2015, http://www.wsj.com/articles/SB11614593350 83063479280458105006142923274.

13 Jackson Diehl, "Eastern Europeans Are Bowing to Putin's Power," *Washington Post*, October 12, 2014, http://www.washingtonpost.com/opinions/jackson-diehl-eastern-europeans-are-bowing-to-putins-power/2014/10/12/2adbf4c2-4fd0-11e4-babe-e91da079cb8a_story.html.

14 Joergen Oerstroem Moeller, "Greece: A Nation Divided—Will Russia Take the Initiative?," *Huffington Post*: "World Post," June 29, 2015, http://www.huffingtonpost.com/joergen-oerstroem-moeller/greece-a-nation-divided-w_b_7689550.html.

15 Henry Meyer, Stepan Kravchenko, and Donna Abu-Nasr, "Putin Defies Obama in Syria as Arms Fuel Assad Resurgence," Bloomberg, April 3, 2014, http://www.bloomberg.com/news/articles/2014-04-02/putin-defies-obama-in-syria-as-arms-fuel-assad-resurgence.

16 Associated Press in Moscow, "Russia to Build Two More Nuclear Reactors in Iran: Deal Reflects Moscow's Intention to Deepen Ties with Tehran before Possible Relaxing of Western Sanctions against Iran," *Guardian*, November 12, 2014, http://www.theguardian.com/world/2014/nov/12/russia-nuclear-reactors-iran.

17 Kim Yonho, "Russia, North Korea Boost Economic Ties," Voice of America, March 22, 2015, http://www.voanews.com/content/russia-north-korea-boost-economic-ties/2690186.html.

18 Thomas Gibbons-Neff, "Pentagon to Boost Military Equipment in Europe amid Moscow Anger," *Washington Post*, June 23, 2015, https://www.washingtonpost.com/world/national-security/pentagon-to-boost-military-equipment-in-europe-amid-moscow-anger/2015/06/23/a2ad65c5-161c-4478-a414-c6da43119b7b_story.html.

19 Maria Tsvetkova, "Putin Says Russia Beefing Up Nuclear Arsenal, NATO Denounces 'Saber-Rattling,'" Reuters, June 26, 2015, http://www.reuters.com/article/2015/06/16/us-russia-nuclear-putin-idUSKBN0OW17X20150616.

20 "Drones Find Russian Base inside Ukraine: Aerial Footage Finds Smoking-Gun Evidence of Russian Army Involvement in the Conflict; More War Is Inevitable," *Daily Beast*, June 30, 2015, http://www.thedailybeast.com/articles/2015/06/30/apparent-russian-base-found-in-ukraine.html.

21 Bill Gertz, "Russia Doubling Nuclear Warheads: New Multiple-Warhead Missiles to Break Arms Treaty Limit," *Washington Free Beacon*, April 1, 2016, http://freebeacon.com/national-security/russia-doubling-nuclear-warheads/.

22 Zbigniew Brzezinski, quoted in Sebastian Fischer and Holger Stark, "Brzezinski on Russia: 'We Are Already in a Cold War,'" Spiegel Online International, July 2, 2015, http://www.spiegel.de/international/world/interview-with-zbigniew-brzezinski-on-russia-and-ukraine-a-1041795.html.

23 Thomas Friedman, "Cold War without the Fun," *New York Times*, June 24, 2015, http://www.nytimes.com/2015/06/24/opinion/cold-war-without-the-fun.html?ref=opinion&_r=1.

24 "From Cold War to Hot War: Russia's Aggression in Ukraine Is Part of a Broader, and More Dangerous, Confrontation with the West," *Economist*, February 14, 2015, http://www.economist.com/news/briefing/21643220-russias-aggression-ukraine-part-broader-and-more-dangerous-confrontation.

25 Edward Lucas, "Buttressing the Front Line against Putin: The U.S. Must Compel Nordic and Baltic States to Put Aside Old Prejudices and Link Arms against the Russian Threat," *Wall Street Journal*, June 18, 2015, http://www.wsj. com/articles/buttressing-the-front-line-against-putin-1434669646.

26 Brad Lendon, "U.S. Sending Tanks and Armor to Europe," CNN Politics, last modified June 23, 2015, http://www.cnn.com/2015/06/23/politics/us-armor-tanks-europe-russia-ash-carter/.

27 Yevgeny Lukyanov, quoted in Thomas Barrabi, "Russia Warns Baltic States NATO's Anti-Missile Shield Will Make Them 'Targets,'" *International Business Times*, June 24, 2015, http://www.ibtimes.com/russia-warns-baltic-states-natos-anti-missile-shield-will-make-them-targets-1981588.

28 Walter Russell Mead, "What Greece Means: It's Past Time for a Pivot to Europe," *American Interest*, June 18, 2015, http://www.the-american-interest. com/2015/06/18/its-past-time-for-a-pivot-to-europe/.

29 Stephen Blank, "The West's Failure of Nerve," Atlantic Council, May 19, 2015, http://www.atlanticcouncil.org/blogs/new-atlanticist/the-west-s-failure-of-nerve.

30 Judy Dempsey, "NATO's European Allies Won't Fight for Article 5," Carnegie Europe, June 15, 2015, http://carnegieeurope.eu/strategiceurope/?fa=60389.

31 Rem Korteweg, "Beware the Four Horsemen Circling Europe: Greece, Russia, Migrants and the Brexit; The Risk of a Greek Default and Eurozone Exit Poses the Most Acute Danger," *Independent*, June 24, 2015, http://www.independent. co.uk/voices/comment/beware-the-four-horsemen-circling-europe-greece-russia-migrants-and-the-brexit-10343447.html.

32 Quoted in Nicole Gaouette and Brian Wingfield, "U.S. Creates Russia Sanctions Loophole to Counter Kremlin Spin," Bloomberg, June 4, 2015, http://www. bloomberg.com/news/articles/2015-06-04/u-s-creates-russia-sanctions-loophole-to-counter-kremlin-spin.

33 Jeremy Bender, "Sweden Confirms It Launched a Second Hunt for a Suspected Russian Submarine in October," *Business Insider*, January 15, 2015, http:// www.businessinsider.com/sweden-second-hunt-for-possible-russian-submarine-2015-1.

34 Michael S. Schmidt and David E. Sanger, "Russian Hackers Read Obama's Unclassified Emails, Officials Say," *New York Times*, April 25, 2015, http://www. nytimes.com/2015/04/26/us/russian-hackers-read-obamas-unclassified-e-mails-officials-say.html.

35 Mala Otarashvili, "Russia's Quiet Annexation of South Ossetia," Foreign Policy Research Institute, February 2015, http://www.fpri.org/article/2015/02/russias-quiet-annexation-of-south-ossetia/.

36 Jo Becker and Steven Lee Myers, "Russian Groups Crowdfund the War in Ukraine," *New York Times*, June 11, 2015, http://www.nytimes. com/2015/06/12/world/europe/russian-groups-crowdfund-the-war-in-ukraine.html.

37 "Estonia Angry at Russia 'Abduction,'" BBC.

38 "Transnistria Shapes Up as the Next Ukraine-Russia Flashpoint," *Financial Times*, June 3, 2015, http://blogs.ft.com/the-world/2015/06/transnistria-shapes-up-as-next-ukraine-russia-flashpoint/.

39 Quoted in Douglas E. Schoen, "Colder Temperatures: Ukraine's Situation Continues to Decline," *New Criterion* 33, no. 5 (January 2015), 43, http://www. newcriterion.com/articles.cfm/colder-temperatures-8056.

40 "[Putin names the main task of Russian forces in Syria]," Interfax.ru, October 11, 2015, http://www.interfax.ru/russia/472593.

41 Quoted in "Putin Orders Start of Russian Military Withdrawal from Syria, Says 'Objectives Achieved,'" RT, March 14, 2016, https://www.rt.com/news/335554-putin-orders-syria-withdrawal/.

42 Simon Saradzhyan, "What Russia Won in Syria," *Boston Globe*, March 16, 2016, http://www.bostonglobe.com/opinion/2016/03/15/what-russia-won-syria/6HWcnSUarefPp9hrS4uLQK/story.html.

43 Barack Obama, quoted in "So Much for Putin's Syria 'Quagmire': The Kremlin Has Achieved Its Goal of Propping Up Assad," *Wall Street Journal*, March 14, 2016, http://www.wsj.com/articles/so-much-for-putins-syria-quagmire-1457998429.

44 Michael Crowley and Nahal Toosi, "Did Putin Once Again Outfox Obama?," *Politico*, March 14, 2016, http://www.politico.com/story/2016/03/vladimir-putin-syria-outfox-obama-220745.

45 Saradzhyan, "What Russia Won."

46 Dalibor Rohac, "Putin's Best EU Friends: The Russian Leader Rounds Up the EU's 'Putinistas' to Bring an End to the Sanctions," *Politico*, June 16, 2015, http://www.politico.eu/article/putin-friends-renzi-tsipras/.

47 *Novoye Vremya*, quoted in "Putin's European Extremist Allies (with Infographics)," *Ukraine Today*, March 3, 2015, http://uatoday.tv/politics/putin-s-european-extremist-allies-412846.html.

48 Quoted in Anthony Faiola, "From Russia with Love: An Energy Deal for Hungary," *Washington Post*, February 16, 2015, http://www.washingtonpost.com/world/europe/from-russia-with-love-an-energy-deal-for-hungary/2015/02/16/05216670-b134-11e4-bf39-5560f3918d4b_story.html.

49 Katie Simmons, Bruce Stokes, and Jacob Poushter, "NATO Publics Blame Russia for Ukrainian Crisis, but Reluctant to Provide Military Aid: In Russia, Anti-Western Views and Support for Putin Surge," Pew Research Center, June 10, 2015, http://www.pewglobal.org/2015/06/10/nato-publics-blame-russia-for-ukrainian-crisis-but-reluctant-to-provide-military-aid/.

50 Edward Lucas, "Fix NATO or Risk WWIII: The Balts, Nordics, and Poles Have a Rare Collective Opportunity to Team Up with NATO against Putin. But Will They?," *Daily Beast*, June 24, 2015, http://www.thedailybeast.com/articles/2015/06/24/fix-nato-or-risk-wwiii.html.

51 Quoted in Schoen, "Colder Temperatures," 43.

52 Quoted in ibid., 43.

53 Karoun Demirjian, "Putin Denies Russian Troops Are in Ukraine, Decrees Certain Deaths Secret," *Washington Post*, May 28, 2015, http://www.washingtonpost.com/world/putin-denies-russian-troops-are-in-ukraine-decrees-certain-deaths-secret/2015/05/28/9bb15092-0543-11e5-93f4-f24d4af7f97d_story.html.

54 Paul J. Saunders, "Why America Can't Stop Russia's Hybrid Warfare," *National Interest*, June 23, 2015, http://nationalinterest.org/feature/why-america-cant-stop-russias-hybrid-warfare-13166.

55 James Sherr, quoted in Agence France-Presse, "NATO Allies Brace for Russia's 'Hybrid Warfare,'" *Defense News*, March 18, 2015, http://www.defensenews.com/story/defense/international/europe/2015/03/18/nato-allies-brace-for-russias-hybrid-warfare/24979545/.

56 "Conscious Uncoupling: Reducing Europe's Dependence on Gas Is Possible—But It Will Take Time, Money, and Sustained Political Will," *Economist*, April 3, 2014, http://www.economist.com/news/briefing/21600111-reducing-europes-dependence-russian-gas-possiblebut-it-will-take-time-money-and-sustained.

57 "How Much Europe Depends on Russian Energy," *New York Times*, September 2, 2014, http://www.nytimes.com/interactive/2014/03/21/world/europe/how-much-europe-depends-on-russian-energy.html?_r=1.

58 Leonid D. Kuchma, Boris N. Yeltsin, John Major, and William J. Clinton, "Budapest Memorandums on Security Assistances, 1994," Council on Foreign Relations, first published December 5, 1994, accessed April 18, 2016, http://www.cfr.org/nonproliferation-arms-control-and-disarmament/budapest-memorandums-security-assurances-1994/p32484.

59 Agence French-Presse, "Accidental Conflict Is True Danger of Russia-West Clash," *Defense News*, June 19, 2015, http://www.defensenews.com/story/defense/2015/06/19/experts-accidental-conflict-is-true-danger-of-russia-west-clash/28984329/.

60 "Kasparov to West: Sanctions Not Enough to Stop Putin, He Will Test NATO Further," UNIAN, March 5, 2015, http://www.unian.info/world/1051935-kasparov-to-west-sanctions-not-enough-to-stop-putin-he-will-test-nato-further.html.

61 Molly O'Toole, "One Year Later, Obama Administration Still 'Reviewing' Lethal Aid to Ukraine," *Defense One*, March 10, 2015, http://www.defenseone.com/politics/2015/03/year-later-obama-administration-still-reviewing-lethal-aid-ukraine/107193/.

62 "The Other Battleground: The West Should Do Much More to Help Ukraine's Economy," *Economist*, May 21, 2015, http://www.economist.com/news/leaders/21651819-west-should-do-much-more-help-ukraines-economy-other-battleground.

63 Jack Crone, "Is This the Proof That Russia Shot Down Flight MH17? New Documentary Claims Plane Was Hit by Buk Surface-to-Air Missile Launcher Operated by 53rd Russian Air Defence Brigade," DailyMail.com News, January 11, 2015, http://www.dailymail.co.uk/news/article-2905692/Is-proof-Russia-shot-flight-MH17-New-documentary-claims-plane-hit-Buk-surface-air-missile-launcher-operated-53rd-Russian-Air-Defence-Brigade.html.

64 "Europe Depends on Russian Energy," *New York Times*.

CHAPTER 1 ▪ THE TRANSATLANTIC RELATIONSHIP IN THE TWENTY-FIRST CENTURY

1 Anders Fogh Rasmussen, "'Why NATO Matters to America'" (speech, Brookings Institution, Washington, DC, March 19, 2014), Brookings, accessed June 29, 2016, http://www.brookings.edu/~/media/Events/2014/3/19-rasmussen-nato/20140319_nato_rasmussen_prepared_remarks.pdf?la=en.

2 Helmut Schmidt, quoted in Paul Goble, "Window on Eurasia: From 'Upper Volta with Missiles' to 'Upper Volta with Credits,'" *Window on Eurasia* (blog), December 31, 2013, http://windowoneurasia2.blogspot.com/2013/12/window-on-eurasia-from-upper-volta-with.html.

3 Francis Fukuyama, "At the 'End of History' Still Stands Democracy: Twenty-Five Years after Tiananmen Square and the Berlin Wall's Fall, Liberal Democracy Still Has No Real Competitors," *Wall Street Journal*, June 6,

2014, http://www.wsj.com/articles/at-the-end-of-history-still-stands-democracy-1402080661.

4 "Countries and Regions: United States," European Commission Trade, last modified October 27, 2015, http://ec.europa.eu/trade/policy/countries-and-regions/countries/united-states/.

5 *Secretary General's Annual Report 2012*, North Atlantic Treaty Organization, last modified February 2, 2013, http://www.nato.int/cps/en/natolive/opinions_94220.htm.

6 Andrew Chuter, "NATO Defense Spending Countries to Decline," *Defense News*, June 23, 2015, http://www.defensenews.com/story/defense/policy-budget/budget/2015/06/23/nato-reports-alliance-members-defense-spending-decline/29153965/.

7 Vladimir Putin, quoted in Xavier Lerma, "No Show McCain and the West," Pravda.ru, September 23, 2013, http://english.pravda.ru/russia/politics/23-09-2013/125733-mccain_west-0/#sthash.STjIeHok.dpuf.

8 Vladimir Putin, quoted in ibid.

9 Robert H. Scales, "Our Precarious Defenses in Europe: There Are Fewer American Soldiers Protecting the Continent than There Are New York City Cops," *Wall Street Journal*, November 29, 2015, http://www.wsj.com/articles/our-precarious-defenses-in-europe-1448833504?mod=djemMER.

10 Emmarie Huetteman, "Despite Cuts, U.S. Army Prepares for Threats in Europe," *New York Times*, October 18, 2015, http://www.nytimes.com/2015/10/19/world/europe/despite-cuts-us-army-readies-for-threats-ineurope.html?_r=1.

11 Richard Galpin, "Russian Arms Shipments Bolster Syria's Embattled Assad," BBC News, January 30, 2012, http://www.bbc.com/news/world-middleeast-16797818.

12 Barack Obama, quoted in Alistair Bell and Tom Perry, "Obama Warns Russia's Putin of 'Quagmire' in Syria," Reuters, October 3, 2015, http://www.reuters.com/article/2015/10/03/us-mideast-crisis-syria-airstrikesidUSKCN0RW0W220151003.

13 Central Intelligence Agency, Directorate of Intelligence, "Communist Aid to North Vietnam" (intelligence memorandum, March 7, 1968), Central Intelligence Agency Library, accessed June 29, 2016, http://www.foia.cia.gov/sites/default/files/document_conversions/89801/DOC_0000483828.pdf.

14 Lionel Beehner and Greg Bruno, "Iran's Involvement in Iraq," Council on Foreign Relations, last modified March 3, 2008, http://www.cfr.org/iran/irans-involvementiraq/p12521#p5.

15 Ivan Šimonović, "Statement by Assistant Secretary-General for Human Rights Ivan Šimonović at the Human Rights Council Inter-Active Dialogue on Ukraine" (speech, September 29, 2015), United Nations Human Rights Office of the High Commissioner, accessed June 29, 2016, http://www.ohchr.org/en/NewsEvents/Pages/DisplayNews.aspx?NewsID=16526&LangID=E.

16 "About 2 Million and Half Killed and Wounded since the Beginning of the Syrian Revolution," Syrian Observatory for Human Rights, October 16, 2015, http://www.syriahr.com/en/?p=35137.

17 Reuters, "More than Four Million Refugees in Neighbouring Countries, UN Says," *Telegraph*, July 9, 2015, http://www.telegraph.co.uk/news/worldnews/

middleeast/syria/11728266/More-than-four-million-Syrian-refugees-
inneighbouring-countries-UN-says.html.

18 Mikhail Gorbachev, "Europe as a Common Home" (speech, Council of Europe,
Strasbourg, July 6, 1989), Roy Rosenzweig Center for History and New Media:
Making the History of 1989, accessed June 29, 2016, https://chnm.gmu.
edu/1989/items/show/109.

CHAPTER 2 ▪ THE RUSSIAN CENTURY: PUTIN'S PLAN FOR THE FUTURE

1 Vladimir Putin, quoted in Mike Eckel, "Putin Calls Soviet Collapse a
'Geopolitical Catastrophe,'" *U-T San Diego*, April 26, 2005, http://www.
utsandiego.com/uniontrib/20050426/news_1n26russia.html.

2 Vladimir Putin, quoted in Justin Huggler, "Putin 'Privately Threatened to
Invade Poland, Romania and the Baltic States,'" *Telegraph*, February 4, 2016,
http://www.telegraph.co.uk/news/worldnews/europe/russia/11106195/Putin-
privately-threatened-to-invade-Poland-Romania-and-the-Baltic-states.html.

3 "Crimea Crisis: Russian President's Speech Annotated," BBC News, March 19,
2014, http://www.bbc.com/news/world-europe-26652058.

4 Barack Obama, quoted in CBS/Associated Press, "Russia Leader Vladimir
Putin Says He'll Protect Russians in Ukraine by Any Means, but Hopes Force
Not Required," CBS News, last modified March 4, 2014, http://www.cbsnews.
com/news/putin-reportedly-orders-troops-near-ukraine-border-back-to-
bases-after-military-exercises/.

5 Ralph Peters, "Putin's Plan to Reclaim the Old Russian Empire," *New York
Post*, May 3, 2014, http://nypost.com/2014/05/03/putins-vengeful-plan-to-
recapture-the-old-russian-empire/.

6 *In the 2008 Georgia War 844 lives lost*: "2008 Russia Conflict Fast Facts,"
CNN, last modified April 12, 2015, http://www.cnn.com/2014/03/13/world/
europe/2008-georgia-russia-conflict/; *in Ukraine around seven thousand
civilian deaths*: Volodymyr Verbyany, "Ukraine's Poroshenko Says Fighting
Killed 7,000 as Truce Strains," Bloomberg, May 8, 2015, http://www.bloomberg.
com/news/articles/2015-05-08/ukraine-s-poroshenko-says-fighting-killed-7-
000-as-truce-strains; *more than two thousand Ukrainian soldiers killed*: Olena
Goncharova and *Kyiv Post*, "At Least 2,180 Soldiers Killed in Russia's War
against Ukraine," *Kyiv Post*, June 19, 2015, https://www.kyivpost.com/content/
ukraine/at-least-2180-soldiers-killed-in-russias-war-against-ukraine-391453.
html; *deaths of hundreds of Ukrainian separatists*: Frank Jordans, "Ukraine
Conflict Death Toll Passes 6,000, UN Human Rights Office Says," *Huffington
Post*: "World Post," March 2, 2015 (*all as of mid-2015).

7 Andrew Osborn, "Putin a Threat to Baltic States, Western Officials Say,"
Reuters, February 19, 2015, http://www.reuters.com/article/2015/02/19/us-
britain-russia-baltics-idUSKBN0LN0FV20150219.

8 "The Abominable Gas Man: How Technological Change and New Pipelines
Improve Energy Security," *Economist*, October 14, 2010, http://www.
economist.com/node/17260657.

9 "[The distribution of the population by nationality and mother tongue,
Ukraine]," State Statistics Committee of Ukraine, accessed April 15th, 2016,
http://2001.ukrcensus.gov.ua/.

10 Krishnadev Calamur, "Why Ukraine Is Such a Big Deal for Russia," NPR, February 21, 2014, http://www.npr.org/sections/parallels/2014/02/21/280684831/why-ukraine-is-such-a-big-deal-for-russia.

11 David Remnick, quoted in Jason Fields, "'In Putin's Mind, Ukraine Is Not a Nation,'" Reuters blog, October 14, 2014, http://blogs.reuters.com/great-debate/2014/10/14/in-putins-mind-ukraine-is-not-a-nation/.

12 Vladimir Putin, quoted in Kevin Drum, "Putin: Eastern Ukraine Is Really 'Novorossiya,'" *Mother Jones*, April 17, 2014, http://www.motherjones.com/kevin-drum/2014/04/putin-eastern-ukraine-really-novorossiya.

13 Paul Kirby, "Russia's Gas Fight with Ukraine," BBC News, October 31, 2014, http://www.bbc.com/news/world-europe-29521564.

14 Alexandros Koronakis, "With Fewer Lifelines Available, and Opportunities Wasted, Ukraine Has Options Which It Must Take Advantage Of," *New Europe*, July 6, 2015, http://www.neurope.eu/article/ukraines-economy-turning-greek-while-eu-monitors-closely/.

15 Sigrid Rausing, "Belarus: Inside Europe's Last Dictatorship," *Guardian*, October 7, 2012, http://www.theguardian.com/world/2012/oct/07/belarus-inside-europes-last-dictatorship.

16 Alexander Lukashenko, quoted in Lidia Kelly, "Belarus's Lukashenko: 'Better a Dictator than Gay,'" Reuters, March 4, 2012, http://www.reuters.com/article/2012/03/04/us-belarus-dicator-idUSTRE8230T320120304.

17 "[Informational-analytic portal of the union state]," Standing Committee of the Union State, April 15, 2016, http://www.soyuz.by/.

18 "2004 Population Census," National Bureau of Statistics of the Republic of Moldova, accessed April 18, 2016, http://www.statistica.md/pageview.php?l=en&idc=263&id=2208.

19 "Trans-Dniester Profile—Overview," BBC News, last modified March 17, 2015, http://www.bbc.com/news/world-europe-18284837.

20 Nicholas Kristof, "Moldova, the Next Ukraine," *New York Times*, April 23, 2014, http://www.nytimes.com/2014/04/24/opinion/kristof-moldova-the-next-ukraine.html.

21 Quoted in Andrew Higgins, "Moldova Eyes Russia's Embrace as Flirtation with Europe Fades," *New York Times*, May 21, 2015, http://www.nytimes.com/2015/05/22/world/europe/moldova-eyes-russias-embrace-as-flirtation-with-europe-fades.html.

22 "Estonia Hit by 'Moscow Cyber War,'" BBC News, May 17, 2007, http://news.bbc.co.uk/2/hi/europe/6665145.stm.

23 Umberto Bacchi, "Vladimir Putin Hybrid War in Baltics: Lithuania Calls for EU Unity amid Cyberattacks," *International Business Times*, April 2, 2015, http://www.ibtimes.co.uk/vladimir-putin-hybrid-war-baltics-lithuania-calls-eu-unity-amid-russian-cyberattacks-1494820.

24 Ben Hoyle and Michael Evans, "Putin Threat of Nuclear Showdown over Baltics," *Times*, last modified April 2, 2015, http://www.thetimes.co.uk/tto/news/world/europe/article4399758.ece.

25 Liis Kangsepp and Juhana Rossi, "Estonia Says Officer Abducted near Russian Border: Security Services Accuses Individuals Coming from Russia; Moscow Says Arrest Occurred in Russia," *Wall Street Journal*, September 5, 2014, http://www.wsj.com/articles/estonian-officer-abducted-near-border-with-russia-1409928475.

26 Radio Free Europe/Radio Liberty, "Estonian Kohver Thanks Supporters after Exchange with Russian Spy," Radio Free Europe/Radio Liberty, last modified September 26, 2016, http://www.rferl.org/content/russia-estonia-eston-kohver-swapped/27272168.html.

27 Barbara Tasch, "Russia Is Reviewing the 'Legality' of Baltic States' Independence," *Business Insider*, June 30, 2015, http://www.businessinsider.com/russia-reviews-baltic-states-independence-2015-6.

28 "The Geopolitics of Pipeline Democracy," ETH Zürich, October 10, 2012, http://www.isn.ethz.ch/Digital-Library/Articles/Special-Feature/Detail/?lng=en&id=153580&tabid=1453347044&contextid774=153580&contextid775=153575.

29 Zulfugar Agayev, "Putin Stirs Azeri Angst That Russia Is Set to Extend Sway," Bloomberg, April 7, 2014, http://www.bloomberg.com/news/articles/2014-04-06/putin-stirs-azeri-angst-russia-will-seek-to-extend-sway.

30 Arastun Orujlu, quoted in ibid.

31 Zahir Rahimov, quoted in ibid.

32 Rayhan Demytrie, "Unrest Tilts Georgia towards Russia," BBC News, May 21, 2015, http://www.bbc.com/news/world-europe-32795249.

33 Vladimir Putin, quoted in Agayev, "Putin Stirs Azeri Angst."

34 Demytrie, "Unrest Tilts Georgia."

35 Associated Press, "Russian Pilot Shot Flares at Swedish Jet," *Real Clear Defense*, July 1, 2015, http://www.realcleardefense.com/articles/2015/07/01/russian_pilot_shot_flares_at_swedish_jet_108156.html/.

36 Bender, "Suspected Russian Submarine."

37 Tom Parfitt, "Russia Plants Flag on North Pole Seabed," *Guardian*, August 2, 2007, http://www.theguardian.com/world/2007/aug/02/russia.arctic.

38 Jonathan Masters, "The Thawing Arctic: Risks and Opportunities," Council on Foreign Relations, December 16, 2013, http://www.cfr.org/arctic/thawing-arctic-risks-opportunities/p32082.

39 "EU Relations with the Western Balkans," European Union External Action, accessed April 18, 2016, http://eeas.europa.eu/western_balkans/index_en.htm.

40 David M. Herszenhorn and Liz Alderman, "Putin Meets with Alexis Tsipras of Greece, Raising Eyebrows in Europe," *New York Times*, April 8, 2015, http://www.nytimes.com/2015/04/09/world/europe/putin-russia-alexis-tsipras-greece-financial-crisis.html?_r=0.

41 MacDougal, "Putin Targets Pro-Western Bulgaria."

42 Andrew MacDowall, "Putin in Serbia: The EU Candidate Welcomes 'Our President,'" *Telegraph*, October 16, 2014, http://www.telegraph.co.uk/news/worldnews/europe/serbia/11166408/Putin-in-Serbia-the-EU-candidate-country-welcomes-our-president.html.

43 Viktor Orban, quoted in Zoltan Simon, "Orban Says He Seeks to End Liberal Democracy in Hungary," Bloomberg, July 28, 2014, http://www.bloomberg.com/news/articles/2014-07-28/orban-says-he-seeks-to-end-liberal-democracy-in-hungary.

44 Adam Halasz, "Orban Gives Putin Warm Welcome," *EUobserver*, February 18, 2015, https://euobserver.com/beyond-brussels/127693.

45 Diehl, "Eastern Europeans Are Bowing."

46 Jan Lopatka and Martin Santa, "Slovakia Nurtures Special Ties to Russia,

despite EU Sanctions," Reuters, May 22, 2014, http://uk.reuters.com/
article/2014/05/22/ukraine-crisis-slovakia-idUKL6N0O847Y20140522.

47 "Europe Depends on Russian Energy," *New York Times*.

48 "Election 2015; Results: Conservatives Win 12-Seat Majority," BBC News, May
8, 2015, http://www.bbc.com/news/election/2015/results.

49 "Obama: Putin se jen tak nezměni: Děsi sousedy k smrti" [Obama: Putin is
not going to change; he scares the neighbors to death], Tyden.cz, December 3,
2014, http://www.tyden.cz/rubriky/zahranici/amerika/obama-putin-se-jentak-
nezmeni-desi-sousedy-k-smrti_326162_diskuze.html.

50 "Russia's European Supporters: In the Kremlin's Pocket; Who Backs Putin,
and Why," *Economist*, February 12, 2015, http://www.economist.com/news/
briefing/21643222-who-backs-putin-and-why-kremlins-pocket.

51 Ibid.

52 Alana Horowitz, "Marine Le Pen Leads French Presidential Poll," *Huffington
Post*, January 29, 2015, http://www.huffingtonpost.com/2015/01/29/marine-
lepen-president-poll-_n_6573356.html.

53 "Russia's European Supporters," *Economist*.

54 Michael Segall, "How Iran Views the Fall of Sana'a, Yemen: 'The Fourth
Arab Capital of Our Hands,'" Institute for Contemporary Affairs 14, no. 36
(November 3, 2014), Jerusalem Center for Public Affairs, http://jcpa.org/
article/iran-sanaa-yemen/.

55 Bruce Riedel, "Saudi's Star Price Keeps Rising, Visits Putin in St. Petersburg,"
Brookings, June 19, 2015, http://www.brookings.edu/blogs/markaz/
posts/2015/06/19-saudi-arabia-russia-mohammad-bin-salman-putin.

56 "Russia and Egypt Planning Definitive Military Cooperation Agreement,"
Moscow Times, March 3, 2015, http://www.themoscowtimes.com/
article/516948.html.

57 "Russia, Egypt to Hold Joint Naval Drill in Mediterranean," RT, March 3, 2015,
http://rt.com/news/237373-russia-egypt-naval-drill/.

58 Joshus Dysart, "Home on the Red Range. The Ostern," Joshuadysart.com
(blog), accessed June 29, 2016, http://www.joshuadysart.com/wp/home-on-
the-red-range-the-ostern/.

59 "Russia, China Agree to Integrate Eurasian Union, Silk Road, Sign Deals," RT,
May 10, 2015, http://rt.com/business/256877-russia-china-deals-cooperation/.

60 Douglas Ernst, "Russia, China Sign Infrastructure Deals Worth Billions,"
Washington Times, May 8, 2015, http://www.washingtontimes.com/news/2015/
may/8/vladimir-putin-xi-jinping-sign-infrastructure-deal/.

61 Ben Blanchard, "Rivals Pakistan, India Start Process of Joining China Security
Bloc," Reuters, July 6, 2015, http://www.reuters.com/article/2015/07/06/us-
china-russia-pakistan-india-idUSKCN0PG09120150706.

62 Julian Ryall, "Russia and North Korea Declare 2015 a 'Year of Friendship':
Regimes Ostracised by International Community and Targeted by UN Decide
to Team Up," *Telegraph*, March 11, 2015, http://www.telegraph.co.uk/news/
worldnews/asia/northkorea/11463265/Russia-and-North-Korea-declare-2015-
a-year-of-friendship.html.

CHAPTER 3 ▪ HOW NATO IS FAILING ITSELF, EUROPE, AND AMERICA

1 Joe Biden, "Remarks by Vice President Joe Biden to Joint United States and
Romanian Participants in Carpathian Spring Military Exercise" (speech,

Otopeni Military Airbase, Bucharest, May 20, 2014), White House President Barack Obama, accessed June 29, 2016, https://www.whitehouse.gov/the-press-office/2014/05/20/remarks-vice-president-joe-biden-joint-united-states-and-romanian-partic.

2 Interview with European diplomat, August 3, 2015. The interviews in the manuscript were conducted in confidentiality, and by mutual agreement interviewees' names are not disclosed.

3 Anders Fogh Rasmussen, quoted in Lincoln Mitchell, "Is NATO Still Relevant?," *Observer* Opinion, February 10, 2015, http://observer.com/2015/02/natos-relevance-the-view-from-georgia/.

4 Alberto Nardelli and George Arnett, "Nato Reports Surge in Jet Interceptions as Russia Tensions Increase: In Europe, over the Aegean and in the Asia-Pacific Region, Interceptions Are 'Almost Routine' but the Sheer Volume of Incidents Risks Escalation," *Guardian*, August 3, 2015, http://www.theguardian.com/world/2015/aug/03/military-aircraft-interventions-have-surged-top-gun-but-for-real.

5 Oliphant, "Incursions into Nato Airspace."

6 Eben Blake, "NATO Jet Interceptions Increase: Russian Planes Responsible for Bulk of Airspace Violations, Members Say," *International Business Times*, August 3, 2015, http://www.ibtimes.com/nato-jet-interceptions-increase-russian-planes-responsible-bulk-airspace-violations-2035969.

7 Interview with senior European diplomat, August 3, 2015.

8 Christopher P. Cavas, "Resurgent Russia Drawing Northern Nations Closer," *Defense News*, September 8, 2015, http://www.defensenews.com/story/defense/2015/09/08/resurgent-russia-drawing-northern-nations-closer/71869042/.

9 Ibid.

10 Dalia Grybauskaite and Raimonds Vējonis, quoted in Jaroslaw Adamowski, "Lithunia, Latvia Eye Joint Weapon Acquisition," *Defense News*, July 15, 2015, http://www.defensenews.com/story/defense/land/weapons/2015/07/15/lithuania-latvia-joint-weapon-acquisition-air-defense/30195659/.

11 Juozas Olekas, quoted in ibid.

12 Daniel Greenfield, "Ukraine Asks for Military Aid, Obama Offers MREs: Let Them Eat MREs," *FrontPage Magazine*, March 16, 2014, http://www.frontpagemag.com/point/221124/ukraine-asks-military-aid-obama-offers-mres-daniel-greenfield.

13 "Lithuania Agrees to Supply Ukraine with Military Aid, Poroshenko Says," RT, November 24, 2014, http://www.rt.com/news/208311-lithuania-ukraine-military-aid/.

14 Thomas Barrabi, "Amid Russian Aggression, Poland Approves Russian-Lithuanian-Ukrainian Military Brigade," *International Business Times*, May 4, 2015, http://www.ibtimes.com/amid-russian-aggression-poland-approves-polish-lithuanian-ukrainian-military-brigade-1906989.

15 "Lithuania to Become First Country to Arm Ukraine against Russia," *Ukraine Today*, June 21, 2015, http://uatoday.tv/politics/lithuania-to-become-first-country-to-arm-ukraine-against-russia-442955.html.

16 Robert Menendez, quoted in Jeremy Herb, "Obama Pressed on Many Fronts to Arm Ukraine," *Politico*, last modified May 11, 2015, http://www.politico.com/story/2015/03/obama-pressed-on-many-fronts-to-arm-ukraine-115999.

17 Ashton Carter, quoted in ibid.

18 Ben Rhodes, quoted in Tara McKelvey, "Ukraine Crisis: US Struggles with Question of Arms," BBC News, February 3, 2015, http://www.bbc.com/news/world-us-canada-31013452.

19 Martin Dempsey, quoted in "'We Should Absolutely Consider Lethal Aid to Ukraine—US General Martin Dempsey,'" RT, March 4, 2015, http://www.rt.com/usa/237601-ukraine-lethal-aid-dempsey/.

20 Cory Fritz, quoted in Herb, "Obama Pressed on Many Fronts."

21 Jonathan Tirone, "Vienna Forum Hears Warning of a New U.S.-Russia Nuclear Arms Race," Bloomberg, June 24, 2015, http://www.bloomberg.com/news/articles/2015-06-24/u-s-risks-weapons-race-as-russia-adds-warheads-senate-stalls.

22 Kedar Pavgi, "NATO Members' Defense Spending, in Two Charts: The Alliance's Easternmost Members Are Racheting Up Their Budgets as Russian Threats Loom," *Defense One*, June 22, 2015, http://www.defenseone.com/politics/2015/06/nato-members-defense-spending-two-charts/116008/.

23 Ibid.

24 Ibid.

25 Ibid.

26 Ibid.

27 Ibid.

28 Andrey Biryukov, "The Secret Money behind Vladimir Putin's War Machine," Bloomberg, June 2, 2015, http://www.bloomberg.com/news/articles/2015-06-02/putin-s-secret-budget-hides-shift-toward-war-economy.

29 "Russia Forced to Reduce 2015 Defence Budget, Further Cuts Possible, IHS Says: Defence Budget Expected to Fall in Real Terms for the First Time since 2010," IHS Newsroom, June 17, 2015, http://press.ihs.com/press-release/aerospace-defense-security/russia-forced-reduce-2015-defence-budget-further-cuts-possi.

30 Igor Sutyagin, quoted in Biryukov, "Vladimir Putin's War Machine."

31 "Countries Ranked by Military Strength (2016)," Global Firepower, accessed June 30, 2016, http://www.globalfirepower.com/countries-listing.asp.

32 Quoted in Nancy A. Youssef, "Pentagon Fears Its Not Ready for a War with Putin: The U.S. Military Has Run the Numbers on a Sustained Fight with Moscow, and They Do Not Look Good for the American Side," *Daily Beast*, August 14, 2015, http://www.thedailybeast.com/articles/2015/08/14/pentagon-fears-it-s-not-ready-for-a-war-with-putin.html.

33 "Heritage Foundation Releases First Annual 'Index of U.S. Military Strength,'" Heritage Foundation, February 24, 2015, http://www.heritage.org/research/reports/2015/02/heritage-foundation-releases-first-annual-index-of-us-military-strength.

34 Michèle Flournoy, quoted in Jonah Bennett, "Report: U.S. Military Capabilities Are Surprisingly Weak," Daily Caller, February 24, 2015, http://dailycaller.com/2015/02/24/report-us-military-capabilities-are-surprisingly-weak/.

35 David Alexander, "U.S. to Cut European Military Bases as Budgets Shrink," Reuters, January 8, 2015, http://www.reuters.com/article/2015/01/08/us-usa-defense-europe-idUSKBN0KH18O20150108.

36 Oliphant, "Incursion into Nato Airspace."

37 David Alexander, "Factbox: Pentagon Planned Cuts in Europe Include

Bases, Waterworks," Reuters, January 8, 2015, http://www.reuters.com/
article/2015/01/08/us-usa-defense-europe-factbox-idUSKBN0KH1ZS201501 0
8?mod=related&channelName=domesticNews.

38 Joe Gould, "US Army Cutting Helos, Troops in Europe," *Defense News*,
May 7, 2015, http://www.defensenews.com/story/defense/land/army-
aviation/2015/05/02/us-army-cutting-helicopters-troops-in-europe/26650767/.

39 Ibid.

40 Zachary Cohen, "Size Matters: Is the U.S. Navy Really Too Small?," CNN
Politics, September 8, 2015, http://www.cnn.com/2015/09/08/politics/us-navy-
size-military-election-2016/.

41 William J. Perry and John B. Abizaid, *Ensuring a Strong U.S. Defense for the
Future: The National Defense Panel Review of the 2014 Quadrennial Defense
Review* (Washington, DC: United States Institute of Peace, 2014), United
States Institute of Peace, June 30, 2016, http://www.usip.org/sites/default/files/
Ensuring-a-Strong-U.S.-Defense-for-the-Future-NDP-Review-of-the-QDR.
pdf.

42 Jim Talent, "Yes, the Navy Really Is Too Small," *National Review*, August 26,
2015, http://www.nationalreview.com/corner/423122/navy-decline-size.

43 Roland Oliphant, "Putin Eyes Russian Strength in Atlantic and Arctic in New
Naval Doctrine," *Telegraph*, July 27, 2015, http://www.telegraph.co.uk/news/
worldnews/europe/russia/11765101/Putin-eyes-Russian-strength-in-Atlantic-
and-Arctic-in-new-naval-doctrine.html.

44 Vladimir Putin, "[Maritime doctrine of the Russian federation]," President
of Russia, July 26, 2015, http://static.kremlin.ru/media/events/files/ru/
uAFi5nvux2twaqjftS5yrIZUVTJan77L.pdf.

45 Dmitry Rogozin, quoted in Oliphant, "Putin Eyes Russian Strength."

46 Dmitry Rogozin, quoted in "Russia Sees Arctic as Naval Priority in New
Doctrine," BBC News, July 27, 2015, http://www.bbc.com/news/world-
europe-33673191.

47 Ryan Faith, "Russia's Massive Military Exercise in the Arctic Is Utterly
Baffling," Vice News, March 20 2015, https://news.vice.com/article/russias-
massive-military-exercise-in-the-arctic-is-utterly-baffling.

48 Franz-Stefan Gady, "Russia and China in the Artic: Is the US Facing an
Icebreaker Gap? Among Other Things, Russia Will Introduce the Design for
a New Super-Nuclear Icebreaker by the End of 2015," *Diplomat*, September 7,
2015, http://thediplomat.com/2015/09/russia-and-china-in-the-arctic-is-the-
us-facing-an-icebreaker-gap/.

49 "Putin: Russia to Boost Nuclear Arsenal with 40 Missiles," BBC News, June 16,
2015, http://www.bbc.com/news/world-33151125.

50 Anatoly Antonov, quoted in ibid.

51 Jens Stoltenberg, quoted in ibid.

52 Paul D. Shinkman, "Top GOP Lawmaker: US Must Consider Building New
Nukes," *U.S. News & World Report* News, June 23, 2015, http://www.usnews.
com/news/articles/2015/06/23/us-must-consider-building-new-nuclear-
weapons-amid-aging-arsenal-russian-aggression-says-hasc-chairman.

53 Clark Murdock, Samuel J. Brannen, Thomas Karako, and Angela Weaver,
*Project Atom: A Competitive Strategies Approach to Defining U.S. Nuclear
Strategy and Posture for 2025–2050* (Lanham, MD: Rowman & Littlefield,

2015), 12, Center for Strategic and International Studies, accessed June 29, 2016, http://csis.org/files/publication/150601_Murdock_ProjectAtom_Web. pdf.

54 Gertz, "Russia Doubling Nuclear Warheads."

55 *Greece*: Matthew Campbell, "Greece: Putin's Trojan Horse," *Sunday Times News*, February 1, 2015, http://www.thesundaytimes.co.uk/sto/newsreview/ features/article1513431.ece?shareToken=b89570f0910ccde9b945486e736dc bde; *Hungary*: Georgi Gotev, "Romanian Spy Chief Warns of 'Threat for EU from Hungary,'" EurActiv.com, February 20, 2015, http://www.euractiv.com/ sections/global-europe/romanian-spy-chief-warns-threat-eu-hungary-312302.

56 "Russia's Friends in Black: Why Europe's Populists and Radicals Admire Vladimir Putin," *Economist*, April 16, 2014, http://www.economist.com/news/ europe/21601004-why-europes-populists-and-radicals-admire-vladimir-putin-russias-friends-black.

57 Interview with senior European diplomat, August 3, 2015.

58 Ibid.

CHAPTER 4 ▪ THE NEW WARFARE: RUSSIA'S ARSENAL OF AGGRESSION

1 Quoted in Youssef, "Pentagon Fears Its Not Ready."

2 Kim R. Holmes, "Putin's Asymmetrical War on the West," *Foreign Policy*, May 5, 2014, http://foreignpolicy.com/2014/05/05/putins-asymmetrical-war-on-the-west/.

3 Vladimir Putin, quoted in Huggler, "Putin 'Privately Threatened to Invade.'"

4 Stephen J. Blank, "Imperial Ambitions: Russia's Military Buildup," *World Affairs* (May/June 2015), http://www.worldaffairsjournal.org/article/imperial-ambitions-russia%E2%80%99s-military-buildup.

5 Joseph Dunford, quoted in Paul McCleary, "More Pentagon Generals Line Up to Proclaim Russia's 'Existential' Threat to U.S.," *Foreign Policy* "The Cable," July 14, 2015, http://foreignpolicy.com/2015/07/14/more-pentagon-generals-line-up-to-proclaim-russia-existential-threat-to-u-s/.

6 Vladimir Putin, quoted in Fred Weir, "Fearing West, Putin Pledges Biggest Military Buildup since Cold War," *Jewish World Review*, 2012, http://www. jewishworldreview.com/0212/putin_pledges_biggest_military_buildup.php3#. VetDcxFVikp.

7 "Russian Defense Budget to Hit Record $81 Billion in 2015," *Moscow Times*, October 16, 2014, http://www.themoscowtimes.com/business/article/russian-defense-budget-to-hit-record-81bln-in-2015/509536.html.

8 Biryukov, "Vladimir Putin's War Machine."

9 "Military Expenditure (% of GDP)," World Bank, accessed June 29, 2016, http://data.worldbank.org/indicator/MS.MIL.XPND.GD.ZS.

10 Biryukov, "Vladimir Putin's War Machine."

11 Weir, "Putin Pledges Biggest Military Buildup."

12 Blank, "Imperial Ambitions."

13 Nikolas K. Gvosdev, "The Bear Awakens: Russia's Military Is Back," *National Interest*, November 12, 2014, http://nationalinterest.org/commentary/russias-military-back-9181.

14 Biryukov, "Vladimir Putin's War Machine."

15 "Russia to Introduce Army Reserve Force—Report," RT, October 13, 2014, http://www.rt.com/news/195376-russian-army-reserve-units/.

16 Christian Beekman, "Why Russia's New Tanks Are a Wake-Up Call for the US," *Task & Purpose*, May 22, 2015, http://taskandpurpose.com/why-russias-new-tanks-are-a-wake-up-call-for-the-us/.

17 Chris Pleasance, "It's 20 Years ahead of the West—and It WON'T Blow Up 'Like Its Predecessor': Brains behind Russia's New Robotic Tank Reveals Secrets of Machine at Centre of $500BILLION Military Upgrade," DailyMail.com, June 12, 2015, http://www.dailymail.co.uk/news/article-3121195/20-years-ahead-West-WON-T-blow-like-predecessor-Brains-Russia-s-new-robotic-tank-reveals-secrets-machine-forefront-country-s-250BILLION-military-modernisation.html.

18 Ibid.

19 Quoted in Alexei Druzhinin, "Men in Uniform: Latest Military News," Sputnik, May 25, 2015.

20 Dave Deptula, quoted in Dave Majumdar, "The Russian Air Force's Super Weapon: Beware the PAK-FA Stealth Fighter," *National Interest*, November 26, 2014, http://nationalinterest.org/feature/the-russian-air-forces-super-weapon-beware-the-pak-fa-11742.

21 Larry Bell, "Indefensible Policies: Our Commander-in-Chief Retreats as Putin's Missile Programs Advance," *Forbes*, July 14, 2013, http://www.forbes.com/sites/larrybell/2013/07/14/indefensible-policies-our-commander-in-chief-retreats-as-putins-missile-programs-advance/print/.

22 Vladimir Putin, quoted in Laura Smith-Spark, "Russia Was Ready to Put Nuclear Forces on Alert over Crimea, Putin Says," CNN, last modified March 16, 2015, http://www.cnn.com/2015/03/16/europe/russia-putin-crimea-nuclear/.

23 Blank, "Imperial Ambitions."

24 Ibid.

25 Vladimir Putin, quoted in Carol J. Williams, "Kremlin Officials Say Russian Nuclear Buildup Is Forced by West," *Los Angeles Times*, June 17, 2015, http://www.latimes.com/world/europe/la-fg-russia-nuclear-missiles-20150617-story.html.

26 "Russia to Pass into Service 100 Ton Ballistic Missile Sarmat," Missilethreat.com, December 27, 2014, http://missilethreat.com/russia-pass-service-100-ton-ballistic-missile-sarmat/.

27 Valery Gerasimov, quoted in David Axe, "The Russian Navy Is on the Verge of Collapse: Big Ships Age Out and Moscow Can't Replace Them," War Is Boring, accessed June 29, 2016, https://warisboring.com/the-russian-navy-is-on-the-verge-of-collapse-b0ce344ebf96#.3lilfxh7i.

28 Sergei Shoigu, quoted in Blank, "Imperial Ambitions."

29 Gvosdev, "Russia's Military Is Back."

30 Alexander Vitko, quoted in Vladimir Soldatkin, "Russia Will Add 80 New Warships to Black Sea Fleet: Fleet Commander," Reuters, September 23, 2014, http://www.reuters.com/article/2014/09/23/us-russia-navy-ships-idUSKCN0HI16K20140923.

31 Steven Lee Meyers, "U.S. Is Playing Catch-Up with Russia in Scramble for the Arctic," *New York Times*, August 29, 2015, http://www.nytimes.com/2015/08/30/world/united-states-russia-arctic-explorationhtml?ref=todaypaper&_r=0.

32 Ibid.

33 Paul F. Zukunft, quoted in Jeremy Bender, "U.S. Coast Guard Chief: We Are

'Not Even in the Same League as Russia' in the Arctic," *Business Insider* Military & Defense, July 6, 2015, http://www.businessinsider.com/us-not-even-in-the-same-league-as-russia-in-arctic-2015-7.

34 Jen Judson, "The Icebreaker Gap: Russia Has 40 Powerful Ships to Clear Lanes through Crucial Arctic Waters. America Is Down to 2," *Politico*, September 1, 2015, http://www.politico.com/agenda/story/2015/09/the-icebreaker-gap-000213.

35 William E. Gortney, quoted in Meyers, "U.S. Is Playing Catch-Up."

36 Paul F. Zukunft, quoted in ibid.

37 Tony Wesolowsky, "Kalingrad, Moscow's Military Trump Card," Radio Free Europe/Radio Liberty, June 18, 2015, http://www.rferl.org/content/kaliningradrussia-nato-west-strategic/27079655.html.

38 Vladimir Zaritsky, quoted in Adrian Blomfield, "Russia Piles Pressure on EU over Missile Shield," *Telegraph*, November 15, 2007, http://www.telegraph.co.uk/news/worldnews/1569495/Russia-piles-pressure-on-EU-over-missileshield.html.

39 Aleksandras Matonis, quoted in Edmundas Jakilaitis, "Russia's Militarization of Kaliningrad—Sign of Forthcoming Military Stand-Off?," "Delfi" by the *Lithuania Tribune*, April 5, 2015, http://en.delfi.lt/lithuania/defence/russias-militarization-of-kaliningradsign-of-forthcoming-military-stand-off.d?id=67619696.

40 Umberto Bacchi, "Russia Issues Nuclear Threat over Crimea and Baltic States," *International Business Times*, April 2, 2015, http://www.ibtimes.co.uk/russiaissues-nuclear-threat-over-crimea-baltic-states-1494675.

41 Andrius Kubilius, quoted in Wesolowsky, "Moscow's Military Trump Card."

42 Linas Linkevičius, quoted in Bacchi, "Hybrid War in Baltics."

43 Vladimir Putin, quoted in Vitaly Shevchenko, "'Little Green Men' or 'Russian Invaders'?," BBC News, March 11, 2014, http://www.bbc.com/news/world-europe-26532154.

44 Sam Jones, "Estonia Ready to Deal with Russia's 'Little Green Men,'" *Financial Times*, May 13, 2015, http://www.ft.com/cms/s/0/03c5ebde-f95a-11e4-ae65-00144feab7de.html#axzz3l9IwhGYc.

45 Anders Fogh Rasmussen, quoted in "Russia Engaging in 'Hybrid War' with Europe, Says Former NATO Chief," *Ukrainia: A Blog Collecting News about Ukraine and Russia . . . . . from Australia*, April 17, 2015, http://ukrainia.com.au/2015/04/17/russia-engaging-in-hybrid-war-with-europe-saysformer-nato-chief/.

46 Valery Gerasimov, quoted in Fiona Hill, "Hybrid War—the Real Reason Fighting Stopped in Ukraine—for Now," Reuters, February 26, 2015, http://blogs.reuters.com/great-debate/2015/02/26/hybrid-war-the-real-reasonfighting-stopped-in-ukraine-for-now/.

47 "Russia's New Tactics of War Shouldn't Fool Anyone," *Washington Post*, August 27, 2014, https://www.washingtonpost.com/opinions/russias-newtactics-of-war-shouldnt-fool-anyone/2014/08/27/0cb73b3a-2e21-11e4-9b98-848790384093_story.html.

48 Hill, "Hybrid War."

49 Ibid.

50 Steven Pifer, "Watch Out for Little Green Men," Brookings, July 7, 2014, http://www.brookings.edu/research/opinions/2014/07/07-watch-out-little-greenmen-pifer.

51 Judith Miller, "Chilly Neighbors: Vladimir Putin Tries to Keep Former Soviet Republics in Moscow's Economic Orbit," *City Journal*, September 24, 2013, http://www.city-journal.org/2013/eon0924jm.html.

52 Dmitry Rogozin, quoted in ibid.

53 Carl Bildt, quoted in Justyna Pawlak and Adrian Croft, "Sweden Lashes Out at Russian 'Economic Warfare' in Europe," Reuters, September 6, 2013, http://www.reuters.com/article/2013/09/06/us-eu-east-idUSBRE9850XA20130906.

54 Mihaela Rodina, "Ex-Soviet Moldova Is Feeling the Squeeze from Russian Fruit Embargo," *Business Insider* Finance, April 8, 2015, http://www.businessinsider.com/afp-ex-soviet-moldova-feels-squeeze-from-russian-fruit-embargo-2015-4#ixzz3ku0NvYom.

55 Quoted in Andrew Higgins, "Increasingly Frequent Call on Baltic Sea: 'The Russian Navy Is Back,'" *New York Times*, June 10, 2015, http://www.nytimes.com/2015/06/11/world/europe/intrusions-in-baltic-sea-show-a-russiachallenging-the-west.html.

56 Rokas Masiulis, quoted in ibid.

57 Masiulis, quoted in ibid.

58 Yury Yakubov, quoted in Karoun Demirjian, "Missile for Missile, Tank *Endnotes* 157 for Tank: Putin Says He Will Match Any Western Military Buildup in Eastern Europe," *National Post*, June 16, 2015, http://news.nationalpost.com/news/world/missile-for-missile-tank-for-tank-putin-says-he-will-match-anywestern-military-buildup-in-eastern-europe.

59 Holmes, "Putin's Asymmetrical War."

CHAPTER 5 ▪ SHADOWBOXING THE KREMLIN: SPIES, PROPAGANDA, AND CYBERWARFARE

1 Quoted in Tom Batchelor, "M16 Chiefs Warn British Agents They Are Being Targeted by Russian Spies in the UK," *Express*, April 26, 2015, http://www.express.co.uk/news/uk/573052/Russian-spies-UK-Vladimir-Putin-British-agents-MI6.

2 Dmitry Kiselyov, quoted in Miriam Elder, "Russia Has a New Propaganda Outlet and It's Everything You Thought It Would Be," BuzzFeed News, November 10, 2014, http://www.buzzfeed.com/miriamelder/russia-has-a-new-propaganda-outlet-and-its-everything-you-th#.juAd9lJjY.

3 Ed Royce, "Countering Putin's Information Weapons of War: Kremlin Propaganda Is Far Outstripping Our Ability to Get the Truth Out. The U.S. Needs a New Approach," *Wall Street Journal*, April 14, 2015, http://www.wsj.com/articles/countering-putins-information-weapons-of-war-1429052323.

4 Quoted in Owen Matthews, "Russia's Greatest Weapon May Be Its Hackers," *Newsweek*, May 7, 2015, http://www.newsweek.com/2015/05/15/russias-greatest-weapon-may-be-its-hackers-328864.html.

5 Peter Pomerantsev and Michael Weiss, "The Menace of Unreality: How the Kremlin Weaponizes Information, Culture and Money," *Interpreter*, November 22, 2014, http://www.interpretermag.com/the-menace-of-unreality-how-the-kremlin-weaponizes-information-culture-and-money/.

6 Scott Shane and Charlie Savage, "In Ordinary Lives, U.S. Sees the Work of Russian Agents," *New York Times*, June 28, 2010, http://www.nytimes.com/2010/06/29/world/europe/29spy.html?pagewanted=all.

7 Quoted in ibid.

8   Quoted in ibid.

9   Mark Lowenthal, quoted in Greg Miller and Philip P. Pan, "Alleged Spy Ring Seen as 'Throwback to the Cold War,'" *Washington Post*, June 30, 2010, http://www.washingtonpost.com/wp-dyn/content/article/2010/06/29/AR2010062905249.html.

10   Randall C. Coleman, quoted in Adam Goldman, "FBI Breaks Up a Russian Spy Ring in New York City," *Washington Post*, January 26, 2015, https://www.washingtonpost.com/world/national-security/fbi-breaks-up-a-russian-spy-ring-in-new-york-city/2015/01/26/d3f8cee8-a595-11e4-a2b2-776095f393b2_story.html.

11   Batchelor, "British Agents Are Being Targeted."

12   Quoted in ibid.

13   Von Dirk Banse, Florian Flade, Per Hinrichs, and Uwe Müller, "Verfassungsschutz warnt vor russischen Spionen" [Secret service warns of Russian spies], *Die Welt*, April 20, 2014, http://www.welt.de/politik/deutschland/article127121099/Verfassungsschutz-warnt-vor-russischen-Spionen.html.

14   Jens Stoltenberg, quoted in "NATO Reportedly Expels Dozens of Alleged Russian Spies from Brussels Headquarters," FoxNews.com World, May 12, 2015, http://www.foxnews.com/world/2015/05/12/nato-reportedly-expels-dozens-alleged-russian-spies-from-brussels-headquarters/.

15   Oleg Kalugin, quoted in Richard Byrne Reilly, "Former KGB General: Snowden Is Cooperating with Russian Intelligence," VentureBeat, May 22, 2014, http://venturebeat.com/2014/05/22/former-kgb-general-snowden-is-cooperating-with-russian-intelligence/.

16   Barry Levine, "Newly Revealed Emails Show Google Met Regularly with NSA," VentureBeat, May 6, 2014, http://venturebeat.com/2014/05/06/newly-revealed-emails-show-google-met-regularly-with-nsa/.

17   *Sunday Times*, quoted in Ewen MacAskill, "Snowden Files 'Read by Russia and China': Five Questions for UK Government," *Guardian*, June 14, 2015, http://www.theguardian.com/us-news/2015/jun/14/snowden-files-read-by-russia-and-china-five-questions-for-uk-government.

18   Philip Breedlove, quoted in Gould, "Breedlove: Intel Gaps Critical."

19   Breedlove, quoted in ibid.

20   Jon Merritt, quoted in Adrian Chen, "The Agency: From a Nondescript Office Building in St. Petersburg, Russia, an Army of Well-Paid 'Trolls' Has Tried to Wreak Havoc All around the Internet—and in Real-Life American Communities," *New York Times*, June 2, 2015, http://www.nytimes.com/2015/06/07/magazine/the-agency.html?_r=0.

21   Ibid.

22   L. Gordon Crovitz, "Putin Trolls the U.S. Internet: A Group in Russia Uses Social Media to Spread Phony News Stories and Propaganda in America," *Wall Street Journal*, June 7, 2015, http://www.wsj.com/articles/putin-trolls-the-u-s-internet-1433715770.

23   Spiegel Staff, "The Opinion-Makers: How Russia Is Winning the Propaganda War," Spiegel Online International, May 30, 2014, http://www.spiegel.de/international/world/russia-uses-state-television-to-sway-opinion-at-home-and-abroad-a-971971.html.

24   Edward Lucas, "Russia Has Published Books I Didn't Write! A Dodgy Imprint Has Compiled Old Material by Several U.S. and British Analysts, without

Their Permission. The Aim Is Pro-Putin Spin," *Daily Beast*, August 20, 2015, http://www.thedailybeast.com/articles/2015/08/20/russia-turned-me-into-propaganda.html.

25　Crovitz, "Putin Trolls U.S. Internet."

26　Philip Breedlove, quoted in Pomerantsev and Weiss, "Menace of Unreality."

27　Ibid.

28　Dmitry Kiselyov, quoted in Elder, "Russia Has a New Propaganda Outlet."

29　Quoted in Spiegel, "Opinion-Makers."

30　Andrew Weiss, quoted in ibid.

31　John McCain, quoted in "'Winning the Cold War with Propaganda': New Dutch-Polish 'Content Factory' to Challenge Russia," RT, July 22, 2015, https://www.rt.com/news/310416-content-factory-propaganda-russia/.

32　Philip Breedlove, quoted in Joe Gould, "Breedlove: Intel Gaps 'Critical,'" *Defense News*, April 30, 2015, http://www.defensenews.com/story/defense/policy-budget/policy/2015/04/30/breedlove-russia-intel-gaps/26642107/.

33　Royce, "Putin's Information Weapons of War."

34　Chris McGreal, "Vladimir Putin's 'Misinformation' Offensive Prompts US to Deploy Its Cold War Propaganda Tools: Pressure Grows from Congress to Counter Slick Russian Media That Erodes Support for Nato," *Guardian*, April 25, 2015, http://www.theguardian.com/world/2015/apr/25/us-set-to-revive-propaganda-war-asputin-pr-machine-undermines-baltic-states.

35　Kadri Liik, quoted in ibid.

36　Jeffrey Carr, quoted in Matthews, "Russia's Greatest Weapon."

37　Ibid.

38　Franz-Stefan Gady, "Russia Tops China as Principal Cyber Threat to US: A Recent Report Singles Out Russia as One of the Most Sophisticated Nation-State Actors in Cyberspace," *Diplomat*, March 3, 2015, http://thediplomat.com/2015/03/russia-tops-china-as-principal-cyber-threat-to-us/.

39　Radio Free Europe/Radio Liberty, "Russian Hacking Network Found Spying on U.S., Europe for Years," Radio Free Europe/Radio Liberty, September 8, 2015, http://www.rferl.org/content/russia-hacking-network-spying-us-europe-dukesfsecure/27254920.html.

40　Artturi Lehtiö, quoted in Anthony Cuthbertson, "Russia: 7-Year Cyberwar against NATO, EU and US by Kremlin-Sponsored Hackers the Dukes Exposed," *International Business Times*, September 17, 2015, http://www.ibtimes.co.uk/russia-7-year-cyberwar-againstnato-eu-us-by-kremlin-sponsored-hackers-dukes-exposed-1520065.

41　Matthews, "Russia's Greatest Weapon."

42　Radio Free Europe, "Russian Hacking Network."

43　Quoted in Evan Perez and Shimon Prokupecz, "How the U.S. Thinks Russians Hacked the White House," CNN Politics, last modified April 8, 2015, http://www.cnn.com/2015/04/07/politics/how-russians-hacked-the-wh/.

44　Evan Perez and Shimon Prokupecz, "Sources: State Dept. Hack the 'Worst Ever,'" CNN Politics, last modified March 10, 2015, http://www.cnn.com/2015/03/10/politics/statedepartment-hack-worst-ever/index.html.

45　Perez and Prokupecz, "Russians Hacked White House."

46　Schmidt and Sanger, "Obama's Unclassified Emails."

47　Quoted in Courtney Kube and Jim Miklaszewski, "Russia Hacks Pentagon Computers: NBC, Citing Sources," CNBC, August 6, 2015, http://www.cnbc.com/2015/08/06/russia-hacks-pentagon-computers-nbc-citing-sources.html.

48 Ibid.
49 Michael Rogers, quoted in Matthews, "Russia's Greatest Weapon."
50 Quoted in ibid.
51 Matthews, "Russia's Greatest Weapon."
52 Leon Panetta, quoted in Gopal Ratnam, "Cyberattacks Could Become as Destructive as 9/11: Panetta," Bloomberg Technology, October 12, 2012, http://www.bloomberg.com/news/articles/2012-10-12/cyberattacks-could-becomeas-destructive-as-9-11-panetta.
53 Leon Panetta, quoted in Elisabeth Bumiller and Thomas Shanker, "Panetta Warns of Dire Threat of Cyberattack on U.S.," New York Times, October 11, 2012, http://www.nytimes.com/2012/10/12/world/panetta-warns-of-direthreat-of-cyberattack.html?hp&pagewanted=print.
54 Quoted in Spiegel, "Opinion-Makers."
55 Crovitz, "Putin Trolls U.S. Internet."

CHAPTER 6 ▪ SOWING DISORDER: RUSSIA, ROGUE REGIMES, AND TERROR

1 Vladimir Putin, quoted in "Putin Makes Accusation against U.S. over Syria Policy," CBS News, December 3, 2015, http://www.cbsnews.com/news/vladimir-putin-us-western-powers-zone-of-chaos-syria-iraq-libya/.
2 Quoted in Michael Weiss, "Russia Is Sending Jihadis to Join ISIS: Even as Washington Touts Its Counterterrorism Partnerships with Moscow, Evidence Points to Putin's Intelligence Service Practically Helping the Islamic State," Daily Beast, August 23, 2015, http://www.thedailybeast.com/articles/2015/08/23/russia-s-playing-a-double-game-with-islamic-terror0.html.
3 Vladimir Putin, quoted in "Putin Makes Accusation against U.S.," CBS News.
4 Vladimir Putin, quoted in Associated Press, "Putin Calls for 'One Powerful Fist' to Confront Terrorism in State of Nation Speech," Los Angeles Times, December 3, 2015, http://www.latimes.com/world/europe/la-fg-russia-putin-speech-20151203-story.html.
5 Igor Eidman, quoted in Paul A. Goble, "'Putin Not Interested in Fighting Islamism but Promoting Instability and Undermining the West,' Eidman Says," Euromaidan Press, November 19, 2015, http://euromaidanpress.com/2015/11/19/putin-not-interested-in-fighting-islamism-but-promoting-instability-and-undermining-the-west-eidman-says/.
6 Eidman, quoted in ibid.
7 James F. Jeffrey, quoted in Michael R. Gordon, "U.S. Begins Military Talks with Russia on Syria," New York Times, September 18, 2015, http://www.nytimes.com/2015/09/19/world/europe/us-to-begin-military-talks-with-russia-on-syria.html.
8 Roland Oliphant and Lousia Loveluck, "Russian Arms to Syria Prevent 'Even Bigger' Refugee Flow to Europe, Says Putin: Russian President Defends Support for Bashar al-Assad, Insisting that the Fall of the Syrian Leader Would Worsen Europe's Migration Crisis," Telegraph, September 15, 2015, http://www.telegraph.co.uk/news/worldnews/europe/russia/11866779/Russian-arms-to-Syria-prevent-even-bigger-refugee-flow-to-Europe-says-Putin.html.
9 Zaidoun Alzoabi, quoted in Kareem Fahim and Maher Samaan, "Violence in Syria Spurs a Huge Surge in Civilian Fight," New York Times, October 26, 2015,

http://www.nytimes.com/2015/10/27/world/middleeast/syria-russian-air-strike-refugees.html?_r=0.

10 US Embassy in Damascus, quoted in Michael Weiss, "Russia's Giving ISIS an Air Force: Putin's Air Campaign in Syria Is Not Only Suppoting Assad, It's Giving Cover to Fighters from the So-Called Islamic State," *Daily Beast*, October 8, 2015, http://www.thedailybeast.com/articles/2015/10/08/russia-s-giving-isis-an-air-force.html.

11 Quoted in ibid.

12 Ibid.

13 Weiss, "Russia Sending Jihadis."

14 Kate Brannen, "Russians Are Joining ISIS in Droves: Jihadists from Russia and Central Asia Are Pouring into the Caliphate, Four Times More than a Year Ago," *Daily Beast*, December 7, 2015, http://www.thedailybeast.com/articles/2015/12/07/russians-are-joining-isis-in-droves.html.

15 Weiss, "Russia's Giving ISIS Air Force."

16 Quoted in Weiss, "Russia Sending Jihadis."

17 Glen Howard, quoted in ibid.

18 James Miller, "Putin's New Axis of Resistance: Russia, Iran, Iraq, Syria, and Hezbollah; The Russian Leader Just Told the UN That State Sponsors of Terrorism Are the West's Only Partners for Fighting Terrorism," *Daily Beast*, September 28, 2015, http://www.thedailybeast.com/articles/2015/09/28/putin-s-new-axis-of-resistance-russia-iran-iraq-syria-and-hezbollah.html.

19 Quoted in Weiss, "Russia Sending Jihadis."

20 Mark N. Katz, "Why Russia Won't Play Ball on Iran," *Diplomat*, June 23, 2012, http://thediplomat.com/2012/06/why-russia-wont-play-ball-on-iran/.

21 Amir Taheri, "An Iran-Russian Axis," *New York Post*, December 7, 2014, http://nypost.com/2014/12/07/an-iran-russia-axis/.

22 Sergey Chemesov, quoted in Peggy Hollinger, Kathrin Hille, and John Reed, "Russia Breaks Deadlock over Sale of S-300 Missile System to Iran," *Financial Times*, November 9, 2015, http://www.ft.com/intl/cms/s/0/7f701684-86d0-11e5-90de-f44762bf9896.html#axzz3u9GyIiSv.

23 Michael Eisenstadt and Douglas Shaffer, "Russian S-300 Missiles to Iran: Groundhog Day or Game-Changer?," Washington Institute, September 4, 2015, http://www.washingtoninstitute.org/policy-analysis/view/russian-s-300-missiles-to-iran-groundhog-day-or-game-changer.

24 Ibid.

25 Associated Press in Moscow, "Two More Nuclear Reactors."

26 Alessandria Masi, "Putin's Latest Moves: The Military Alliance among Iran, Hezbollah and Russia in Syria Could Spread to Yemen," *International Business Times*, September 25, 2015, http://www.ibtimes.com/putins-latest-moves-military-alliance-among-iran-hezbollah-russia-syria-could-spread-2113386.

27 Dion Nissenbaum and Carol E. Lee, "Russia Expands Military Presence in Syria, Satellite Photos Show: Apparent Development near Latakia Is Latest Sign Moscow Is Preparing to Intervene in Syrian War," *Wall Street Journal*, last modified September 22, 2015, http://www.wsj.com/articles/russia-expands-military-its-presence-in-syria-satellite-photos-show-1442937150.

28 Kathrin Hille and John Reed, "Russia to Deploy 2,000 in Syria Air Base Mission's 'First Phase,'" *Financial Times* Politics & Society, September 21, 2015,

http://www.ft.com/intl/cms/s/0/95971a4e-607d-11e5-a28b-50226830d644.
html#axzz3mgDIAs2e

29 Nissenbaum and Lee, "Russia Expands Military Presence."

30 Weiss, "Russia Sending Jihadis."

31 Michael Pregent, quoted in Erick Stakelbeck, "Russia-Iran 'Nightmare'
    Alliance: Why You Should Be Concerned," CBN News, November 5, 2015,
    http://www1.cbn.com/cbnnews/world/2015/November/Russia-Iran-
    Nightmare-Alliance-Why-You-Should-Be-Concerned/.

32 Ibid.

33 Quoted in Masi, "Putin's Latest Moves."

34 Ibid.

35 Quoted in ibid.

36 Matthew Levitt, quoted in Stakelbeck, "Russia-Iran 'Nightmare' Alliance."

37 Julian Ryall, "Isolated North Korea Looks for New Allies," DW, July 9, 2015,
    http://www.dw.com/en/isolated-north-korea-looks-for-new-allies/a-18697433.

38 Doug Bandow, "Friends with Benefits: Russia and North Korea's Twisted
    Tango," National Interest, February 29, 2016, http://nationalinterest.org/print/
    feature/friends-benefits-russia-north-koreas-twisted-tango-12369.

39 Fidel Castro Ruz, "Fidel's Message to President Nicolás Maduro," Granma,
    December 11, 2015, http://en.granma.cu/cuba/2015-12-11/fidels-message-to-
    president-nicolas-maduro.

40 Sergei Shoigu, quoted in "Russia Seeks Several Military Bases Abroad—
    Defense Minister," Sputnik Military & Intelligence, February 26, 2014, http://
    sputniknews.com/military/20140226/187917901/Russia-Seeks-Several-
    Military-Bases-Abroad--Defense-Minister.html.

41 Vladimir Putin, quoted in Girish Gupta and David Blair, "Hugo Chávez
    Divides Venezuela in Death as in Life amid Fears of Violence," Telegraph,
    March 6, 2013, http://www.telegraph.co.uk/news/worldnews/southamerica/
    venezuela/9912556/Hugo-Chavez-divides-Venezuela-in-death-as-in-life-amid-
    fears-of-violence.html.

42 Daniel Ortega, quoted in Ramiro Sebastián Fúnez, "Russia's Military Power in
    Latin America," America's Quarterly, March 11, 2014, http://americasquarterly.
    org/content/russia-military-power-in-latin-america.

CHAPTER 7 ▪ BLACK-GOLD BULLY: RUSSIA'S OIL AND GAS

1 Quoted in Faiola, "From Russia with Love."

2 Jude Clemente, "How Much Energy Does Africa Have Anyways?," Forbes,
    March 25, 2015, http://www.forbes.com/sites/judeclemente/2015/03/25/how-
    much-energy-does-russia-have-anyways/print/.

3 John P. Millhone, Russia's Neglected Energy Reserves (Washington,
    DC: Carnegie Endowment for International Peace, 2010), http://
    carnegieendowment.org/files/russia_energy_reserve.pdf.

4 Ibid.

5 Clemente, "How Much Energy Does Africa Have?"

6 Reuters, "Russian Oil, Gas Reserves Jump Most in BP League Table," Hurriyet
    Daily News, June 10, 2015, http://www.hurriyetdailynews.com/russian-oil-gas-
    reserves-jump-most-in-bp-league-table.aspx?pageID=238&nID=83770&News
    CatID=348.

7   Ibid.

8   Stephen Bierman and Julian Lee, "Russia Oil Production Poised for Record as Industry Defies Slump," Bloomberg, October 29, 2015, http://www.bloomberg.com/news/articles/2015-10-29/russia-oil-production-poised-for-record-as-industry-defies-slump.

9   Clemente, "How Much Energy Does Africa Have?"

10 Ibid.

11 Maria van der Hoeven, quoted in James Crisp, "EU Dependent on Russian Gas for 'Foreseeable Future,' Warns IEA," EurActiv.com, last modified December 7, 2014, http://www.euractiv.com/sections/energy/eu-dependent-russian-gas-foreseeable-future-warns-iea-310469.

12 Ibid.

13 Robert Lea, "Europe Plunged into Energy Crisis as Russia Cuts Off Gas Supply via Ukraine," DailyMail.com, last modified January 7, 2009, http://www.dailymail.co.uk/news/article-1106382/Europe-plunged-energy-crisis-Russia-cuts-gas-supply-Ukraine.html.

14 Alexander Novak, quoted in Elena Mazneva, "Russia to Shift Ukraine Gas Transit to Turkey as EU Cries Foul," Bloomberg, January 14, 2015, http://www.bloomberg.com/news/articles/2015-01-14/russia-to-shift-ukraine-gas-transit-to-turkey-as-eu-cries-foul.

15 Randall Newnham, "Oil, Carrots, and Sticks: Russia's Energy Resources as a Foreign Policy Tool," *Journal of Eurasian Studies* 2, no. 2 (July 2011), http://www.sciencedirect.com/science/article/pii/S187936651100011X.

16 Ibid.

17 Péter Szijjártó, quoted in Faiola, "From Russia with Love."

18 Ibid.

19 Quoted in ibid.

20 Simon, "Liberal Democracy in Hungary."

21 "Europe Depends on Russian Energy," *New York Times.*

22 Ibid.

23 Chi-Kong Chyong and Vessela Tcherneva, "Europe's Vulnerability on Russian Gas," European Council on Foreign Relations, March 17, 2015, http://www.ecfr.eu/article/commentary_europes_vulnerability_on_russian_gas

24 Paul Craig Roberts, quoted in Kenneth Schortgen Jr., "If Putin Shut Off Oil to Europe It Would End Ukrainian Crisis Instantly," examiner.com, September 13, 2014, http://www.examiner.com/article/if-putin-shut-off-oil-to-europe-it-would-end-ukrainian-crisis-instantly.

25 "Europe Depends on Russian Energy," *New York Times.*

26 Elena Mazneva, Irina Reznik, and Dina Khrennikova, "Putin Seeks Chinese Gift as Oil Slump Sours Second Gas Deal," Bloomberg, August 23, 2015, http://www.bloomberg.com/news/articles/2015-08-23/putin-hopes-for-chinese-gift-as-oil-slump-sours-second-gas-deal.

27 Monica Crowley, "Monica Crowley: Putin's Real Target," Newsmax, October 15, 2015, http://www.newsmax.com/Newsfront/Monica-Crowley-Putin-Russia/2015/10/15/id/696377/.

28 Ibid.

29 Ibid.

30 Larry Jeddeloh, quoted in Leslie P. Norton, "Get Ready for a Shaky EU and Higher Oil, Dollar and Gold: Institutional Strategist's Larry Jeddeloh on the

Mideast, a Rising Dollar, Stocks and Commodities," *Barron's*, November 21, 2015, http://www.barrons.com/articles/get-ready-for-a-shaky-eu-and-higher-oil-dollar-and-gold-1448082682.

31 "Russia Submits Arctic Claim to UN in Move to Seize Oil and Gas Rights," FoxNews.com World, August 5, 2015, http://www.foxnews.com/world/2015/08/05/russia-submits-claim-for-vast-arctic-seabed-territories-at-united-nations/.

32 Gary Roughead, "In the Race for Arctic Energy, the U.S. and Russia Are Polar Opposites; The Obama Administration Dithers while Moscow—with China Close Behind—Revs Up Offshore Oil Production," *Wall Street Journal*, August 25, 2015, http://www.wsj.com/articles/in-the-race-for-arctic-energy-the-u-s-and-russia-are-polar-opposites-1440542608?alg=y.

33 Judson, "Icebreaker Gap."

34 Patrick McLoughlin, "Norway, Russia on Collision Course over Arctic Oil Drilling," ed. Maurice Geller, Platts, May 27, 2015, http://www.platts.com/latest-news/oil/london/norway-russia-on-collision-course-over-arctic-26102429.

35 Roughead, "Race for Arctic Energy."

36 Angus Miller and Shamil Yenikeyeff, "Oil's Well in Central Asia: China, Kazakhstan, and Russia Make a Deal," *Foreign Affairs*, May 19, 2015, https://www.foreignaffairs.com/articles/china/2015-05-19/oils-well-central-asia.

37 Ibid.

38 James Kanter and Stanley Reed, "European Leaders Seek Tighter Cooperation on Energy," *New York Times*, February 25, 2015, http://www.nytimes.com/2015/02/26/business/international/european-leaders-push-for-energy-union.html.

39 Petr Polak, "How to Beat Goliath: An EU Energy Union to Fight Russia's Gas Monopoly," *Foreign Affairs*, December 10, 2014, https://www.foreignaffairs.com/articles/russia-fsu/2014-12-10/how-beat-goliath.

40 "EU Proposes Much-Needed Energy Union," *American Interest*, March 1, 2015, http://www.the-american-interest.com/2015/03/01/eu-proposes-much-needed-energy-union/.

41 Polak, "How to Beat Goliath."

42 Paul Driessen, "Breaking Russia's Energy Stranglehold," Townhall.com, September 29, 2014, http://townhall.com/columnists/pauldriessen/2014/09/29/breaking-russias-energy-stranglehold-n1897826/print.

43 Anders Fogh Rasmussen, quoted in ibid.

44 Dalibor Rohac, "Time to End Europe's Dependence on Russian Energy," *Financial Times* blog, May 5, 2015, http://blogs.ft.com/beyond-brics/2015/05/05/time-to-end-europes-dependence-on-russian-energy/#.

45 Crisp, "EU Dependent on Russian Gas."

46 "How the EU Can Progress towards an 'Energy Union,'" International Energy Agency, December 1, 2014, http://www.iea.org/newsroomandevents/pressreleases/2014/december/how-the-eu-can-progress-towards-an-energy-union.html.

47 David Hunt, "Obama Should Open the Arctic to Counter Russia on Energy," *Washington Examiner*, June 16, 2015, http://www.washingtonexaminer.com/obama-should-open-the-arctic-to-counter-russia-on-energy/article/2566167.

48 Ibid.

49 Ibid.

CHAPTER 8 ▪ PUTIN'S PROXIES: HOW RUSSIA INFLUENCES EUROPE

1   Marine Le Pen, quoted in "Le Pen: I Admire 'Cool Head' Putin's Resistance to West's New Cold War," Euronews, January 12, 2014, http://www.Euronews. com/2014/12/01/le-pen-i-admire-cool-head-putin-s-resistance-to-west-s-new-cold-war/.

2   "Latvijas iedzīvotāju etniskais sastāvs" [Latvian ethnic composition], Centrālā statistikas pārvalde, August 18, 2015, http://www.csb.gov.lv/sites/default/files/skoleniem/iedzivotaji/etniskais_sastavs.pdf.

3   "Latvian Communist Jailed for Coup Role," *Spokesman-Review*, January 28, 1995, http://www.spokesman.com/stories/1995/jul/28/latvian-communist-jailed-for-coup-role/.

4   Eszter Zalan and Nikolaj Nielsen, "Jobbik MEP Accused of Working for Russia," *EUobserver*, May 15, 2014, https://euobserver.com/eu-elections/124156.

5   "Pro Russia Party Signs Major Deal with Crimea Group," *Baltic Times*, August 13, 2014, http://www.baltictimes.com/news/articles/35355/#.VA97mRbgJHU.

6   Latvian Union of Russians [Latvian Russian Union], quoted in ibid.

7   Kristīne Jarinovska, "Popular Initiatives as Means of Altering the Core of the Republic of Latvia," *Juridica Interational* (2013), http://www.juridicainternational.eu/index.php?id=15331.

8   "For Human Rights in a United Latvia Party's Program for the Elections of the 11th Saeima," Latvian Russian Union, November 14, 2012, http://www.rusojuz.lv/en/party/Programs/25945-/.

9   Luke Harding, "Latvia: Russia's Playground for Business, Politics—and Crime; Mystery of Missing Tycoon Shows How Russian Influence Is Growing Again in Small Baltic Nation," *Guardian*, January 23, 2013, http://www.theguardian.com/world/2013/jan/23/latvia-russian-playground.

10 Aleksei Gunter, "Center Party Signs Cooperation Protocol with Kremlin-Controlled United Russia," *Baltic Times*, December 15, 2004, http://www.baltictimes.com/news/articles/11595/.

11 Valery Bogomolov, quoted in ibid.

12 "Savisaar Suspended from Mayor's Office," ERR.ee, September 30, 2015, http://news.err.ee/v/politics/2b68a0b6-7636-4070-8389-f9751d5874a4/savisaar-suspended-from-mayors-office.

13 "A Political Scandal in Estonia and Russian Influence in the Baltics," Stratfor Global Intelligence, December 27, 2010, https://www.stratfor.com/analysis/political-scandal-estonia-and-russian-influence-baltics.

14 "[Notable deputies that are in Russia 'defending the interests of the Russian world']," Ukrainian Pravda, September 18, 2014, http://www.pravda.com.ua/news/2014/09/18/7038181/.

15 "Opposition Bloc Boosts Rating by Distancing Itself from Yanukovych Era," *KyivPost*, October 24, 2014, http://www.kyivpost.com/content/kyiv-post-plus/opposition-bloc-boosts-rating-by-distancing-itself-from-yanukovych-era-369312.html.

16 Nestor Shufrych, quoted in ibid.

17 Nikolas Kozloff, "Ukraine: Insider Oligarchs Derail Maidan Revolution," *Huffington Post*: "World Post," last modified April 30, 2015, http://www.huffingtonpost.com/nikolas-kozloff/ukraine-insider-oligarchs-derail-maidan-revolution_b_6773856.html.

18 "Gutted: A Banking Scandal Is Set to Bankrupt Europe's Poorest Country," *Economist*, August 1, 2015, http://www.economist.com/news/finance-and-economics/21660165-banking-scandal-set-bankrupt-europes-poorest-country-gutted.

19 "[Population by main nationalities, in territorial aspect]," National Bureau of Statistics of the Republic of Moldova, last modified 2004, http://www.statistica.md/public/files/Recensamint/Recensamintul_populatiei/vol_1/6_Nationalitati_de_baza_ro.xls.

20 Tim Whewell, "The Great Moldovan Bank Robbery," BBC News, June 18, 2015, http://www.bbc.com/news/magazine-33166383.

21 "Moldovan Prime Minister Accused of Forging High School, College Diplomas," Sputnik, last modified June 7, 2015, http://sputniknews.com/europe/20150607/1023047693.html.

22 Mark Baker, "Moldova's Mysterious Magnate," Radio Free Europe/Radio Liberty, last modified May 6, 2016, http://www.rferl.org/content/moldova-mysterious-magnate-ilan-shor-scandal/26998388.html.

23 Associated Press, "Moldovans Choose between Russia, Europe in Local Elections," *Economic Times*, June 28, 2015, http://economictimes.indiatimes.com/news/international/world-news/moldovans-choose-between-russia-europe-in-local-elections/articleshow/47856450.cms.

24 Reuters, "Big Wins Expected for Moldova's Pro-Russia Parties in Local Elections," Voice of America, June 14, 2015, http://www.voanews.com/content/big-wins-expected-for-moldova-pro-russian-parties-in-local-elections/2821213.html.

25 Melodie Bouchad, "Leaked Messages Allegedly Show Kremlin Paid for French Far Right Leader to Endorse Crimea Annexation," Vice News, April 5, 2015, https://news.vice.com/article/leaked-messages-allegedly-show-kremlin-paid-for-french-far-right-leader-to-endorse-crimea-annexation.

26 Ibid.

27 Marine Le Pen, quoted in "'Cool Head' Putin's Resistance," Euronews.

28 DowneastDem, "Putin Supporting Europe's Far-Right Parties," *Daily Kos*, November 28, 2014, http://www.dailykos.com/story/2014/11/28/1348031/-Putin-supporting-Europe-s-Far-Right-Parties.

29 Viktor Orbán, "Full Text of Viktor Orbán's Speech at Băile Tuşnad (Tusnádfürdő)," (speech, Bálványos Free Summer University and Youth Camp, Băile Tuşnad, Romania, July 26, 2014), compiled by Csaba Tóth, *Budapest Beacon*, July 29, 2014, http://budapestbeacon.com/public-policy/full-text-of-viktor-orbans-speech-at-baile-tusnad-tusnadfurdo-of-26-july-2014/10592.

30 Vladimir Soldatkin and Krisztina Than, "Putin Finds Warm Welcome in Hungary, Despite European Chill," Reuters, February 17, 2015, http://uk.reuters.com/article/2015/02/17/uk-hungary-putin-idUKKBN0LL1XP20150217.

31 Andrew Byrne, "Orban Defies EU to Host Putin in Hungary," *Financial Times*, February 17, 2015, http://www.ft.com/intl/cms/s/0/fc6c4590-b674-11e4-a5f2-00144feab7de.html#axzz3ftfFsjLn.

32 Ibid.

33 Faiola, "From Russia with Love."

34 Ibid.

35 Péter Szijjártó, quoted in ibid.

36 Gábor Vona, quoted in Elisabeth Braw, "Putin Seeks to Influence Radical Parties in Bid to Destabilise Europe," *Newsweek*, January 9, 2015, http://www.newsweek.com/2015/01/16/putins-envoys-seek-influence-european-radicals-297769.html.

37 Ibid.

38 Zalan and Nielsen, "Jobbik MEP Accused."

39 Ibid.

40 Mitchell A. Orenstein, "Putin's Western Allies: Why Europe's Far Right Is on the Kremlin's Side," *Foreign Affairs*, March 25, 2014, https://www.foreignaffairs.com/articles/russia-fsu/2014-03-25/putins-western-allies.

41 Golden Dawn, quoted in ibid.

42 "Alternative for Germany's New Leader Promises Closer Ties with Russia," Sputnik, July 5, 2015, http://sputniknews.com/politics/20150705/1024234752.html.

43 Justin Huggler, "Germany's Eurosceptic Party Begin Selling Gold; Alternative for Germany (AfD) Has Started Selling Gold Bars and Coins Online, to Raise Funds for Its Operations," *Telegraph*, November 3, 2014, http://www.telegraph.co.uk/news/worldnews/europe/germany/11205562/Germanys-eurosceptic-party-begin-selling-gold.html.

44 Braw, "Putin Seeks to Influence Radical Parties."

45 "22% of Bulgarians Want to Join Russia's 'Eurasian Union,'" EurActive.com, May 15, 2014, http://www.euractiv.com/sections/eu-elections-2014/22-bulgarians-want-join-russias-eurasian-union-302163.

46 Orenstein, "Putin's Western Allies."

47 Ibid.

48 Gabrielle Tétrault Farber, "Greek Election Wins Putin a Friend in Europe," *Moscow Times*, January 26, 2015, www.themoscowtimes.com/news/article/greek-election-wins-putin-a-friend-in-europe/514923.html.

49 Ibid.

50 Ibid.

51 Ibid.

52 Vladimir Putin, quoted in ibid.

53 "Russia's European Supporters," *Economist*.

54 Pablo Iglesias, quoted in Eduardo Suárez, "Pablo Iglesias acusa a la UE de usar 'un doble rasero' con Rusia e Israel" [Pablo Iglesias accuses the EU of applying "a double standard" with Russia and Israel], *El Mundo*, September 9, 2014, http://www.elmundo.es/espana/2014/09/09/540f0faf22601d76308b4574.html.

55 Ibid.

56 Raphael Minder, "Spanish Upstart Party Said It Could, and Did. Now the Hard Part Begins," *New York Times*, May 29, 2014, http://www.nytimes.com/2014/05/29/world/europe/spanish-upstart-party-said-it-could-and-did-now-the-hard-part-begins.html?_r=2.

57 Paul Ames, "Europe Looks Left; Pablo Iglesias: Nobody's Servant," GlobalPost, November 15, 2014, http://www.globalpost.com/dispatch/news/regions/europe/141114/europe-left-spain-podemos-iglesias-euro-crisis.

58 Francisco Mercado, "La fundación relacionada con Podemos cobró 3,7 millones de Chávez en 10 años" (Foundation related to Podemos took 3.7 million from Chavez in ten years), *El País*, June 17, 2014, http://politica.elpais.com/politica/2014/06/17/actualidad/1403039351_862188.html.

59 Randeep Ramesh, "London Estate Agents Caught on Camera Dealing with 'Corrupt' Russian Buyer," *Guardian*, July 7, 2015, http://www.theguardian.com/uk-news/2015/jul/07/london-estate-agents-caught-on-camera-russian-buyer.

60 Gerhard Schröder, quoted in Tony Paterson, "Putin's Far-Right Ambition: Think-Tank Reveals How Russian President Is Wooing—and Funding—Populist Parties across Europe to Gain Influence in the EU," *Independent*, November 25, 2014, http://www.independent.co.uk/news/world/europe/putins-farright-ambition-thinktank-reveals-how-russian-president-is-wooing--and-funding--populist-parties-across-europe-to-gain-influence-in-the-eu-9883052.html.

61 Luke Harding, "We Should Beware Russia's Links with Europe's Right," *Guardian*, December 8, 2014, http://www.theguardian.com/commentisfree/2014/dec/08/russia-europe-right-putin-front-national-eu.

CHAPTER 9 ▪ THE UNITED STATES AND EUROPE: HOW AND WHY WE MUST FIGHT BACK

1 Petro Poroshenko, quoted in Christopher Harress, "House Votes in Favor of US Lethal Aid for Ukraine, but Obama's Tipping Point Not Reached Yet," *International Business Times*, March 24, 2015, http://www.ibtimes.com/house-votes-favor-us-lethal-aid-ukraine-obamas-tipping-point-not-reached-yet-1857848.

2 Condoleezza Rice and Robert M. Gates, "How America Can Counter Putin's Moves in Syria," *Washington Post*, October 8, 2015, https://www.washingtonpost.com/opinions/how-to-counter-putin-in-syria/2015/10/08/128fade2-6c66-11e5-b31c-d80d62b53e28_story.html.

3 Adam Withnall, "Russia Threatens Denmark with Nuclear Weapons If It Tries to Join NATO Defence Shield: The Russian Ambassador in Copenhagen Says Danish Warships Would Become 'Targets for Russian Nuclear Missiles,'" *Independent*, March 22, 2015, http://www.independent.co.uk/news/world/europe/russia-threatens-denmark-with-nuclear-weapons-if-it-tries-to-join-nato-defence-shield-10125529.html.

4 Steven Pifer, "Russia's Rising Military: Should the U.S. Send More Nuclear Weapons to Europe?," *National Interest*, July 21, 2015, http://nationalinterest.org/feature/russias-rising-military-should-the-us-send-more-nuclear-13381.

5 Ibid.

6 John Herbst, quoted in Katie Engelhart, "Ex-US Ambassador Calls American Military Commitment to Baltics a 'Joke,'" Vice News, June 11, 2015, https://news.vice.com/article/would-russia-really-invade-a-nato-country-ex-us-ambassador-to-ukraine-says-maybe.

7 Eric Schmitt and Steven Lee Myers, "U.S. Is Poised to Put Heavy Weaponry in Eastern Europe," *New York Times*, June 13, 2015, http://www.nytimes.com/2015/06/14/world/europe/us-poised-to-put-heavy-weaponry-in-east-europe.html?emc=edit_th_20150614&nl=todaysheadlines&nlid=55833253&_r=1.

8 Max Boot, "Obama's Move Won't Deter Russian Aggression," *Commentary*, June 15, 2015, https://www.commentarymagazine.com/foreign-policy/europe/obamas-move-russian-aggression/.

AFTERWORD

1   Nicholas Eberstaft, *North Korea's 'Epic Economic Fail' in International Perspective* (Seoul: Asan Institute for Policy Studies, 2015), http://en.asaninst. org/contents/north-koreas-epic-economic-fail-in-international-perspective.

2   Vladimir Putin, quoted in Rebecca Kheel, "Russia Names US as Security Threat," *Hill*, January 2, 2016, http://thehill.com/policy/defense/264570-russia-names-us-as-national-security-threat.

INDEX

White, Jeffrey, 82

Xi Jinping, 26, 91

Yakubov, Yury, 57
Yanukovych, Viktor, 53, 111
Yatsenyuk, Arseniy, 112
Yemen, 87–88, 100

Yousafzai, Malala, 7
YouTube, 68
Yushchenko, Viktor, 96

Zaritsky, Vladimir, 50
Ždanoka, Tatjana, 109
Zukunft, Paul F., 49